Different Kind of Great:

Reflections for Christians Who Lead

Tim Way

Cover Design by the Amazing Rachelle Rummage.

DEDICATION

I joyfully and gratefully dedicate this book to Jesus, with the prayer that He will be glorified.

I further dedicate it to all the wonderful servants of Jesus who have provided such powerful examples for me of what a gospel leader truly is. I will not attempt to list them here, but hopefully I have expressed my gratitude in one way or another.

In addition, I dedicate this work to Oli, Heidi, Micah, and Sarah, with gratitude for their exemplary servanthood as they lead the spiritual family and work of God that I love so much.

During the process of writing this book, I've found myself wandering in my mind back to when my parents were alive. As I have aged, I have begun to see, in their parenting and leadership, traits of godliness that I had overlooked in my youth. So I specifically dedicate this to the memory of my Dad and Mom, Peter and Elizabeth Way, with the comforting expectancy that I will see them again.

Table of Contents

GRATITUDE

As I bring this project to a close after some seven years of work, I am overwhelmed with the support and encouragement I have received along the way from those who mean the most to me. First, I want to thank my wife, Jill. You have believed in me from page one and given me the encouragement I needed to persevere and keep writing. There is so much more to say, but this is all I will include here. I love you. To my kids, especially Philip and Hannah, who put up with me taking so much time on this, thank you. Thank you for your patience and your support.

Thank you, Abby Bibeau, for editing, and more than editing. Thank you for the words of encouragement along the way that boosted my sometimes discouraged heart. Thank you, too, for helping me to say things better and for challenging my ideas in a grace-filled way. You are incredible and I really am so grateful.

I'm thankful to you, Bob Burch, for your unequaled insight and your labor to make this book readable, accurate, and helpful. I have enjoyed our long discussions and have implemented, to the best of my ability, so many of your suggestions. You always make my work better. Thank you for your unfailing friendship.

Thank you to others who read all or parts of the manuscript and offered very helpful feedback, especially Richard Coleman, Jonathan Fruh, Keith Hill, Travis Remple, and, of course, Jill Way. I appreciate each one of you.

PREFACE
A Letter to You, My Reader

Dear Reader,

Thank you for picking up this book. My prayer for you and for me is that we will come to know Jesus more as we consider these reflections on greatness. I pray that we will glorify Him in our lives and in our leadership. I pray that we will faithfully make Him known to others.

It feels redundant to put yet another book about leadership out there. We as Jesus followers seem obsessed with the topic. Like His first disciples, we all want to be great. And maybe that's not so bad — as long as we allow Him to mold our understanding of greatness; as long as we are prepared to reject the seemingly wise ways of the world that so brazenly contradict the teachings and example of our Lord.

Over the years of writing this, I've often questioned my decision to do so. There are so many books, written by better leaders and better writers and better Christians than me. This is not false humility or even true humility. It is just the clear truth. Yet all through the long months and the changing seasons of writing this book, I can only say I have felt compelled.

I am fully aware that there has already been a lot written on this subject, but perhaps all has not yet been said. The pursuit of greatness is an exercise in becoming more and more conformed to Christ. In fact, the pursuit of greatness is nothing less than a pursuit of Jesus Himself. And He is infinite and wondrous beyond description! There is no getting to the end of Him. We could be writing such books from now til forever and still not fully describe Him or understand Him. My sincere hope is that this book will be a refreshing and challenging look at a well-worn subject.

In the preface to his classic work, *The Pursuit of God*, A.W. Tozer wrote something that resounds with me as I begin the process of offering my own book to you, my reader:

This book is a modest attempt to aid God's hungry children so to find Him. Nothing here is new except in the sense that it is a discovery which my own heart has made of spiritual realities most delightful and wonderful to me. Others before me have gone much farther into these holy mysteries than I have done, but if my fire is not large it is yet real, and there may be those who can light their candle at its flame.[1]

I pray that you will find my fire to be real and that some will be able to light their candles at its flame.

Tim Way
Masaka, Uganda
September, 2024

---

[1] A.W. Tozer, *The Pursuit of God* (Christian Publications, Inc, 1948), pg 5.

FIRE WORDS

O God, my words are cold:
The frosted frond of fern or feathery palm
Wrought on the whitened pane—
They are as near to fire as these my words;
Oh, that they were as flames!"
    Thus did I cry.

    And thus God answered me:
"Thou shalt have words, but at this cost:
That thou must first be burnt—
Burnt by red embers from a secret fire,
Scorched by fierce heats and withering winds that sweep
Through all thy being, carrying thee afar
From old delights. Doth not the ardent fire
Consume the mountain's heart before the flow
Of fervent lava? Wouldst thou easefully,
As from cool, pleasant fountains, flow in fire?
Say, can thy heart endure, or can thy hands be strong
In the day that I shall deal with thee?

"For first the iron must enter thine own soul,
And wound and brand it, scarring awful lines
Indelibly upon it; and a hand
Resistless in a tender terribleness,
Must thoroughly purge it, fashioning its pain
To power that leaps in fire.
Not otherwise, and by no lighter touch,
Are fire-words wrought."[2]

---

[2] Amy Carmichael, quoted in *Amy Carmichael of Dohnavur* by Frank Houghton (Fort Washington, PA: CLC Publications, 1953), Kindle loc 1965.

THE GREATEST

When I think of that day, I imagine it to have been hot and dusty. A ragged and testy group of men and women are slowly making their way to the big city, every day bringing them a little closer. To say the tension among them is thick would be a gross understatement. The leader, stubbornly determined, entertains no alternative views in this matter. The others follow. Some hold their doubts close, silently and grimly putting one foot in front of the other. Others, more bold, cannot help making their dissent known. This journey is foolish, after all. Dangerously so. They are playing into their enemies' hands. Conflict will be inevitable; their very survival hanging in the balance. And what if they don't make it? What of the great dreams of God's deliverance and salvation? What of the movement that was even now sweeping the nation so powerfully? It would all be crushed. Yes, there was plenty of tension that day.

But there was hope, too. These unlikely friends had seen too much to fully give in to despair. So much had happened that seemed more than unlikely just a few years ago. Something was stirring. Everywhere they went, there was a change. They could feel it. Something was in the air. The tired and oppressed people of this great land were coming awake. If they survived, this thing could not be stopped. This movement was going to overtake the nation. There was hope, and something more. Ambition. There would be opportunities for loyal men; opportunities few could have dreamed of. Great influence was just around the corner. Prestige. Honor. Power. It was right there. It was so close.

Hot. Dusty. Fatigued. Afraid. Hopeful. Proud. Ambitious. Tense. And the leader of this motley band tells a story that is probably actually relevant, but to be honest nobody finds it worth the effort just now to figure

1

out how. He tells them of a wealthy farmer seeking day laborers to work his land, and how he hires groups of men throughout the day. He concludes the parable with this cryptic punchline: "So the last will be first, and the first will be last." (Matthew 20:16).

Nice story, Jesus.

A little later, with a somber look, He pulls the twelve aside — these apostles of a new age and messengers of the Day of the Lord; possibly even rulers of a new Kingdom? Jesus looks at His distracted friends and tries to get through to them yet again. He tells them He is going to die. Soon. In fact, He is going to be murdered in a cruel, humiliating, and excruciatingly painful way. But don't worry! He is going to rise from the dead. The disciples are understandably worried and not a little confused. What does it all mean?

Something big is going to go down in Jerusalem. That much seems clear. But what does He mean? Surely there is some spiritual significance to all this talk of death that He will explain eventually. Jesus is like that. He loves to speak in riddles and shadows. Yes, something is about to happen — perhaps the great culmination, the Great Beginning. Maybe this will be the moment they have been waiting for. Perhaps this is the time faithful and courageous and bold men will be rewarded.

And so we come to this moment, saturated with doubt and confusion, hope and ambition. Heedless of Jesus' warnings and ignorant of the message He has been trying to get across, the disciples approach what will prove to be a watershed moment. Jesus is about to redefine leadership for all time, upending the systems of power and authority that have dominated human society for millennia. He will announce that in the coming age, all ideas of leadership will not be simply tweaked or improved or fixed, but will be scrapped and replaced with something completely new. In nothing will the Kingdom make a more profound difference than in the way people exercise influence over one another, than in the way power is gained and wielded.

Matthew tells us that a zealous mother approaches Jesus with a request — at once both igniting the indignation and jealousy of the others and revealing the full extent of their lack of comprehension regarding all Jesus has been telling them. She petitions for her sons to receive the top two positions under Jesus in His new government. Jesus is not shocked by the request. He asks first if they are truly willing to pay the price in suffering that would be necessary. They enthusiastically — and perhaps naively — affirm that they are. He then tells them plainly that He cannot do what they ask because it is His Father who will make such decisions. The other ten followers of course do not appreciate this power play by the sons of Zebedee, and they let their displeasure be known. Things deteriorate. And then Jesus pulls them together and upends everything:

> "You know that the rulers of the Gentiles lord it over them, and their high officials exercise authority over them. Not so with you. Instead, whoever wants to become great among you must be your servant, and whoever wants to be first must be your slave— just as the Son of Man did not come to be served, but to serve, and to give his life as a ransom for many." — Matthew 20:25-28

We know how leadership works. The leader is in control. The leader has authority. The leader makes decisions. The leader sets the vision. The leader... leads.

Not so with you.

How does one lead without lording? How rule without exercising authority or be great by becoming less? How can one influence by becoming a slave?

How indeed?

Wrestling with these questions will form the basis for much of this book. In these few chapters from the Gospel of Matthew, Jesus gives the ultimate leadership instructions for His Kingdom. But before we can even attempt to understand, much less act on, Jesus' directives, we have to take a step back. We must examine what Jesus has said within the immediate context of scripture.

When writing his gospel, Matthew, led by the Holy Spirit, compiled and presented Jesus' actions and teachings to us in a particular order; regularly grouping material under a unifying heading or theme (for example, the collection of parables of the Kingdom in Matthew 13). This allows us to see a variety of Jesus' actions and teachings on the same general subject all together in one place. By presenting different lessons and events that are related to the same theme together, Matthew gives us a deeper and more multi-faceted understanding of what Jesus is teaching. The group of teachings, parables, and happenings that are found in Matthew 18:1 — 20:28 all combine to reveal what greatness and leadership in the Kingdom of Heaven is.

This section is book-ended by two verses that provide us with the context for everything that lies between. In Matthew 18:1, the disciples ask Jesus who is the greatest in Heaven's Kingdom. In Matthew 20:28, Jesus summarizes His radical plan for leadership by saying that even He Himself did not come to be served but to serve. Between these two verses are a number of stories, interactions, and short teaching moments that the former tax collector has intentionally included to show us what greatness in the Kingdom means.

The core of this book will be made up of us walking together through the intriguing passages that lie between the disciples' question and Jesus' ultimate answer. While we may want to just get to the point so we can start doing something for Jesus, the truth is that we must give time for the Holy Spirit to change our hearts and minds so that we can do what our Lord is telling us. Jesus' instructions are so contrary to our human understanding that it is easy for us to ignore or downplay or water them down. We do this to our detriment, no matter how practical or worldly-wise our alterations may be.

It takes trust and grace to understand and accept what Jesus is teaching. It is comforting, perhaps, that the twelve did not get it at this point; that they were unwilling or unable to grasp this dangerously revolutionary idea. It seems that they only began to understand what Jesus was saying sometime after His death, resurrection, and ascension and the coming of the Holy Spirit to dwell within them.

This now brings me to the use of words such as "greatness" and "leadership." Is it a stretch to turn the question of greatness into a series of lessons on leadership? I maintain that the idea of leadership is a good way of thinking about the questions brought up by the original disciples. When they seek greatness, it becomes fairly clear that what they are after is power, influence, position, and authority. They are not asking about greatness as a moral quality — something that could be re-worded as "Who is the best person in the Kingdom? How can I become a really good person?" This is neither their ultimate intent here nor is it the question to which Jesus seems to be responding. They are getting at prestige and honor and recognition and power. In our day, a fair way of considering that intent is with the concept of leadership. The question, at least partially (if not wholly), is "Who will be the top leaders in the Kingdom?" Thus, in this work, I will often use "leadership" terms rather than or alongside "greatness" terms. I think in doing so I am being faithful to the intention of the text.

It is important, perhaps, to also add a note about my intended audience. This is not a book intended solely for those with leadership positions. All of us as disciples of Jesus are people with some level of influence in the lives of others. All of us, indeed, are called to greatness in the way Jesus defines the term. I do hope and believe that these musings will be beneficial to pastors, teachers, missionaries, and people with all kinds of leadership positions. However, I believe it will be equally helpful to people who love Jesus and serve Him faithfully apart from position. This should become obvious as you progress through the book.

We have in these three chapters of Matthew an incredible store of treasures from Jesus' teaching on greatness. Even if this is not an intentional grouping by the inspired author, the number and importance of the issues that arise in this section of scripture will prove to be greatly beneficial to us as we seek to be leaders in Jesus' movement. Regardless, we have a deep well of insights and challenges into Kingdom leadership to draw from in Matthew 18:1 — 20:28. Indeed, in these verses Jesus teaches the very essence of what it means to be a Christian leader. I encourage you to meditate on these three chapters as you read this book. My prayer is that we will all grow in this kind of greatness for the sake of glorifying Jesus and making Him known in the nations.

In Part Two, I will initiate a discussion about leadership as discipleship. I hope to convince you that making disciples is in fact the heart of all true Christian leadership, and I will attempt to give some practical handles on how to do this. We will look at some broad, biblically informed ideas regarding how to make disciples. I will end by taking the process one step further by considering the idea of leadership development as an essential element in true discipleship.

PART ONE
JESUS LEADERSHIP

1 - WHO IS THE GREATEST?
(Matthew 18:1 - 19:15)

At that time the disciples came to Jesus and asked, "Who, then, is the greatest in the kingdom of heaven?" — Matthew 18:1

Little Children
(Matthew 18:1-14)

He called a little child to him, and placed the child among them. And he said: "Truly I tell you, unless you change and become like little children, you will never enter the kingdom of heaven. Therefore, whoever takes the lowly position of this child is the greatest in the kingdom of heaven. And whoever welcomes one such child in my name welcomes me." — Matthew 18:2-5

It was the disciples, for their own reasons, who brought up the subject. I imagine them putting on a casual face, attempting to mask the fervency of their desire. At any rate, I am pretty sure that they had no idea, though by now they probably should have, how Jesus would turn their words on end, unsettle all they thought they knew on the subject, and countermand all that the wise of their day taught. But here they are. "Who is the greatest in the kingdom of heaven?" And it is here that we, too, begin our journey. Who is the greatest in the Kingdom?

What is even meant by greatness? As we read, that comes into more focus. As mentioned in the introduction, the disciples were interested in power, influence, and prestige. These are the kinds of ambitions we ourselves know full well. They wanted to know what type of person would be promoted and who would attain the highest rank. In this book, we will consider greatness to be something akin to influence and power. Again, the word that, for us, best summarizes the idea expressed would be leadership. Who are the leaders in the Kingdom? Jesus does not bother with definitions here but simply responds to the loaded question. As our journey continues, we will see that the Lord re-directs both the definition of greatness and the means to attaining it. The disciples are thinking about worldly power and renown. Jesus bypasses those destinations and takes us to higher ground.

What motivated these twelve students to ask such a question of their rabbi? It seems apparent that they each wanted to be great, or even the greatest. I can relate to this ambition. I, too, desire to be well-known; to wield power; to be honored. Like the apostles, I want to have great authority and influence over many people. Perhaps you do, too. I want to be special. And, to be clear, I do not mean special in an ordinary way either. I am aware that "everyone is special." But that isn't enough. I want to be unique. I think this desire may be a fundamental part of the human condition, at least to some degree. In any case, though I am a little bit uncomfortable with the voicing of the disciples' question, I am not at all shocked by the sentiment. Jesus does not seem to be either, and He has a ready answer.

First, He tells them, you must change. You are not currently on the path to greatness. You are not walking in the way of the Kingdom of Heaven. Your fundamental ideas about leadership and about how to become significant and successful are wrong. Your very ideas about what success itself is must be radically dismantled. You are immersed in the world's ways of thinking and acting and getting ahead. None of that is going to work here. You have to change.

As you read this, perhaps you are like me. I sit in smug comfort, thinking about how much Peter, James, John, and the rest of them needed to learn. But the truth is that today we are in the midst of a global leadership crisis. Organizations and ministries all over the world report a desperate unmet need for qualified and godly leaders. *They* must change. *You* must change. Could it be? *I* must change. If these meditations are to be in the least bit worthwhile, we are going to need to approach them with the conviction that we need to change. We must come to grips with the reality that our leadership and our pursuit of greatness are not what they need to be. Jesus has something to say to us through His Word and His Spirit, and in order to hear Him we must be committed to change. We must be ready to admit our failures and our wrongness and to repent. I am ready to try. In fact, I am desperate. Are you with me?

You may be wondering why the dramatic preamble. It is because what Jesus says immediately after *change* is so shocking. It is because the specific change He calls us to is so radical. Our Lord tells us that if we want to become real leaders then we must "become like little children." And He does not leave us guessing about how He wants us to be like children; He makes it clear exactly what He intends. "Whoever takes the lowly position of this child…" It is the lowly position of the child that is being highlighted, and the exhortation of Jesus is for you and me to do something; to decide and to act. We are to *take* the lowly position. We are not merely to accept it if offered. We are not simply to allow it to be bestowed on us if someone would be so bold as to suggest such a thing. But we are to take it. We are to insist on it and to maneuver for it. We are to grasp it. Jesus' command is not passive.

The disciples are asking what they must do to be great and in so doing they are already making moves to take the exalted position. Yet Jesus tells them to use those efforts instead to grab the low place. The paradox is almost too much. To be great, you must change and use your efforts to be *not* great. In order to lead, you must use all your efforts to attain the lowest rank in the room.

I also note that it is a *position* Jesus tells us to take. In this moment He does not say to do the lowly task or to have a lowly attitude, but to take the lowly position and to put ourselves fully under others. A position is something that gives value and reveals a part of who we are. Whether that position is earned through achievement or granted through birth or the bestowing of a title, it speaks to identity. It is a handle for others as they seek to define us, assess our worth, and perhaps determine how they should treat us. So, of course, we prefer the higher position. It is part of our nature. We can accept an admonition to patiently accept where we are, as long as we sense that there is hope of advancing. But to actually seek out the lowly position and claim it for ourselves? How is this greatness?

Lowly is certainly a good way of describing the position of a child. Children are not taken seriously. Their voices are dismissed and their opinions disregarded. They are not placed in positions of honor. Children are vulnerable and weak. There is nothing important or glorious about the tasks they are assigned. They must always defer to the grown-up in the room, for they have no power, no control. To choose this position, then, is to not grasp for these things — having a voice or being honored or wielding power. It is to avoid worrying about being taken seriously or getting your way. On a deeper level, it is to not let the desire to be taken seriously or the need for control influence how you live or what you say or who you befriend. Be willing to do things that will open yourself up to ridicule or reveal your weakness. Do not fight or manipulate to be seen as important. Take the lowly place. It is one thing to hold this position by default, to persevere through this season out of necessity, but it is an entirely different thing to choose this; to choose dishonor, disrespect, weakness, and helplessness; to choose to give up control.

Yes, we need to change.

Second, Jesus says we are to not only take the low position but also to welcome the one who is in that place. If we want to be Kingdom-great we will be intentional about who we notice, recognize, and embrace, and it will not be the usual ones that the world (or the Church) seeks out. Though to take the lowly position is to choose to be unheard and dishonored and unknown, we will actively seek to hear and to honor and to know the very ones that others do not. In giving up our own voice, we give volume to theirs. In laying down our own honor, we lift another in glory. In giving up our own need to be known, we truly see and acknowledge one who has been invisible. We become lowly and we welcome the lowly. We do not surround ourselves with the great or the famous so that we can bask in their reflected glory. We do not ingratiate ourselves to the powerful so that we can rise and become like them. We, instead, open our arms to the ones who cannot aid our advance or boost our position. We welcome the lowly.

Thirdly, and here Jesus gets very intense indeed, we do not cause "such a one" to stumble into sin. Greatness is about influence. Those with the desire to be great are those who want to be able to exert influence over other people and over society. Jesus seems to have no problem with this desire. However, He gives such a fierce and solemn warning regarding the use of that influence that it must have startled the disciples. If you are going to come to a place where you exercise influence in the life of another, particularly in the life of one who belongs to Jesus, you had better make sure that your influence is leading them towards Jesus and not away from Him. If you, in your pursuit of greatness, cause another to stumble, the consequences are terrible in their devastation. Poking out your eye or cutting off your foot would be much preferred to facing God having used your influence to ruin another. Be very careful that you do not, through your attempts to gain influence, cause another to stumble. If we promote sin in any way in the life of another, we are guilty of a horrible betrayal, and we will face the very fires of Hell in consequence.

Why do you want to be great? If it is for selfish motives, beware. Those who seek to be great out of lust for power or longing for comfort or to boost self-esteem or for any reason other than the glory of Jesus will end up using other people to get what they want. In so doing, they will inevitably cause someone else to stumble. The issue of what we want to use our influence for is no small matter, and Jesus highlights this through shocking and even grotesque imagery. He is urging us, *"Pay attention to this!"* This is big. Leadership can be a blessing if harnessed for the good of others, but it will be the deadliest curse if wielded wrongly.

Finally, Jesus admonishes us to not despise the lowly because the Father has determined that the very ones who seem insignificant to the world are of immense value to Him. Their angels always see the face of God. They are important. They are a big deal. The Father rejoices if even one of them is found after wandering off and getting lost. Do not despise who the world despises. Do not underestimate or undervalue those whom the Father has called important. Kingdom greatness comes clothed in lowliness and weakness. It comes dressed in the disguise of a mere child.

Forgive
(Matthew 18:15-35)

If another believer sins against you… — Matthew 18:15 (NLT)

The primal cry erupted from a place of great anguish in my soul. I felt that something in me was being ripped apart and that I would not make it out of this experience fully whole. Shame and anger and disappointment and humiliation filled me. I was confused, groping around in a soul-darkness that felt almost physical. Dear God, what was happening?

Life had been difficult for some time. Finances were worse than tight and the lack of funds was causing a great deal of stress. Things with Jill, my wife, were strained; not to the point of breaking, but enough to add to the anxiety. For the past several weeks I had been nursing an offense and rejection that had caused me deep pain and anger. And now I had learned that one of my best friends was dead. The paradoxical sweetness that comes with grief as we remember and celebrate the life of one close to us had given way to something darker and more hopeless.

My wife and kids had gone out for the evening, and I was happy to be left alone with my sadness and gloom. But as I sat in the room alone, I remembered again my last interactions with my recently departed friend, and the shame and regret became unbearable. In a burst of insight that descended too late, I became aware that I was guilty of the very same thing (and even worse) as those who had hurt me and caused such righteous offense in me over the previous weeks. Whatever had been done to me to cause this emotional pain was small compared to how I had treated him. And now there was no making amends. No asking for forgiveness. No making things right. He had died before I even realized how I must have hurt him.

As I sat in the mess of my guilt and shame and grief and despair, an unsettling thought penetrated the deep fog of my soul. I was forgiven. Fully. Jesus has the authority to do that, and in truth, He had done it for me. Even for me. I did not welcome this revelation. I saw it, for the first time in my life, as unfair. That I should be so cleansed with such little personal cost was unbearably unjust. That the shame and guilt could be simply removed, gone forever, felt profoundly and wholly not right. It was not fair to my friend and it certainly was not fair to Jesus. I could not accept these terms! How could I? To escape unscathed from the guilt of my misdeeds? To get off scot-free after treating my friend so badly and causing him such pain? And to have treated him like that while all the time brooding over a lesser offense perpetrated against me without even seeing the irony of it?

The ingratitude! The willful blindness! The selfishness and arrogance! The insensitivity and callousness.

No, Jesus. Let me at least do something to earn Your forgiveness. Let me suffer for my meanness.

In no uncertain terms, it became clear to me that it was no use. There was not one thing I could do to pay for this wrong. I had to accept His offer of free forgiveness and cleansing, and I had to give up any thought of making it up to my friend.

And that's when the scream came. I had never before seen the utter vileness of my own sin, and I had certainly never grasped to such a degree the scandal of His grace and mercy.

What came next was no more welcome than the original revelation of my sin or the reality of my forgiveness by Jesus' grace alone. It was joy. Pure, unadulterated joy. I fought against this rising tide of euphoria that threatened to overrun my soul and make a mockery of my sin and failure and grief but to no avail. Finally, I gave in to its unrelenting encroachment on my self-pity and anger and shame, and I abandoned myself to shameless delight and happiness. I rejoiced and shouted praises to Jesus my Savior as I jumped about the room. Weeping joyful tears of gratitude, I basked in my freedom and the truly unimaginable love of the Father.

At some point during this uncharacteristic celebration, I thought about the people who had offended me and on whom I had focused such anger and resentment. To my wonder, I found that the sting was completely gone. What was it that had made me so upset? It had dispersed like a wispy cloud in a gust of wind. Where was the offense? Where the righteous outrage? All gone. Forgive them? Of course I would — if there was even anything to forgive. What had I been thinking? I felt nothing but love and even gratitude towards these people.

In our journey to greatness with Jesus, after calling us to the low position of a child, He speaks to us about offense. Curious. It almost seems like He has changed the subject, that after giving a brief but troubling answer to the disciples' awkward query, He is ready to move on. But maybe not. I wonder if perhaps nothing hinders the rise to greatness so much as offense, or more to the point, how we handle offense. Maybe forgiving is one of the clearest signs of Kingdom-greatness that there is. And perhaps the opposite is also true: that unforgiveness is a sure sign we are still on the wrong track, headed full steam away from the greatness that Jesus is seeking to develop in us.

"If another believer sins against you," Jesus begins. If, indeed. He then gives very practical guidance on how to handle being sinned against. It is clear that Jesus' aim here is restoration and reconciliation. Do not let offense sit in your soul, a simmering, venomous stew of bitterness, pain, and resentment.

Talk it out. Get others to help if necessary. Do the hard relational work. Value the person who sinned enough to take the dreaded first step. Most of the time, repentance and relief will follow. But even when it does not, do not allow the situation to mark you. If sin continues unabated and without remorse, separate yourself from the person — not in hatred but in hope. Perhaps the drastic action will shake the offender out of his sinful ways and even yet bring restoration. Of course, the implied command here is to forgive (as shown in verse 21 by Peter's question, "How often should I forgive...?"). And there is the rub.

Matthew places this teaching in the immediate context of the question about greatness, and it seems likely that this is intentional. Even if it is not, the truth remains that Kingdom-greatness is bound up with the issues of offense and forgiveness. Jesus calls us to deal with offense in a different way from the world. The wisdom of the day calls us to first protect ourselves. Forgiveness is important, they say, but the primary motive for that is your own well-being and emotional health. You would certainly not forgive beyond a reasonable point, and you would not forgive to the extent that it would cause loss or trouble for yourself. But Jesus pushes us beyond these self-centered approaches to handling relationships and the offenses we feel, and He moves us into the arena of the Kingdom. In Jesus' Kingdom, we forgive to a virtually unlimited degree, and we do so because we ourselves have been forgiven even more. Our forgiveness of others is a reflection of the Father, who forgives us at the great personal cost of the blood of Jesus. We forgive, not to achieve some kind of personal wholeness or health, but because we are children of our Father.

The very nature of true forgiveness is sacrificial. It is sacrificial because it is abundantly not about me or for me, but is for the other. I may, and in fact typically do, reap benefits from forgiving, but that must not be my motive. God forgives me at a cost to Himself. He forgives me, not to get a load of stress or bitterness out of His soul, but because He loves me and wants good for me. His forgiveness benefits me, the sinner. That is how we are to forgive. We forgive out of sacrificial love.

The story Jesus tells in Matthew 18 brings insight into the experience I related at the beginning of this section. A king calls in one of his subjects who owes him a great sum of money — "ten thousand bags of gold" in the NIV. The king demands payment, but there is no way the debt could ever be repaid. At first, it seems that the king will deal harshly with his servant, but in the end, he shows mercy and actually forgives the entire debt. The forgiven servant then goes and finds someone who owes him a far smaller sum — "a hundred silver coins" — and demands immediate payment. When this unfortunate man begs for mercy, it is not granted and he is thrown into prison. The brazen wickedness of this act in the light of the servant's so recent and great deliverance is hard to fathom. How could one who has been forgiven so much act in such a way? The whole situation is too much for others in the story who know all that has taken place, and they bring word of the forgiven servant's vile actions to the king, who responds as expected. That servant is "handed over to the jailers to be tortured, until he should pay back all he owed" (18:34). Jesus concludes with the somber words, "This is how my heavenly Father will treat each of you unless you forgive your brother or sister from your heart" (18:35).

In my life, I found it impossible to forgive others until I had a revelation of what I myself had been forgiven and what that forgiveness cost. This lesson has served me well over the years, and I have had many opportunities to thank the Lord for the awful and enlightening revelations of that emotional night. Forgiveness still does not come easy, and I have certainly struggled to give it at times since that day. However, in His mercy, the Father has given me a glimpse of the impossible debt I owed and has enabled me to experience the boundless joy of that debt being wiped away at no cost to myself. Whenever I begin to rehearse the sins of another against me, I am forced to recognize that I have been forgiven far, far more.

That experience has also helped me in another way. I now recognize this disturbing but liberating truth: whatever evil has been done to me is something I have either done to another or am capable of doing apart from the grace of God. My bent towards righteous indignation and taking offense cannot stand up to the simple experience of God's grace in my own life. When I examine the most painful hurts I have received from the actions or words of others, I know without a doubt that I could easily have done the same as they did, and even worse. Easily — and without even noticing it. Such is the evil in my own heart. Oh! How great is the grace and mercy of God! How wonderful is His forgiveness and His love towards me! Even me.

As a leader in God's Kingdom work, people will sin against you. You will be offended. You will face rejection and betrayal. You will be lied to, taken advantage of, and mocked. You will be hated for no reason. Please understand this: It is okay. These things do not need to mark you or debilitate you. You will even do some of this to others. In fact, you already have. But Jesus has forgiven you. Your guilt is gone. Furthermore, He has given you the power — and the responsibility — to forgive others.

That Jesus longs for unity in His people is abundantly clear in the Scriptures. People who are great in His Kingdom are forces for oneness in the body of Christ. They work for unity. One of the ways they do this most powerfully is through forgiveness. They bring people together in reconciliation and genuine fellowship. They absolutely refuse offense or sin or anything that would separate them from brothers and sisters in God's family. Sometimes this is costly, and it would be so much easier to hold the offense or to push people away. Such is not the way of greatness.

The world warns us to keep "toxic" people out of our lives for our own good and wholeness. But what if, through the cross, we have been given the antidote to the toxicity of human relationships? What if forgiveness is the secret weapon that not only protects you from the poison in another's heart but even brings deliverance to them — through extending grace and love? Just as Jesus did for me. Just as He has done for you. The way to greatness lies through offense. There is no getting around it. How will you respond? Will you self-protect and harbor resentment and push troublesome people away in your rise to the top? Or will you take the lowly path of lifting up others through forgiveness and freely bestowing grace and mercy?

Divorce
(Matthew 19:1-12)

What God has joined together, let no one separate. — Matthew 19:6

Having challenged His ambitious followers to take the lowly position of a child and to continually forgive others who offend them, Jesus now gives us further insight into greatness with this question about divorce: "Is it lawful for a man to divorce his wife for any and every reason?" (19:3).

Before getting into heady discussions about Kingdom leadership and authority, Jesus confronts us with a more mundane kind of greatness. Mundane, but very significant. Family is the training program, the proving grounds, and the very atmosphere in which people are developed and leaders are formed. Family is the original and foundational structure in society and was created by God Himself. "What God has joined together…" Not only did God create the whole idea of marriage and family, but He is actively involved in forging and creating these unique and powerful relational ties. Fidelity to one's spouse is basic to greatness. Indeed, some decades later the Apostle Paul would write that leading a family well is an important indicator pointing to a person's qualifications to lead God's people. He says: "If anyone does not know how to manage his own family, how can he take care of God's church?" (1 Timothy 3:5).

Now, this may at first seem like a stretch, considering Jesus' audience of twelve (probably) mostly unmarried young men. They were in a training program with Jesus apart from wives and children. Paul, too, was likely single — not to mention Jesus Himself. So being married is certainly not an essential qualification for greatness. Furthermore, a few verses later Jesus goes on to say that there are people who will choose to be single for the sake of devoting themselves to God's Kingdom (we will discuss that more in a moment). However, Jesus still introduces this point, and the churches established by the great apostle took it as a maxim that one's ability to lead a family was an important indicator regarding fitness to lead God's church. Certainly, one who proves himself unfaithful in family leadership is disqualified from Kingdom leadership.

The previous statement of course opens up another whole can of worms to which I do not intend to devote significant time here. Suffice it to say that there are different reasons that people get divorced and there are a variety of factors to be taken into account when considering such a one for leadership roles. In what season of life did the divorce occur? What growth has occurred since then? What were the factors related to the divorce itself? The grace of Jesus is a marvelous and powerful force and we need not give up hope for anyone ready to receive His grace and turn to Him. All of this, however, is a side note, a parenthesis that Jesus Himself does not consider in this passage. So, with that behind us, let us return to the text.

God's intention for marriage is that it is permanent and that it is the bedrock of all human relationships and institutions. As already mentioned, the Creator Himself is the founder of marriage and is actively involved in its development. Whenever two people are joined together in matrimony, we are to understand that God Himself seals the union. It is therefore a uniquely sacred relationship and one that should not be broken under any save the most severe of circumstances.

This brings us back to the big idea of faithfulness. Marriage provides perhaps the clearest test of a person's commitment to this essential virtue. Faithfulness can be seen as simply keeping one's promises. God Himself is continually displayed in the scriptures as the Faithful One. He has made promises and over millennia has proven that He keeps His Word, often in spite of the ongoing lack of faithfulness of those to whom He has made these promises:

"If we are faithless,
he remains faithful,
for he cannot disown himself." (2 Timothy 2:13)

God's faithfulness extended all the way to the giving of His Son to die to reconcile and redeem this lost world. Nothing can stand in the way of God keeping His promises. He is the One who joins a husband to his wife, and His is the kind of faithfulness that is expected as they together build a family.

Faithfulness is built on commitment, which is not a trendy topic in our day. There are much more exciting things to discuss and more spectacular ways to show our devotion and our value. Jesus drags our exalted aspirations of greatness into the mud and grit of day-to-day living. Kingdom leadership is built block by block on the back of hard commitments and a doggedly tenacious determination to keep them, no matter what. The greatness of faithfulness is revealed in the seemingly bland, behind-the-scenes loyalty to a holy promise. It requires guts to make the kind of commitments that build greatness. In marriage, you are making a promise that is to stand true for the rest of your life, over decades of unforeseen challenges and year upon year of temptations and trials. You are making a commitment even though you have no idea how it will be tested or whether or not you will regret it after ten, twenty, or fifty years. Yet you do so in the faith that God Himself joins you together and that He will also supply the grace needed to keep you together. The marriage covenant is an audacious promise. And although we often make it in the naivety of romance and impulse, we still recognize it as a holy and God-breathed commitment.

The marriage commitment is a strong indicator of greatness because it is one that tests faithfulness over long years and varied circumstances. It is called upon to weather storms of conflict and emotional pain. It must endure the cooling of passions, the stresses of family life, and the surfacing of unaligned values and aspirations. To be successful, the husband and wife must make their relationship a consistent priority over an ever-changing landscape of responsibilities and hopes and disruptions and temptations. They are committed to one another over jobs, differences of opinion, extended family, and deeply held personal dreams. This is a commitment that will be tested because many times the emotions and attractions that birthed the sacred promise will seem to disappear in the face of the onslaughts of temptation, boredom, anxiety, and other more glamorous or exciting pursuits. Through all of this and more, the Kingdom-minded husband and wife stay true to one another and to the promise made to their Creator and Lord. They are faithful. And, in that faithfulness, they reflect the goodness of God and the character of our Father.

Of course, this is not meant to imply that marriage is only a dry struggle and drudgery. Not in the least! On the contrary, a marriage built on the kind of faithfulness that would endure any hardship is inevitably one filled with sweetness and beauty and romance and life. Dry seasons will certainly come — and they will as certainly go. Whenever faithfulness is seriously put to the test and proves to be true, an infusion of grace, affection, and strength is poured into the marriage relationship. Passions are rekindled and old dreams are re-engaged. Maturity and grace settle in as youth and idealism dissipate.

Even so, it seems that God's people found this insistence on faithfulness in marriage a standard too high to be true: "Moses permitted you to divorce your wives because your hearts were hard. But it was not this way from the beginning" (Matthew 19:8). Even Jesus' disciples were shocked by the force of His stance, exclaiming, "If this is the situation between a husband and wife, it is better not to marry" (Matthew 19:10).

As in the days of Moses and the days of Jesus, many today, even among His followers, find the standard too high. The faithfulness required is considered impossible. Or, at least, very much undesirable. Unwavering fealty to such a commitment could ruin a life! It could hinder an on-fire follower of Jesus from the great deeds he is meant to accomplish. It could bring years of unfulfillment or regret. The death of Kingdom dreams. The squandering of spiritual gifts. And worst of all (dare I mention it?), it could mean the loss of personal fulfillment romantically, sexually, vocationally, and in every way imaginable. And this is precisely where true greatness is tested in the lonely fires of anonymity and sacrifice. Will you be faithful to your commitment? Will you keep the sacred promise? Will you allow God to determine in what way greatness will be demonstrated in your life? Will you accept the apparently lesser path of prioritizing your marriage over other more public calls to so-called greatness and influence? Are you faithful? This is the burning question. Not are you gifted. Not are you called. Not are you zealous. Not are you knowledgeable or skilled or well-placed or fearless. Are you faithful? Will you be true to Jesus no matter what comes?

Marital fidelity tests one's self-control and proves what one truly values. It tests self-control by insisting on absolute sexual and emotional commitment to one person, without ever entertaining the thought or possibility of another. It means saying "no" to the temptation to be faithless, not most of the time, but absolutely every time. It also means demonstrating the preeminence of the marriage partner by ordering one's life around that commitment. A husband does not allow himself to even be in a position in which his self-control may fail. A wife does not begin to entertain thoughts of a more romantic or ideal mate. Fidelity means to be pure in the face of any temptation that may come. Such faithfulness to a spouse is a key indicator that reveals a person's true character. Infidelity in marriage is akin to idolatry or unfaithfulness to God.

Jesus also reveals another path to Kingdom greatness for those who are not married. When the apostles conclude that it is best not to marry at all because of the high standard God has for that commitment, Jesus responds positively:

> There are eunuchs who were born that way, and there are eunuchs who have been made eunuchs by others—and there are those who choose to live like eunuchs for the sake of the kingdom of heaven. The one who can accept this should accept it. — Matthew 19:12

Singleness, too — within the confines of sexual abstinence — is an honored way of life in the Kingdom and one that can also produce Jesus-style leaders. Some people are single not by their own choice. For others, it is a conscious decision that comes out of a desire to be fully consecrated to Jesus and set aside for His work. Obviously, this was the path of Jesus Himself, as well as the Apostle Paul and many others. Their lack of marital commitment only served to deepen their commitment to God and to His mission in the world. In fact, their choice to live a single life is a reflection of their sole focus on the Lord and desire to be wholly given over to Him. Whether you are single by choice or by any undesired or un-chosen reality in your own life, there is still a way to be great in the Kingdom and to lead and serve others in faithfulness and zeal.

Whatever path Jesus leads you on, you can be great in His Kingdom. However, you cannot be great apart from a faithfulness that supersedes all selfish ambition and need for personal fulfillment. You are called to sexual purity, to relational loyalty, and to a life of radical commitments that are fulfilled in sacrificial faithfulness.

Children Again
(Matthew 19:13-15)

The kingdom of heaven belongs to such as these. — Matthew 19:14

It was only one chapter ago that Jesus had said, "Whoever welcomes one such child in my name welcomes me" (Matthew 18:5). Now an opportunity arises that would allow the disciples to put Jesus' words into action. Children are brought to Jesus to receive a blessing. And the disciples, having heard Jesus' exhortation about welcoming children, utterly fail to do so. Sadly, they do the opposite. They go so far as to rebuke those who bring the children. Jesus again uses the opportunity to allow the children to teach a lesson about the Kingdom: *"The kingdom of heaven belongs to such as these."* (19:14).

Like the original twelve, we who follow Jesus today may have missed the point the first time around, and so Jesus gives us another chance. Welcome the children. Make way for the lowly. Honor the weak. Do not become too impressed with your own importance. Do not harbor self-important thoughts or ambitions at all. Do you want to belong in the Kingdom? Divert your eyes from the great and choose to see the small. Open your arms wide to them.

Who are you seeking out? To whom do you offer the gift of your time? Who captures your attention? In your rush to be great, are you bypassing, in a headlong pursuit of the influential and the impressive, those whom Jesus values? "Let them come," Jesus insists. Those who become like children are the greatest. Children themselves will inherit the Kingdom.

There have been many times when I was absorbed in my "very significant" work, feeling all the weight and stress and importance of it, only to be interrupted by one of my children. They would approach, reminding me of a commitment I had made to them — maybe to play a game, watch a movie, or go to the park. Inevitably a thousand excuses would force their way into my consciousness and I would be close to uttering them, or sometimes actually in the midst of uttering them, when I'd look again at the child before me. I would reluctantly put my things down and join them in the "unimportant, insignificant, meaningless" activity. And in so doing they would once again rescue me from my self-importance and misguided priorities. As I entered into their world — the small, unimpressive world of a child — I would remember who I am and whose I am, and the Father would give me peace. As I welcomed my own child, I would recall that I myself am welcomed into the presence and the heart of my Father in Heaven. Entering into what is small I would become better. And I would again be living and experiencing the beautiful and utterly right Kingdom of God.

2 - COST AND REWARD
(Matthew 19:16-30)

And everyone who has left houses or brothers or sisters or father or mother or wife or children or fields for my sake will receive a hundred times as much and will inherit eternal life. — Matthew 19:29

The Rich Ruler
(Matthew 19:16-26)

Jesus answered, "If you want to be perfect, go, sell your possessions and give to the poor, and you will have treasure in heaven. Then come, follow me." — Matthew 19:21

As Jesus finishes praying for the children, a rich man approaches Him and asks what he must do to gain eternal life. It is interesting, as a by-the-way, to note this contrast: apparently nobody attempted to stop him from coming to Jesus. Unlike the insignificant children, everyone knows that the rich are "important" and worth Jesus' time. Anyway, you know how it turns out. Jesus tells him to follow the commands. The man assures the Lord that he does so. Then Jesus shocks him (not to mention his disciples) by telling him that he must sell his possessions, give to the poor, and come follow. The man cannot bring himself to do it. It is just too much. Everything?

And so we come, very early in our study, to the crux of the matter. What does it mean to be great? What does it mean to even follow Jesus? It means that He is Master. He is over all. He is your boss. But He is so much more than that. He demands absolute allegiance and obedience, and He must be Lord of all of your life. Whatever sits enthroned in your heart must be overthrown. Whether that be riches or relationships or power or your own righteousness or pleasure or any other thing, Jesus will find it out and He will demand it be abolished forever; thrown down never to rise again. Jesus is Lord.

This all may seem rather extreme, and it is meant to. Kingdom greatness is not a tame pursuit. But there is another element that we also must recognize to truly follow Him. Jesus demands everything and He has full authority over your life. True. But you must also realize that He is worth it. It is His right, not only because He is God and all-powerful, but because He is utterly good and He loves you like nobody else ever will or even could. The truth is that the rich man was not simply defiant or greedy; he was blind. He refused Jesus' offer not because it was too harsh but because he failed to see the One asking it of him. This young seeker did not recognize the glory of Jesus. He missed the wonder of Who was speaking to him. He saw his riches clearly, and he even had a decent grasp of the commandments. But Jesus Himself eluded him, though He stood there in full daylight. He saw the man but he missed the essence of Who He was. In another place, Jesus had described the Kingdom like this:

> The kingdom of heaven is like treasure hidden in a field. When a man found it, he hid it again, and then in his joy went and sold all he had and bought that field.
> — Matthew 13:44

"In his joy."

The man in this story, unlike the rich youth standing before Jesus, perceived the truth. He saw the value of the Kingdom and joyfully sold all he had to inherit it. The emphasis is not so much on the cost as on the worth. It is not on what is lost but on what is gained. How can it be otherwise when the treasure to be won is Jesus Himself?

When we think about this encounter that Jesus had with the rich man, we understandably stagger at the weight of Jesus' response. But in focusing on the massive requirements laid down, we often miss the promise that is tucked into this demand. Jesus says, "Go, sell your possessions and give to the poor, *and you will have treasure in heaven*" (emphasis added). To our over-accustomed mind, this little nugget is often ignored. But consider it! Jesus promises treasure in heaven! The implications are breathtaking. The man is being called upon to lay down his earthly treasure, but there will be a heavenly treasure waiting for him. Clearly, the heavenly one is better than the earthly one. The heavenly one will be without toil, without sadness, and without greed or anxiety of any kind. It will be utterly pure and good and beautiful. It will be eternal. The earthly one that this man so valued will be gone one day. It will decay. But the heavenly one will last forever and will never diminish. Yes, Jesus makes a big demand. But He offers something in return that is far more glorious.

Several decades ago, I was on a short-term mission trip in the nation of Uganda. As a young man just learning what it meant to know and follow Jesus, I had a zeal to do great things for Him. My heart had been captured. But not fully. One day I had a thought that came in the form of a question: "Would you be willing to be lonely for My sake?" I was troubled by this and tried to ignore it, but it persisted. I could not get the idea out of my head. Was God asking this of me? So I began to ponder it. Would I really be willing? A theme of my life so far had been the longing for true friendship, and this question hit a tender place. I continued trying to shake it without facing it but to no avail. I felt compelled to answer. After a day or two I finally gave a simple "*Yes.*"

To my chagrin, this was not followed by a "Congratulations, you passed the test," but by another question.

"Would you be willing to not get married for My sake?" Again I spent a day or two dodging and agonizing before answering in the affirmative. Then, another question.

"Would you be willing to serve Me in an isolated place, where nobody would ever know what you do for Me?" More deep thinking. More discomfort and discouragement, but eventually a weak, "*Yes.*"

The questions continued, and now I do not even remember them all. Finally after more than a week of this, another came that provoked me more than all the others, "Would you be willing to go to some place dangerous for My sake? To give your life for Me?"

By this time I was utterly convinced that these questions were coming from God Himself, and it did not feel like He was joking. Still, I could barely wrap my mind around the implications, and I was becoming deeply troubled. There was a war being waged within my soul, and I could not predict what would happen if the victory went one way or the other. I knew I was facing a moment of great significance for my life, and I strove to fix my eyes on Jesus rather than the cost. Finally, in near exasperation, but utter sincerity, I responded, *"My answer is 'Yes.' To every question, it is 'Yes.' Whatever You would ask of me, my answer is 'Yes.' I just want to be Yours and to follow You always."*

And with that, I sensed that this particular time of questioning was over. I felt His delight and my heart soared into joy and relief. My immediate response was to volunteer to be a missionary, telling God I would not only be willing to serve Him in the nations but that I was asking for the privilege of doing so. I felt at that very moment that my offer was accepted, and from that night I set my gaze on becoming a missionary to Uganda.

As the years and the decades have rolled by, I regret that I have not always been true to my commitments made during those wonderful and awful days of surrender. But all in all, this encounter has set the tone and the trajectory of my life. I cannot escape the fact that I have already said "Yes" to questions that even now perhaps have yet to be asked. I have given Him a blank check and a limitless book full of blank checks, all with my signature at the bottom, waiting for Him to write in the details above. Regarding some of the questions I faced, He has given back the very thing I surrendered. I have a wonderful wife and five amazing children. This is a wonder to me. He is so good! With others, my "Yes" has been tested, and with other questions perhaps the trials are yet ahead of me. As I contemplate that, I can only pray for the grace and the true vision to be faithful to the word I have given to my Creator, my Savior, my Lord.

What about you? With what cost is Jesus confronting you today?

> Suppose one of you wants to build a tower. Won't you first sit down and estimate the cost to see if you have enough money to complete it? For if you lay the foundation and are not able to finish it, everyone who sees it will ridicule you, saying, "This person began to build and wasn't able to finish." — Luke 14:28-30

Whatever it is, He knows the thing that you tend to hold tightly. He knows where the competition lies for the affections of Your heart, and He will not let it be. There can be no rival.

Twelve Thrones
(Matthew 19:27-30)

Jesus said to them, "Truly I tell you, at the renewal of all things, when the Son of Man sits on his glorious throne, you who have followed me will also sit on twelve thrones, judging the twelve tribes of Israel. And everyone who has left houses or brothers or sisters or father or mother or wife or children or fields for my sake will receive a hundred times as much and will inherit eternal life. But many who are first will be last, and many who are last will be first." — Matthew 19:28-30

A rich man has just sadly turned away from Jesus. The price demanded to follow this itinerant teacher is too high. In the aftermath of the tragic encounter, Jesus utterly perplexes His followers by making a blanket statement about the practical impossibility of the rich entering the Kingdom of God. Unable to let such an astonishing claim go unchallenged, the disciples ask who then could enter the Kingdom. Jesus assures them that with God all things are possible.

Peter, heartened by this encouragement, offers his credentials: he has left everything to follow Jesus. What will he and the other disciples receive in exchange for such sacrifice?

Jesus promises them each a throne.

He does not even hesitate. Nor does He elaborate. He just leaves it sitting there. Twelve thrones for the twelve apostles. And then, since He is on the subject, Jesus dramatically broadens the recipients of His rewards to include any who would leave all for Him. This presumably could include you and me, if we meet the conditions (which, to be honest, are pretty steep). These will receive a hundred times as much as they've surrendered, with eternal life thrown into the bargain. Lofty promises to be sure. For now, though, let us return to those twelve thrones.

Jesus has promised tremendous authority and power to these men. They will judge the twelve tribes of Israel. They will sit on cosmic thrones, ruling under and along with the King of Everything.

Here is an interesting addition to our study of Kingdom leadership: Jesus shares His authority. He gives positions of leadership to others; others who are of course very inferior to Himself. He raises common people to extraordinary heights of prestige, power. and authority. These men — these unimpressive, often faithless, sometimes outright dense students — will sit on heavenly thrones.

Jesus shares His authority. At the risk of indulging in unwarranted speculation, consider for a moment why He does so. It is rather unlikely that Jesus shares His authority because the responsibility is too much for Him to carry and He needs help. The burden of leadership is not too heavy a weight for God to bear. If not out of necessity, then, it must be out of desire. God shares authority because He wants to. Could it be that our King simply wants to include others, people like you and me, in the leadership of His creation? Looking back at the Garden of Eden, God commissioned mankind to steward this new world, to rule it on His behalf:

> God blessed them and said to them, "Be fruitful and increase in number; fill the earth and subdue it. Rule over the fish in the sea and the birds in the sky and over every living creature that moves on the ground." — Genesis 1:28

Jesus shares His authority, I suspect, not for expediency but for relationship. The invitation to lead is not primarily an invitation to prestige or power or to help Him get things done, but it is an invitation to know Jesus more deeply. The ultimate goal and reward for leading, when done right, is closeness with Jesus. Is it possible that His gain in sharing authority with you is not all the wonderful things you will accomplish in His Name, but that you will know Him more?

Jesus shares authority to lead and govern His people, and He does this for the sake of relationship. With whom does He share this authority?

It seems clear that He shares it with those He chooses. We are never given a list of the qualities that induced Jesus to choose the twelve. We are simply told that, after a night of prayer, Jesus called them to Himself and appointed them to be apostles (see Luke 6:12-16 and Mark 3:13-19). After spending a full night in communion with the Father, Jesus knew who He was to choose. This choice had unfathomable implications. On that fateful morning on the side of the mountain, the chosen twelve certainly had no idea they were being selected as under-sovereigns in the Kingdom of God. But they were. The Father chose them out of His perfect knowledge and wisdom. No other explanation is offered. Jesus prayed and then He appointed.

God chooses leaders.

He chooses people for specific roles and tasks. This means, logically, that He does not choose others for those roles and tasks. There are twelve thrones for the twelve apostles. A specific and limited number. This is strangely comforting. The Father may place you in a position of leadership or He may choose to appoint someone else instead. You are simply expected to respond when your name is called and to be faithful in the role assigned to you. In the words of Oswald Sanders, "Spiritual leadership is not a calling we choose to pursue; it is a calling we choose to answer."[3]

Another thing we notice about those with whom Jesus chooses to share His authority is that they "have left everything to follow [Jesus]" (Matt 19:27). Jesus shares His authority with those who demonstrate a willingness to turn their backs on all that is not Jesus, including the things most precious to them. I think it is safe to state a principle here. Jesus gives authority to those who follow Him without condition and who hold nothing back from Him. God demands everything from His leaders (as indeed He does of all His followers). Fortunately for us, He works with us in a process of ever-increasing surrender, filling our failures with His grace. He is so good! But let us not miss the point all the same: the standard is absolute surrender and complete obedience.

Jesus' list of what may be left behind to follow Him is formidable. "Houses or brothers or sisters or father or mother or wife or children or fields..." Do you want to be one of Jesus' leaders? Do you want to be His follower? His demands are not to be taken lightly. Nothing can be held back. Nothing is more sacred than following Him and doing His work. There is no part-time or part-way position in the Kingdom. You have to be all in. This is not something you can do on the side. Maybe you run a business, look after your family, engage in community service, have fun with your friends, and do some Kingdom work when you can fit it in. No.

Of course, it is not that you cannot or should not work or have a family or be involved in your community or enjoy your friends. It is not even a matter of priorities per se. Jesus is not merely the highest on a list of priorities. He is everything. This means that you need to consider what it means for Jesus to be the center of your work and your family and all of it. You do those things as part of your Kingdom work, which means you do them in Kingdom ways and with Kingdom priorities. Your business is no

---

[3] J. Oswald Sanders, <u>Spiritual Leadership</u> (Moody Publishers, Chicago, 2007), 171.

longer primarily about making money. It is about making disciples. Your family and friends are not primarily for your enjoyment or fulfillment. They are people you are sent to influence for the Kingdom. Community service is not merely about caring for the marginalized. It is about leading people to Jesus.

And sometimes, as Jesus makes clear, following Him does mean outright leaving other things. He is not calling you to divorce your wife or abandon your children, but He is insisting that God is supreme. You and they will have to make sacrifices for the mission of Jesus. Maybe you will be called to leave your job or your home and journey into an uncertain future as you follow Jesus. Floyd McClung issues this challenge:

> By dying to our rights, we find life. That means dying to our opinions, dying to the right to be understood, the right to be represented, the right to be loved, the right to be treated justly, and all of our other rights. Very few leaders understand this truth. They strive to find their role, their ministry, how they fit on the team, and so on. It is sad to watch men and women strive to keep what they have to give up anyway if they are to be part of God's mission.[4]

The cost is high indeed. But we cannot forget that Jesus made some extraordinary promises to go along with these intense demands. Those who leave everything to follow Him "will receive a hundred times as much and will inherit eternal life" (Matthew 19:29b). Whatever it is that you give, God promises to return in greater abundance. God rewards those who follow Him.

Twelve thrones! A hundred-fold return! Eternal life! It cannot be overstated or denied that the expectations are high. But the rewards! Impossible as it would seem, they actually make the cost appear small. He is very generous with us. He gives infinitely more than we are even capable of offering.

Are you ready for Him to call your name? How will you respond?

---

4 Floyd McClung, *You See Bones, I See An Army* (YWAM Publishing, Seattle, 2008), Kindle loc 1504.

First Will be Last
(Matthew 19:30)

But many who are first will be last, and many who are last will be first. — Matthew 19:30

Jesus continues training the twelve in issues of power, authority, and leadership with a bit of foreshadowing. In this somewhat cryptic phrase, He sounds the second note of discord with the expectations of the day. The first was that it is hard (impossible for all practical purposes) for the rich to enter the Kingdom. Conventional wisdom would have put them among the first in line. And now Jesus says simply that "many who are first will be last, and many who are last will be first." He is going to make this point increasingly clearly and controversially. But for now, just know that things with Him and His rule are... *different*. His ways are not what we would expect. His teachings are not like those of anyone else. Jane Overstreet says it this way:

The values of the kingdom of God are countercultural to every earthly culture. God's values go against our human nature.[5]

Remember that Jesus was telling His disciples about leaving everything to follow Him and the great rewards that would come to those who did so. He summarizes this teaching with the statement we are now considering: "But many who are first will be last, and many who are last will be first." People who tend to be first are not likely the ones to turn their back on everything for the risky proposition of following Jesus. They are the ones for whom life is pretty good. They tend to be satisfied. And it is difficult indeed to induce a satisfied person to take great risks. The last, on the other hand, are ready for something different. They are discontented. They feel they have little to lose.

I suspect that Jesus is leading His disciples to embrace a certain skepticism with satisfaction. Yes, He does want us to be content, but only in Him. The more our contentment is based on things other than Jesus (possessions or security or friends or fulfilling work or pleasure or whatever you can think of), the more of a "first" we will consider ourselves to be, and the less likely to lay it all down to follow Him. And, of course, if we do not lay it all down to

---

[5] Jane Overstreet, *Unleader* (Biblica, Colorado Springs, 2011), pg 3.

follow Him, we are not worthy of Him and cannot truly know Him. We certainly cannot be useful in the supreme work of His mission. So, to be in a position to be chosen by God for His service, we must cultivate a certain dissatisfaction with the world and all it offers. You may have been chosen by people to be a pastor, bishop, or some other kind of leader, but have you truly been chosen by God? Be ready to lose it all in a moment to follow the call of the Master.

"Many who are first." Who are the firsts? Clearly, they include the rich and the advantaged. We could probably extend this to the educated. The ones voted most likely to succeed. The impressive, the talented, and the connected. Perhaps even the good. The ones we expect to lead. The wise, those who always end up on top, the unusually smart, the freakishly athletic, the privileged and proud, and the blessed and beautiful. The first.

These will be last. That is frankly shocking. We know how the world works. The "firsts" end up *first*.

At this point, it might be helpful to offer some clarification. Jesus does say that "*many* who are first will be last." Not all, but many. So this is not an immutable, heavenly law. He is making a point that is generally true, though not in every case. It is true, not because the intelligent, the wealthy, and the gifted are bad people or that their advantages are automatic grounds for dismissing them. I think that is apparent. Instead, He is saying that the very advantages the "firsts" enjoy usually cause them to not grasp the true nature of the depth of their need and spiritual poverty. Remember, "It is easier for a camel to go through the eye of a needle than for someone who is rich to enter the kingdom of God" (Matthew 19:24). However, "With man this is impossible, but with God all things are possible" (Matthew 19:26).

It is also helpful to understand that, in Jesus' time and culture, riches and worldly success were seen as a sign of divine approval and personal holiness. The opposite was also true. Poverty and misfortune were often absolute signs of God's displeasure. Perhaps it is not so different today. Jesus is forcefully refuting this deeply ingrained way of thinking

Jesus is establishing a new order. In His domain things will be different. You will not make it to the top in the old way, according to the old rules of engagement. You will not have authority or significant influence over others for the same reasons you are used to. If you seek success or greatness according to the world's ways, you will end up last. In fighting to have it all, you will lose everything. Do not put your hope in being a "first" (according to cultural views of what that is). Do not rejoice in the glow of worldly success. This is a warning from the heart of Jesus.

"The last will be first." Who are the lasts? Obviously, they are the opposite of the firsts. They are the poor, the disadvantaged, and the ignorant; the most likely to fail, the overlooked, the awkward, and the forgotten. They are the questionable and the ones of whom we have low expectations; the not-clever ones, the people who find a way to end up at the bottom, the average, the clumsy, the marginalized, the insecure, the unfortunate, and the common. The last.

God is going to use these. We are going to find out that they are first on His list, no matter how unqualified and underwhelming they seem to us. What if you made it your ambition to be a "last" instead of a "first?" What if God called you to embrace your "lastness" so that He could be the One to make you a true first? As you consider that, allow me a spoiler alert: Jesus Himself becomes the ultimate "last" and ends up the absolute first.

This is a ticklish point, so I will again offer some clarification. Am I claiming that Jesus is calling us to mediocrity, laziness, and underachieving? Obviously not. But again, Jesus is turning the accepted order of things on its head. Make no mistake: This idea of the last being first is a radical, controversial teaching. Being unsuccessful in the honest and worthy pursuits that come with living in the world (such as jobs and competitions and wealth and education) is not a sign of failure in the things that God cares about. A lack of intelligence or lack of money or lack of education does not mean that a person is unspiritual or bad or less than others. In fact — and bear with me here — Jesus is saying that it is more likely that these people are approved by God and chosen by God than the rich and powerful. Again, this is not a universal law, but a general truth.

Am I suggesting that all who are considered "lasts" in the world will automatically be "firsts" in the Kingdom? Again, clearly not. "Lasts" must still lay down whatever advantages they do have, however insignificant those advantages seem to be. Jesus is saying, though, that it is far more likely for a "last" to do this than a "first."

The great virtue of the Kingdom is dependence. It is humility. It is acknowledging our need for God. The simple fact is that the "lasts" find it easier to recognize their own lack and to call out to God for help than the "firsts."

Again, this call to pursue or value our lastness is not a call to intentionally do poorly in life. It is not better for you to fail out of school than to do as well as you can. Rather, it is a call to value what Jesus does and to acknowledge that these values are very different from what your culture values. It is also a call to truly distrust worldly ways of viewing people and to not rely on those things that the world uses as proof of worth. Finally, it is a call to recognize your total dependence on God and to not count on yourself for true greatness and life.

For example, imagine two people wandering into your Sunday morning church gathering. One is well-dressed, articulate, and confident. The other is shabbily dressed, difficult to have a conversation with, and clearly uncomfortable. Do you give more attention to the impressive one or the other one? Which of these would you tend to think would be a more beneficial member of your congregation?

This all leads me to two observations.

First, we can see that leadership in God's Kingdom is certainly not something to boast about. It is more humiliating than flattering. Whatever the personal qualities that drive God's choices may be, they are certainly different than the ones I am used to respecting and cultivating. If I discover that God has chosen me for some kind of influence, that is truly nothing to be proud of. Hudson Taylor was once introduced to a congregation as "our illustrious guest." The great missionary's response is noteworthy. He stepped to the podium where he stood silently a moment before beginning, "Dear friends, I am the little servant of an illustrious Master."[6] It is said that Francis of Assisi was once asked the simple question, "Why you?" His unexpected answer was, "He chose me because He could find none more worthless."[7] In the words of the songwriter Don Francisco:

> If the Lord starts using you,
> don't you pay it any mind
> He could have used the dog next door
> if He'd been so inclined[8]

---

[6] Howard Taylor and Mrs Howard Taylor, Hudson Taylor and the China Inland Mission, pg 265

[7] Francis of Assisi, quoted in J. Oswald Sanders, Spiritual Leadership (Moody Publishers, Chicago, 2007), pg 31

[8] "The Steeple Song" by Don Francisco

Oh! That we all might have such awareness! I imagine that Jesus looks with great sadness on God's people strutting around like peacocks, doing our utmost to draw people's attention to our beautiful plumage, rejoicing in feathers of position or money or honor we have won. I have looked in the mirror and seen the same of myself. Dear Lord, forgive us!

Secondly, God can use me! He can use me, not because of my worldly accolades, but in spite of them. This really is great news. In my truest moments, I am painfully aware that I tend to strive to be in the "first" class of people. I like to position myself there. To my shame, I place myself as a "first" because of my education, my relative wealth (as an American living in Uganda), and my experience. I have tendencies to manipulate perceptions and maneuver my way into being noticed. I minimize my weaknesses, spin my failures, conceal my embarrassments, and exaggerate my successes and strengths. And I do all of this so that I might be "first." But God makes all such shenanigans worthless and laughable. He is disturbingly unimpressed. But He loves the "lasts." When I come to terms with the reality of my mediocrity, I am in a great place to be chosen by God.

Today, young men and women fill our seminary and Bible school classrooms, full of hopes and dreams for future usefulness in God's work. Unfortunately for many, this means positioning themselves to climb the ecclesiastical ladder. They will search out the position that promises to look good on their resume so that they can attain higher and higher levels of position and leadership. They are being sucked into a system that is the antithesis of the simple yet forceful teachings of Jesus: "But many who are first will be last, and many who are last will be first."

I have a clear memory of a bright morning on a lonely hillside of a small African town. A few months earlier, I had entered into a work full of faith and passion, and no small degree of idealism and pride. I was gathering leaders to equip and train for the great harvest fields of a waiting continent. At first, all went well. Many people came to the training sessions, and their enthusiasm and zeal were inspiring. But on this day, I gathered with barely a handful. And undoubtedly a handful of "lasts." They were poor and uneducated, coming from small rural churches rather than the influential town ones. Shabbily dressed and of unimpressive appearance, they were the epitome of the unimportant. They were the few not called away for more significant duties; the left-over and passed over. As we futilely waited for others to join us, one of those present timidly suggested we begin with praise, and he began to sing out. A woman moved over to beat the African drum. The only remaining person stood to join in. Together we sang a simple chorus or two.

In that moment of prideful discouragement, I believe the Lord spoke to my heart. He at once revealed the arrogance of my disdain and the hope of His calling. He assured me that His praises would indeed ring throughout this land and that He would use such as these to do His great work. He would again choose the small and the weak — the "lasts" — to accomplish great things. My heart soared with hope and gratitude. In that moment I came to recognize that it was not the three students who were on track to be ultimate "lasts," but that their teacher, in his arrogance, qualified above all. In pride, I had thought of myself as a "first," thus making myself one of the truly "lasts." And what glorious humiliation! This revelation itself was enough to check my downward spiral and help me to begin being small and weak enough for the King's work.

3 - THE LAST WILL BE FIRST
(Matthew 20:1-19)

So the last will be first, and the first will be last. — Matthew 20:16

Made Equal
(Matthew 20:1-16)

You have made them equal to us who have borne the burden of the work and the heat of the day — Matthew 20:12

Elaborating on the idea of the first being last and the last first, Jesus tells a story. The owner of a vineyard goes out early in the morning to hire day laborers. He gathers a crew, agrees on the usual wage, and sets them to work. A little later he recruits more workers and does the same a couple more times after intervals of a few hours each time. Finally at 5:00 in the afternoon, with only one more hour left to work, he returns to the place where men congregate to be chosen. He seems surprised to find some still waiting, claiming that nobody has been willing to hire them all day. The vineyard owner sends them into his vineyard for the day's final hour. And this is where the story becomes odd.

The landowner pays the same amount of money to all the workers, even the ones who worked for just that last hour. True, it is the amount that was originally agreed upon with the first work crew, but the ones who were chosen first feel cheated nonetheless. They naturally assumed that they would receive more than the others because they had worked more. But not so. Even those sluggards who worked only one hour received the same!

> "These who were hired last worked only one hour," they said, "and you have made them equal to us who have borne the burden of the work and the heat of the day." (Matthew 20:12).

You can hear the accusation in their words. "You have made them equal to us!" The landowner chastises them for being envious because he is generous. And then Jesus caps it off by restating what He had said just a few moments before, "So the last will be first, and the first will be last." (20:16).

After a discouraging start, it had been a good day for those half-day workers, and even for the 3:00 ones. But for the 5:00 workers? What a day! They labored for one short hour and yet were paid for a full day. This is the wonder and beauty of grace. People receive blessings that they do not deserve and did not earn. If you were among the 5:00 crew that day, you went home full of gratitude and joy. Can you imagine it? After milling around all day discouraged and sullen, perhaps embarrassed and certainly anxious, this happens. The landowner sees you. He shows kindness to you. You are paid a wage, yet you both know it is in truth a gift in a rather obvious disguise.

But what if you were an all-day worker? You were chosen at dawn, perhaps because you are known to be reliable and hardworking. You are gifted and wanted. You are one of the "firsts." Many of you reading these words are all-day kind of people. You are used to being chosen. How do you respond to this story? It is not fair. You deserve to receive more than the others. You are being cheated and disrespected; your work under-appreciated. "You have made them equal to us!" Such is the scandal of grace.

With this unusual story, could Jesus be setting his unsuspecting followers up for a big lesson about leadership? Considering what follows, I tend to think so. Jesus is about to lay on His apostles — the future occupants of those twelve glorious thrones — some heavy and highly unusual principles regarding what it means to lead in His Kingdom. But before getting to that, He prepares them with this story.

You who are confident in the good you have done must live with the generosity of the Master to others who are less deserving. You have to come to terms with the truth that in His eyes your worth is the same. Your value to the Master is, in fact, no more than anyone else's. And that leads to a disturbing but critical point: The Master does not assign value based on the work done. Even though the whole world judges things in this way, He is different. Everyone knows that the value of a laborer is based on the quality and quantity of his work. But not with this Master. Not with Jesus. The value of each worker that day was derived not based on the service rendered, but from the fact that they were chosen by the landowner.

So what does all this mean, and what does it have to do with leadership?

Grace is indeed a beautiful scandal. It is beautiful when we receive it, but scandalous when applied to others. It is beautiful when we are rewarded with more than we deserve, but scandalous when others receive what we have rightfully earned and they have not. As leaders in God's Kingdom, we are required to receive grace. We are not allowed to relate on the basis of merit. And in God's beautiful Kingdom, we are also required to extend grace to others and to celebrate the grace they receive from the Father.

This leads me to suggest that you, too, need to live out of the Master's values rather than the world's. Do not exult in being a so-called "first." Do not expect greater benefits in the Kingdom because you are capable of greater accomplishments. Being a "first" does not increase your value, so stop trying to do just that (increase your value) through the works that you do in His vineyard. In fact, it may be prudent for you to acknowledge and even rejoice in your "lastness" (that is, your weakness, your need) than to boast in your "firstness," because it is the "lasts" who tend to recognize God's grace in their lives. God is seeking people who thankfully and humbly receive His grace. I like to think of myself as one who would have been on that truck at 5:00 a.m. with the other prized workers. The truth is that I am easily impressed with my own qualifications. However, the rub is that the more impressed I am with myself, the more frustrated I am at God's grace to others. And besides that, the more impressed I am with myself, the more difficult it is to receive God's grace at all.

Your value is not based on your performance. You have to get this from the start, before considering anything else about leadership of Kingdom work. Your value is not based on how others perceive you. It is not based on the usual list of "firsts" accolades. Some days you will be an all-day kind of servant. On other days you will be a 5:00 p.m. kind of one. Probably most days you are going to be somewhere in the middle. Your value to the Father remains the same. Your acceptance is the same. You are loved the same.

> Whatever you become in the eyes of men — even a person of great authority, fame, or title — you will never become more or less than a child in the arms of God.[9]

This is essential to grasp and to receive before moving on to the more challenging lessons Jesus is about to teach. Truly, this is an absolutely necessary foundation for all that will follow. If you try to go ahead with Jesus' more stringent teachings and do not have this firmly in place in your soul, you will not make it. Somewhere along the way, your leadership will collapse, and you will have to begin again right here. Your value is not based on your performance.

Receiving God's love is the only true foundation for Christian leadership.

> We must have the security of resting in God's love in order to lead successfully from God's perspective. It is not optional.[10]

This is no easy task. Brennan Manning claims that "the most difficult thing in mature believing is to accept that I am an object of God's delight."[11] I have found this to be true in my own experience. And yet it is essential for us to accept this great truth.

Do not compare yourself with other people. You are a leader because you were chosen, but you will not always know why you were chosen — or not chosen. Furthermore, you may be a leader today but not tomorrow. In different seasons of life, you may find yourself sometimes leading big and glorious works, and other times serving in apparently small and insignificant ministries. Sometimes you will be sure that you would have been a better candidate than the other guy. Other times you find yourself leading people who are extremely talented and experienced and you begin to doubt the wisdom of your appointment. We all have to learn to trust that God chooses

---

[9] Floyd McClung, *The Father Heart of God* (Harvest House Publishers, Eugene, OR, 1985), *Kindle loc 160.*

[10] Jane Overstreet, *Unleader* (Biblica, Colorado Springs, 2011), pg 13.

[11] Brennan Manning, *The Signature of Jesus* (Multnomah Books, New York, 1996), pg 184.

and that His choices are good and right. You and I were not chosen for those twelve thrones, but we have been given other work, other authority. This is a powerful stress reliever. We can be content with the Father's choices. We do not have to strive to prove that we are better than others. We do not have to convince power brokers that we are legitimate "firsts." We can rest in the good wisdom of our King.

"Call the workers and pay them their wages, beginning with the last ones hired and going on to the first." (20:8)

"So the last will be first, and the first will be last." (20:16).

Jesus is intentionally putting the first workers last, even though they are correct in their claim that they have "borne the burden of the work and the heat of the day." It is a striking point. Jesus does not honor the ones who work more or harder or better than the others. Shockingly, the landowner makes them wait to receive their pay until after He has settled with the less productive workers. You who think you have a lot to offer Jesus and His Kingdom need to know that your contribution does not increase your value and it does not make you more important than others. And those of you who seemingly have less to offer need to know that, in His generosity and kindness, Jesus values you all the same.

Only Jesus is worthy of glory. No matter what honors we receive, all glory comes from Him and will be reflected back to Him. Indeed, "The one thing that transcends all others, the focus we are to have above everything else, is the glory of God. That's all that matters."[12] The truth is that none of us have anything other than what we have received from Jesus. This means that if one person is the leader of a great movement and another an unknown, simple laborer, in the eyes of God they are not very different. The leader receives esteem from men far more than the laborer. But God will one day reverse this, and the laborer will receive in the end the same as the leader. Jesus will ensure that the last become first.

How are you doing at receiving the scandal of grace these days? How aware are you of your need? How are you doing at extending this grace to others? How do you feel when others receive undeservedly what you have rightfully earned?

----

12 Floyd McClung, *You See Bones, I See An Army* (YWAM Publishing, Seattle, 2008), Kindle loc 2239.

One Denarius for Everyone
(Matthew 20:1-16)

Are you envious because I am generous? — Matthew 20:15b

I made the point before that your value is not based on your performance. Jesus makes this abundantly clear in the story He told. But it still refuses to sit right, doesn't it? It is ingrained in us too deeply that our value comes from our status, our position, our performance, our possessions, our influence. Perhaps from our education, job title, or list of responsibilities. We are valuable because of what we have to offer. We are valuable to the degree that we have something significant to bring to the table. But this is not true. Remember, Jesus said, "The workers who were hired about five in the afternoon came and each received a denarius" (Matthew 20:9). You will not receive anything that follows in this book if you do not at least begin to accept this: The first will be last, and the last will be first. Leadership in Jesus' realm is not a pathway to worldly success. Nor is it an indication that you are more important or valuable than others.

The gospel — the good news — is that Jesus has done everything needed for you to be accepted by the Father. He has paid the full price. He lived a life of perfect righteousness and purity and power because you cannot. At the cross, He handed over to you and me the credit for all the goodness and perfection of His life, and, in return, He took your sin and weakness and failure. You earn nothing.

Gospel leadership is leading with nothing to prove. It is leading with nothing to gain except glory for Jesus. It is leading in the confidence and security that you already have all you could possibly desire or need, and so are not tempted to use leadership to grasp anything for yourself. Gospel leadership is good news leadership because it is free of strife and arrogance and striving and boasting and proving and earning.

If leadership for you is a means to be more valued or more loved or more esteemed, then you are off course. Profoundly and dangerously so. Nothing is earned. All is grace. You are valued because of Jesus. You have worth because of Jesus. You are lovable because of Jesus. Your identity is in Jesus. You are accepted because of Jesus. You belong because of Jesus. You are respected because of Jesus. You are important because of Jesus. Do not try to use leadership (position or influence) to gain these things. That is a trap.

You have everything you could want already as a gift from your Father because of Jesus.

Please do not rush over this. Stop and consider. Meditate on these truths.

It is human tendency to strive after the very things God wants to give us. We long to feel valuable. We crave honor. We need an identity. We are desperate to feel like we belong. We would love to believe that we are good. Yet the tragedy is that in seeking to provide for these legitimate needs and desires ourselves, we forfeit the gift. If you use leadership (or anything else) to make yourself important, you lose the far greater importance you already have in Jesus. You cannot rely on both works and grace. It is one or the other.

I have to confess something. I like to be liked. I like for people to think I have something amazing to offer. I like to be special. I do not want to be loved just because everyone is loved but loved a little extra because there is something different about me. I'd like to think that I am something unusual, something great. I want to be respected, and not just because I am created in God's image like everyone else or because Jesus died for me as He did for the whole world. Yes, all that. But just a little bit more too. I desire to be respected because I have proven myself to be a cut above. To be esteemed because I am a little better. To be valued a little more because I have something more to offer.

It feels foolish writing that, but it is all true. Painfully true. And maybe it at least comes close to hitting the mark for you as well.

I graduated from university in 1991 and got married in 1992. When people asked me what I was going to do, I reveled in announcing that I was going to be a missionary to Africa. For the next dozen years or more, that made up a large part of my identity. I felt good about it. I imagined that people saw my calling as something radical and praiseworthy. I would have bet that God Himself viewed it the same way. I was not going to be a run-of-the-mill Christian. I had it in my sights to be a special one, a radical one. People would respect me. God would love me. And best of all, my own heart would approve of me. Finally.

The workers who were hired about five in the afternoon came and each received a denarius. So when those came who were hired first, they expected to receive more. But each one of them also received a denarius. — Matthew 20:9-10

I was there early, waiting for the vineyard owner by 5 a.m. I exulted in being chosen while so many others were just straggling out of their beds. I proudly looked down on those who were clearly less capable or less willing than me.

I was looking forward to my hard work paying off, and having my specialness vindicated by God. But to my dismay, we all get a denarius. No matter who did what for how long, there is one denarius for each of us.

That's not fair!

There is a prideful inclination to recoil from this setup. I want to think that I can earn my way to special status. But when I accept the truth that we all get a denarius, there is a profound freedom. I do not have to earn my way. I have nothing to prove. I can be honest. I can let the truth slip out that, despite all my bravado and radical talk, I have a suspicion deep inside that I am not going to prove to be anything special. To be candid, I have a fear that I will not even be average. I have a past littered with failure and experiences of being not quite good enough. No matter how I try to hide it, my weakness and my lack and my averageness seep through. I cannot earn God's love. When I look in my heart and when I objectively assess my actions, I know that there is no good reason for Him to love me or accept me. Except for Jesus.

One denarius for each of us. That is not fair. Thank Jesus. It is not fair that He would love me, accept me, adopt me, bless me, promote me, and use me. But He does.

When I moved back to the US from Uganda, I could no longer hang my value on the identity of being a missionary. All my pride in being radical or committed or important evaporated, and I was left with nothing. Nothing except what Jesus had wanted to give me all along. It was a merciful, painful, loss. It finally became obvious, even to me, that I had been striving for all the things Jesus had won for me already, and that in so doing I was bankrupt. Without the position or identity to rely on, I was forced to come face to face with my own need, and with Jesus' abundant provision. How good He is!

So why show up? Why bear the burden of the work and the heat of the day? Why go to the hard places? Why agree to lead? Why give everything we have?

Because the Master has chosen us to do so. We labor in the heat of the day not to become worthy but because He is worthy. We bear the burden of the work not to prove that we are special but because He is special. We all get a denarius. Why not just slack our way through life, choosing laziness and complacency over radical and costly service? Because we love Jesus. That is the only reason. He is worth all that we can give Him. He values us all the same because our worth comes from what He has done, not what we do. However, we do not all love Him the same. I choose to bear the burden of the work and the heat of the day because that is how I love Him.

I am a father of five children, and through them, the Lord has driven this lesson home over and over to me. In all other spheres of life, it is natural for value to be tied to performance. In school, in sports, in business, in politics, and in every other field of human endeavor, performance matters most. But not in family. In family, value comes with membership. Performance in a family is inconsistent. Older children are more "useful" in the running of the household than the younger ones. Eventually, the child becomes an adult and moves out. They take on the responsibilities of a household of their own, and so are even less available to us. Beyond the age differences, there are different temperaments, different abilities, and different interests. Some are strong-willed while others are compliant. Some are outgoing and communicative while others are quiet and shy.

All this is simply to say that performance in a family varies according to the person and the season of life. But value is consistent throughout. Each child is endowed with great worth because they are loved. The newborn baby is loved with the same passion and affection as the teenager, even though the baby performs no "useful" function. The baby is demanding and needy and never helps with the dishes. The teenager mows the lawn, does the laundry, and occasionally cooks dinner. They are loved the same. They are valued the same.

The implications are clear and, if you are getting it, staggering. The Kingdom of God is a family, not a sports team. Your value is secure. You are loved, regardless of how useful you are in the work of the Kingdom. Your worth will never be tied to a position or a project or a role. Your worth hangs on the fact of your membership in the family. You are valuable because you are chosen. You are important because the Father loves you. You belong to Him. Jon Petersen writes in his book, *Unveiled*:

> Remember that we're talking about a family relationship, not an organizational
> one. The distinction is critical. In an organization, the goal is to lead and be led,
> do the task and produce an outcome that satisfies the leaders' vision, so the

organization can thrive. The corporate leader hires people to ensure his/her vision is fulfilled, leaving one's sense of value in the hands of the leader's evaluation of one's performance. Corporations tend to employ the many to fulfill the vision of a few. In God's family, the leaders are parents who value maintaining a unified relationship over performance objectives, a vision of Jesus over ministry accomplishments. Such leaders exhibit tenacious loyalty in the face of monumental failures by their disciples. One is assigned value independent of performance and perfection. In the light of failure, fathers and mothers do not patronize, yet they are committed to tell the truth in an atmosphere of grace. The goal is always helping each other grow closer to God.[13]

You cannot fulfill God's dream for your ministry or leadership if you are using those things — the very ministry and leadership you seek — to earn what you have already been freely given in Jesus. Leadership does not make you important. But Jesus has made you important! Ministry does not make you special. But Jesus has made you special! Serving God does not make you lovable or acceptable. But Jesus has already made you lovable and acceptable! He has created you to belong. He has given you an identity. He has given you purpose. It is all in Him and through Him and for Him.

We have to be settled in this, or we will not be able to face what is coming next.

Because what is coming next will knock the wind out of us if we are still trying to increase our worth through our performance.

Condemned to Death
(Matthew 20:17-19)

They will condemn him to death and will hand him over to the Gentiles to be mocked and flogged and crucified. On the third day he will be raised to life! — Matthew 20:18-19

Twice Jesus has insisted that the last will be first and the first last. We are still grappling with that. What does He mean? Who are the firsts? Who are

---

[13] Jon Petersen, *Unveiled: What a Pirate, a Pot Farmer, and a Gaggle of Prostitutes Taught Me About Being the Church* (City Force Media, Castle Rock, CO, 2019) , Kindle location 1871.

the lasts? How will their places be reversed? What does that mean to me? As we struggle with these weighty questions, Jesus adds fuel to the fire by making the preposterous claim that He, too, is a "last."

Jesus is going to be **condemned**.

Human judges will sit and discuss the fate of the Son of God. And in the end, they will pronounce a death sentence on Him. Jesus will be labeled a criminal. Humanity dares to sit in judgment and declare the Creator guilty. The One you and I have chosen to follow is a convicted criminal. The last of the last. He has been relegated to the very bottom of the pecking order.

How do we follow a convict? How do we lead in His movement?

Jesus continues. Not only will He be proclaimed guilty, but He will be handed over to the Gentiles. His own people will give Him over to the ungodly enemy, to the blasphemers, to the oppressors, to the ones who do not know God. The people of God hand God over to godless men. Jesus will be condemned by the so-called righteous and by the unrighteous.

Jesus will then be **mocked**. They will consider Him a buffoon; call Him an idiot; say He is a delusional, powerless failure. And they will ridicule and demean Him for it. They will shame Him with false praise, strip Him naked in public to embarrass Him, satirize and lampoon Him to make Him look foolish. Jesus will be presented to the world as a fraud, a lunatic, an inconsequential and meaningless pretender.

What does it mean to follow one such as that? How does one lead others in a Kingdom whose King is so scorned?

And **flogged**. Jesus predicts that He will not only endure the emotional trauma of being rejected and mocked, but He will undergo severe physical suffering as well. He will be beaten within an inch of His life. He will experience horrendous pain. He will be tortured. He will be rendered helpless and defenseless. He will be exposed and abused.

How do we follow such a vulnerable Savior?

Crucified. Finally, Jesus will be killed. He will die in a humiliating and agonizing way. He will be fully conquered. All His claims of divine power will be thrown back in His face. His so-called wisdom will be revealed as foolishness. His kindness just a show. His righteousness a farce. His promises null and void. His movement defeated. Dead.

How do we follow such a powerless leader? How do we lead others in such a Kingdom, whose King is so utterly overcome?

But... On the third day, He will be raised to life! And in that one glorious display of power, the guilty verdict and the humiliation and the pain and the defeat will be undone. He will rise victorious and vindicated. He will be revealed as innocent. He will be exalted; forever alive and clothed in honor and might. The very last will have become the absolute first.

And this is the curious thing. Jesus was never truly a last, was He? All the condemnation and the mockery and even the death were on false grounds. He was a "last" only because He chose to be. He made Himself a "last." He did not make Himself a "last" by being an underachiever, but by choosing humility, clothing Himself in all the scorn the world could throw His way. He embraced weakness rather than the dominance of power. He surrendered control rather than fight for His rights.

> He made himself nothing
>> by taking the very nature of a servant,
>> being made in human likeness.
> And being found in appearance as a man,
>> he humbled himself
>> by becoming obedient to death -
>> even death on a cross!
> — Philippians 2:7-8

How do we follow a Lord who makes Himself a criminal? A holy one who takes on guilt? An exalted one who chooses to be humiliated?

For some time, it had been dawning on these twelve men who Jesus really was. Peter was the first to speak the word out loud: *Messiah*. They were following the long-awaited Anointed One of ancient prophecy! The hope of their people. The implications were overwhelming. They were chosen as leaders in the Kingdom of Heaven. Twelve thrones!

But now this. This? Of all things, this!? How can Jesus say He will be condemned, mocked, flogged, and crucified? This is not the kind of thing the Messiah of ancient prophecy is supposed to endure.

Like us, these bewildered apostles wanted to follow a powerful and always victorious Lord. They were scandalized by Jesus' talk of suffering and debasement. It was unthinkable. They had a picture of who the Messiah would be; of how He would be received. They had preconceived ideas about His methods and His purposes, and they were on board.

But they were wrong. Jesus had a different plan than the one they assumed. In many ways, He was a different person than they thought He was. After all this time together, they still did not really know Him. Their false expectations blinded them to the reality of Jesus Himself. They simply could not envisage a suffering Messiah, a weak Messiah.

In order to follow Jesus and eventually lead others in His movement, these men would have to turn away from their own expectations and hopes. They would have to embrace Jesus not as they assumed He would be or wanted Him to be, but as He was. You and I face the same challenge.

> In every age and culture we tend to shape Jesus to our own image and make him over to our own needs in order to cope with the stress his unedited presence creates.[14]

Peter and James and John and the others did not expect to serve a humiliated and defeated Messiah. They did not understand. Jesus' ominous predictions were so confusing. Confusing, but sure. It would all happen just as He said.

Of course, all that Jesus is about to endure is heavy with theological significance. This is the very reason He came. These events — the suffering, death, and resurrection of Jesus — would prove to be the center of our faith. By being condemned and crucified, He would provide for our salvation, reconcile us to God, and create a new humanity. And in all of it, He eternally broadcasts and proves His love for fallen people. In this horrible suffering, Jesus shouted His love for you with a roar that echoes throughout the universe. His love is not cold, calculated, and detached. It is not sentimental or flaky. It is passionate, affectionate, and steady. He is for you. He loved you even when you were living as His enemy. He spared no expense, spurned no pain, withheld no part of Himself for you.

Can you lead like that? The suffering of Jesus is central to our theme of leadership because it demonstrates that love is the ultimate Kingdom leadership "principle." You cannot lead in Jesus' movement if you cannot love. And you cannot love unless you are willing to suffer for the objects of your affection. And you cannot suffer for others until you are willing to receive Jesus' love and sacrifice for yourself.

---

[14] Brennan Manning, *The Signature of Jesus* (Multnomah Books, New York, 1996), pg 153.

Jesus allowed Himself to be condemned so that you might be proclaimed innocent. He permitted the humiliation of being mocked so that you could be honored. He endured the horrors of physical torture so that you might be made whole. He suffered the defeat of death so that you might live victoriously forever. This is Jesus leadership. How do you lead?

What would it mean to be a leader after Jesus' heart? Perhaps there will be opportunities for you to bear the responsibility for the failures of those you lead. Instead of pointing fingers and passing the buck, maybe you will have the privilege of taking the heat for another's mistakes. Maybe you will be ridiculed, attacked, or defeated as you seek to lift others. Certainly, you are called to lay down your life for those you lead. You are called to put their interests and good ahead of your own. You are commissioned to love. Henri Nouwen challenges us:

> Here we touch the most important quality of Christian leadership in the future. It is not a leadership of power and control, but a leadership of powerlessness and humility in which the suffering servant of God, Jesus Christ, is made manifest.[15]

How do you follow such a Savior? How do you lead in such a Kingdom? There are implications here, profound ones. Take time to meditate on what Jesus has done and the example He has provided, and to assess your own leadership in the light of His.

In her poem, 'Hast Thou No Scar," Amy Carmichael ponders these very questions:

> Hast thou no scar?
> No hidden scar on foot, or side, or hand?
> I hear thee sung as mighty in the land,
> I hear them hail the bright, ascendant star:
> Hast thou no scar?
>
> Hast thou no wound?
> Yet, I was wounded by the archers, spent.
> Leaned me against the tree to die, and rent

---

[15] Henri Nouwen, *In the Name of Jesus* (Crossroad Publishing, New York, 2002), pg 82.

By ravening beasts that compassed me, I swooned:
Hast thou no wound?

No wound? No scar?
Yes, as the master shall the servant be,
And pierced are the feet that follow me;
But thine are whole. Can he have followed far
Who has no wound? No scar?[16]

---

[16] Amy Carmichael, quoted in J. Oswald Sanders, <u>Spiritual Leadership</u> (Moody Publishers, Chicago, 2007), pg 117.

4 - A BOLD REQUEST
(Matthew 20:20-23)

Grant that one of these two sons of mine may sit at your right and the other at your left in your kingdom. — Matthew 20:21

It is clear that the twelve are dramatically missing the point. Immediately after Jesus shares about His coming agony, His disciples start vying for the highest positions. Matthew is using the power of contrast to bring into sharp focus the differences between worldly and Kingdom leadership. Jesus' teaching about greatness is set against the disciples' still worldly understanding. Jesus had said, "Whoever takes the lowly position of this child is the greatest in the kingdom of heaven" (Matt 18:4) and, "The last will be first, and the first will be last" (Matt 20:16). The disciples respond with the typical power moves of the world. The two approaches to greatness are thus set side-by-side. On the one hand, there is the crucified, mocked, suffering, crucified Jesus, laying down His life in love. On the other hand, we see James and John seeking to rise above their friends, maneuvering for the highest positions. The Kingdom and the world. They could not be more different. To which kind of greatness do you aspire?

The apostles have been promised a seat in the King of the Universe's inner court. Each had been offered one of the twelve highest positions in the Kingdom. So far so good. We'll take it. But among the twelve, what will be the pecking order? James and John are thinking that they have a legitimate shot at the top two spots, and they are not going to take any chances. If they are not careful, Peter is sure to try to land the throne closest to Jesus. And so they make their play.

Maybe, like James and John, you have completely missed the message that everyone gets a denarius. Maybe the fact of the first being last has not truly sunk in. You are still looking for the "deeper spiritual meaning," while all the time fighting your way to the top. I understand James and John a lot more than I like to admit, even to myself. I have been given a lot, but there is always more. What about you?

James and John (through their mother) seek out the two best thrones, the ones closest to Jesus. The ones closest to power. Why? I cannot answer for the Sons of Thunder, but I have some idea of why you and I can relate.

Some want those thrones because of the simple but mighty lure of power. It seems to be part of the human condition to crave control, to want to be in charge, to desire power over our own lives and power over others. For many, Christian leadership is a way to satisfy this primal urge. In fact, Henri Nouwen laments that

> One of the greatest ironies of the history of Christianity is that its leaders constantly gave in to the temptation of power... even though they continued to speak in the name of Jesus, who did not cling to his divine power but emptied himself and became as we are.[17]

Such leaders pay close attention to how people honor and esteem them. They are hurt when they feel disrespected. They are encouraged when people revere them. They demand loyalty and do not encourage questioning or open discussion. They may work very hard and sacrifice significantly in the work of the Kingdom and their accomplishments may be impressive, but they are leading as kings, like lords of their Christian domains. Nouwen adds more insight when he asks,

> "What makes the temptation to power so seemingly irresistible? Maybe it is that power offers an easy substitute for the hard task of love."[18]

---

[17] Henri Nouwen, *In the Name of Jesus* (Crossroad Publishing, New York, 2002), pg 76.

[18] Henri Nouwen, *In the Name of Jesus* (Crossroad Publishing, New York, 2002), pg 77.

Indeed, it is much easier to exercise power over another (for their own good, of course) than to influence them by laying down one's life in love. I know when I am falling into the seduction of power when I care more about how a person respects me (or disrespects me) than about Christ being formed in that person; when I care more about myself being honored than about Jesus being glorified.

Others seek the top spots for more subtle reasons. They are enticed by the desire to be important. They long for significance. They need purpose and value. This is a subtle temptation because of the fact that these are not wicked desires. One could argue that God Himself has put the longing for these things within mankind. You can argue that God actually wants men and women to feel important and to know that they are significant. He desires that we have purpose and realize our value. So the end is right, but the means are all off. The ends (importance, value, significance, purpose) are godly. But these things are not gained by leadership. They are not won by fighting your way up the Christian corporate ladder. As mentioned in a previous chapter, these are freely given by the Father through Jesus. The problem arises when we try to obtain them by any means other than grace, even through good Christian work and leadership. When we attempt to use leadership or ministry to get what God has given freely by His grace, we refuse God's gift and insist on only getting what we can earn. And so, ironically, in the pursuit of significance and purpose and value, we become devalued. We cannot make ourselves more important than God has already made us. We cannot increase our value by our own methods. God has made you significant. Do not grasp for more.

Another thing that draws us in the way of James and John is even more difficult to diagnose. Some want those thrones because of an admirable desire to be near Jesus. They want to be loved by God. They want to belong and to be fully "in." Again, these are wonderful desires to have. God put those longings within you. But He also offers you the fulfillment of them through Jesus. You cannot become closer to Jesus by your positions of leadership. It is Jesus on the cross that allows you to be close to God. It is God who loves you by His own will and grace, not because of what you can do for Him. You belong. You have been accepted. You are deeply loved. All this is because of Jesus. Position, power, or title will not get you any closer. Pastors are not closer to Jesus than bankers. Apostles are not more loved than garbage collectors. Prophets are not accepted into an inner circle beyond that of doctors or butchers or businessmen. There are no degrees of adoption. We are all sons and daughters in the house of our Father if we have put our faith in Jesus.

Jesus tells this ambitious mother, along with her scheming sons, that they do not know what they are asking. Only His Father can give those positions. And He gives them according to His choosing. This is not a competition. There is no need for you to be more holy than another or more fruitful or more successful in ministry, only to be faithful to God and committed in love.

> Do nothing out of selfish ambition or vain conceit. Rather, in humility value others above yourselves, not looking to your own interests but each of you to the interests of the others. — Philippians 2:3-4

When we are motivated to Christian leadership by selfish ambition, we poison our ministries and demean our positions. When we think that our leadership proves that we are more valuable than others, we actually devalue ourselves. When we use our leadership to look after our own interests, we disqualify ourselves from receiving the free gifts of God's grace.

We lead because the Father loves us, and we love Him in return. We lead because He has chosen us to do so. We lead because we want Jesus to be glorified, not ourselves.

Why do you lead?

Can You Drink the Cup?
(Matthew 20:20-23)

> "You don't know what you are asking," Jesus said to them. "Can you drink the cup I am going to drink?" — Matthew 20:22

"You don't know what you are asking," says Jesus to the bold brothers. But perhaps He is also saying it to you. "You don't know what you are asking," says Jesus to you who want to be a leader, to you who want to be a great man or woman of God. The chances are, like our ambitious young disciples in this story, you simply do not know what it is you are asking. Jesus gives two reasons why they do not know; two implications of the request that they do not understand. The first reason is the cup. The second is Who makes those decisions.

"Can you drink the cup I am going to drink?" Clearly, the cup Jesus had in mind is the cup of suffering. The very first thing that comes out of Jesus' mouth when His disciples, whom He loves, ask Him for seats of power and influence is this question about the cup. He is concerned about what it will cost them. He does not first rebuke their ambition or speak of their need for greater maturity or faith. He could have corrected their backroom methods or scolded them for ignoring what He had just shared with them, for responding to the revelation of His coming pain and death with a crass power move. He could have shouted in their faces, "*I said, 'the first will be last!'*" But he did none of that. His first thought, apparently, was the suffering that would be experienced by those who would ultimately occupy those twelve thrones.

Whatever personal, selfish ambition that drove such a request would not be worth it. Whatever misplaced desire for greatness that had compelled them to seek such a thing would not pay off. The cost would be too high. The thrill of power would not be great enough to counteract the terrible suffering that would come. The pride of position would not be worth it. Only love for Jesus and a desire for His glory would be strong enough motivations to get them through the approaching trials. The thrones would not be trophies given to the ambitious or clever or gifted, but authority and responsibility given to the scarred.

Why do you want to lead? You must face this question because a self-centered motive will not give you the strength to endure the suffering. May we heed the warning of Hudson Taylor, coming to us down through the generations:

> In these days of easy-going Christianity, is it not well to remind ourselves that it really does cost to be a man or woman whom God can use? One can not obtain a Christlike character for nothing; one can not do a Christlike work save at great price.[19]

I can almost see Jesus looking at these two young firebrands and perhaps lowering His head a little in sadness. Not sadness because of the request, but

---

[19] Dr and Mrs Howard Taylor, *Hudson Taylor's Spiritual Secret* (2013), pg 14.

distress coming from the knowledge of what they would go through. He loved them. *Oh, my friends, you don't know what you are asking.*

Why is this His immediate response? Very soon He will bring the whole crew together and, in a moment, wreck all their ideas about leadership and power. But before He does that, He reacts in compassion as He looks to the coming years and sees what these precious disciples cannot. We have to grasp this hard truth: Suffering is an indispensable part of Kingdom leadership. In fact, it seems to be inescapable in following Jesus at all.

We must go through many hardships to enter the kingdom of God. — Acts 14:22

Everyone who wants to live a godly life in Christ Jesus will be persecuted. — 2 Timothy 3:12

Dear friends, do not be surprised at the fiery ordeal that has come on you to test you, as though something strange were happening to you. But rejoice inasmuch as you participate in the sufferings of Christ, so that you may be overjoyed when his glory is revealed. — 1 Peter 4:12-13

This is disturbing on more than one level.

First, there is the utter inevitability of it. Over and over again throughout the New Testament, we are warned about hardship and suffering. Following Jesus, according to the scriptures, will not be easy, and it will lead us into significant adversity. The idea that being a Christian will provide an easy and unopposed journey through life is completely false. The thought that being a leader in the Jesus movement will be all rainbows and unicorns is absurd. Jesus and the apostles tell us again and again to expect to suffer. This is a hard pill for us to swallow, but as leaders in His movement, there is simply no other way. This fact demands of you and me a brutal assessment of our own motives and expectations. You must count the cost. And you must take a hard, honest look at your motives. If your motives are anything less than love for Jesus and a response to His calling, you will lose your footing. You will give up or give in. Or, instead of quitting, you could "successfully" lead people away from the life of Jesus rather than into it. The scripture's insistence on the surety of suffering must give you pause. Can you drink this cup?

Second, the Bible's emphasis on suffering is disturbing because of the somewhat embarrassing lack of it in many of our lives and churches. What are you to make of this if your life is pretty easy? Is not all this talk of suffering much more applicable for "back then" and "over there?" Western church leaders often live nice, middle-class lives. Probably nobody has hatched a plan to take your life lately. I have not been stoned or put in prison or beaten. I have not gone hungry or even been decently "reviled and persecuted" (Matt 5:11). What are we to make of all these biblical warnings of hardship and suffering? Frankly, it is awkward.

There are in fact many believers in the world who are facing the same kinds of physical, in-your-face persecution that the early apostles endured. Christians in the West are, for the most part, not those people. At least not now. So what are those who are not suffering to make of the warnings about suffering?

We must begin by acknowledging that many people in our world today are enduring terrible suffering in the cause of Christ. They are being beaten and imprisoned. Many have been expelled from their families. Others face severe financial and material hardship. Others are killed. This is a severity of suffering to which most of us in the West cannot relate. We are to honor our brothers and sisters who face such things, give weight to their words, assist them when we can, and always pray for them. May the words of an ancient suffering disciple haunt our prayers and our pleasures, "Continue to remember those in prison as if you were together with them in prison, and those who are mistreated as if you yourselves were suffering" (Hebrews 13:3).

Then, as long as we are realistic and not overly dramatic about it, those of us in the West can acknowledge and honor a different scale of suffering. This suffering can take different forms. You may have to endure financial stress because of your decision to follow Jesus or be a leader in His work. You may have to face rejection from friends or family and perhaps a diminished status in society. There is definitely plenty of anxiety that will come as you seek to do Kingdom work among broken people, within the church and without. You will be called on to sacrifice things like family time and privacy. You will be made to look or feel foolish at times in public discourse. You will assuredly face some degree of loneliness and exhaustion. You will go long stretches without a "day off" as you minister to those in need. You will face questions and doubts about your leadership and will grieve deeply over those that fall away. You will pass through seasons of discouragement and perhaps even depression. You can acknowledge each of these as true suffering.

In the end, we cannot, nor should we aim to, create suffering for ourselves. Instead, we should simply live a life that makes us vulnerable to it. The decisions that we make must not be motivated by the desire to shield ourselves from hardship. We must be ruthless in not allowing fear to impact our choices. We must cultivate a countercultural willingness to suffer, to not let people talk us out of things that may lead to pain, to take risks, and to be willing to fail. As Brennan Manning says, "When we are seized by the power of a great affection, we are empowered with the courage to risk."[20] Do not neglect to speak the truth because of how someone might be offended by it. Take a stand for the marginalized and oppressed. Do not value your income over your witness, your job more than the gospel. Francis Chan issues this challenge:

> We're busy reassuring one another that God wants us to do what's safest for our families and to pursue God in a way that looks suspiciously similar to what we'd naturally do if our only concern was our own comfort and happiness.[21]

I urge you to examine your leadership and your lifestyle. Is your comfort, security, safety, or ego more of a driving force behind your decisions, relationships, and ministries than the gospel? Are you seeking the authority of Jesus while quietly trying to pour the contents of the cup of suffering under the table, like a child discreetly scheming to get out of taking his medicine? Do not fall for it. Embrace whatever hardship comes as you faithfully carry out the work of the gospel. "Join with me in suffering, like a good soldier of Christ Jesus" (2 Timothy 2:3).

Can you drink the cup?

---

[20] Brennan Manning, *The Signature of Jesus* (Multnomah Books, New York, 1996), pg 184.

[21] Francis Chan, *Letters to the Church* (David C Cook, Colorado Springs, 2018)., pg 156.

You Will Drink the Cup
(Matthew 20:20-23)

You will indeed drink from my cup. — Matthew 20:23

You will indeed drink the cup. If you hope to have any power in your ministry, you will drink the cup. If you love Jesus with all your heart, you will share the bitter brew with Him. Count the cost. It is important that we grasp this so that our expectations will not betray us. On the night before he died, Jesus encouraged His disciples with these words:

> All this I have told you so that you will not fall away. They will put you out of the synagogue; in fact, the time is coming when anyone who kills you will think they are offering a service to God. They will do such things because they have not known the Father or me. I have told you this, so that when their time comes you will remember that I warned you about them. — John 16:1-4

And then,

> I have told you these things, so that in me you may have peace. In this world you will have trouble. But take heart! I have overcome the world. — John 16:33

Forewarned is forearmed. Jesus warns His friends about the difficulties that will come so that they will not give up and so that they can have peace even amid the approaching turmoil. And these warnings are passed down to you and me.

Suffering, for leaders in the ministry of Jesus, is a sure thing. As foreboding as that sounds, you must understand that Jesus and His early apostles did not view suffering (even to the point of physical torture and death) as an entirely negative force. In fact, you will be hard-pressed to find any reference to suffering in the New Testament that does not sound outright positive. The forefathers of our faith actually seem to have considered suffering to be a good thing.[22] For example, after spending a night in jail and

---

[22] See, for example, Acts 5:41, Romans 8:17-18, 2 Corinthians 12:7-10, Philippians 3:10, Colossians 1:24, 2 Timothy 1:8, 1 Peter 2:20-21

then being flogged, "The apostles left the Sanhedrin, rejoicing because they had been counted worthy of suffering disgrace for the Name" (Acts 5:41).

For a servant of Jesus, suffering is inevitable. And suffering is good. How can this be? For one thing, suffering helps us to be stronger in Jesus, to be more like Him.

> Not only so, but we also glory in our sufferings, because we know that suffering produces perseverance; perseverance, character; and character, hope." — Romans 5:3-4

One might argue that character, hope, and perseverance could also develop apart from suffering. Perhaps. But it cannot be denied that it is a well-used tool in God's training methods.

> Endure hardship as discipline; God is treating you as his children. For what children are not disciplined by their father?... No discipline seems pleasant at the time, but painful. Later on, however, it produces a harvest of righteousness and peace for those who have been trained by it. — Hebrews 12:7, 11

We may not fully understand the theology behind what God allows or what He causes, but the point is still clear. When hardship comes, take it as discipline from the Lord. Receive it with the confidence that somehow in some way God is at work in the midst of it, and the work He is doing is good. He is forming you into the image of Jesus. Every difficult thing that you pass through can be used by the Father for a positive outcome, but you must submit to it. Discipline produces a good harvest *"for those who have been trained by it,"* for those who intentionally allow the Lord to use the hard thing for His greater purposes. Suffering is good because it has the potential to make us more like Christ if we submit to God's good work.

Suffering also helps us to know Jesus better — and there is nothing better than that!

> I want to know Christ—yes, to know the power of his resurrection and participation in his sufferings, becoming like him in his death." — Philippians 3:10

There is nothing better to aim for than knowing Jesus! And one essential way we get to know Him is through suffering. Because Paul was so convinced of this, he welcomed trouble. There is a bond that forms between those who pass through trials together that is different from other relationships. There is an intimacy with Jesus that we cannot experience apart from suffering. To know Him deeply, we have to walk with Him through the dark valley. The amazing thing is that, as we journey on the path of suffering, He is there with us. He makes it a holy thing by His presence. He does not promise to shield us from suffering or to make it easy to bear, but He does promise to be with us in it. And what a promise! Yes, He is always with us. But in suffering there is a special camaraderie with Him that we experience. It is beautiful. It is a mysterious but nonetheless sure thing; suffering brings us into deeper and more profound union with Jesus. To know Him in the fellowship of His sufferings. To join Him in draining the cup.

A willingness to suffer also allows us to do the work to which He has called us.

> Now I rejoice in what I am suffering for you, and I fill up in my flesh what is still lacking in regard to Christ's afflictions, for the sake of his body, which is the church. — Colossians 1:24

Paul is happy in the adversity he has to face because it allows him to legitimately participate in Christ's great work of redemption. Obviously, the suffering of Jesus is sufficient to cleanse us from sin and to make us whole. However, this fact does not benefit those who do not know about it. So, in that sense, Paul (and you and me!) can "fill up in [our] flesh what is still lacking in regard to Christ's afflictions." If we want our work to truly lead to the glory of Jesus in the nations through the salvation of lost people, we will have to embrace suffering. It serves the mission.

Suffering is guaranteed. Suffering has positive benefits. You are called to respond to suffering in grace.

When afflictions come, the essential thing is to walk through them in the grace of Jesus. How do we do that? Here are a few thoughts.

First, remember this was expected. Remember the warnings. Envision yourself drinking that cup. Jesus is not surprised by this trouble, and you should not be either. Do not allow yourself the luxury of complaining. Do not tolerate seeds of doubt that call into question the goodness of God.

In His goodness, He has done all He can to prepare you for this moment. It may take a different form than you thought it would. It may hit with greater force than you believed it ever could. Still, this is not something bizarre that is happening to you.

> Dear friends, do not be surprised at the fiery ordeal that has come on you to test you, as though something strange were happening to you. But rejoice inasmuch as you participate in the sufferings of Christ, so that you may be overjoyed when his glory is revealed." — 1 Peter 4:12-13

This is it. This thing you are passing through at this time is the cup of suffering. Maybe when you first considered it, the idea of this precious cup sounded more romantic or heroic than what you are now experiencing. That's okay. Recognize it and name it. This is the cup of Jesus. Drink deeply.

After spending the better part of a decade on the mission field, I had returned to the States with my family to begin anew. Two years later, I was facing trials that threatened to undo me. I was rocked by financial lack and the loss of identity, purpose, and value. I was confused and discouraged, feeling rejected and broken. One day I sat with a wise mentor who listened to my tales of woe. After some time, he simply told me that this was the cup of Jesus for me at this time. This was my dose of suffering. And, if I allowed it, it would help me to be more like Jesus, to know Him more deeply, to be more devoted to Him, and to produce greater fruit for His glory. This revelation filled me with hope and strength. I received courage for the battle. Situations did not immediately change, nor even did my emotional and relational struggles, but I recognized the presence of Jesus. I persevered into better times by His grace, and I lived to look back on this time of testing with deep gratitude.

Secondly, submit to it. Remember that God is at work, and a harvest will come "for those who have been trained by it" (Hebrews 12:11). With the apostles of old, rejoice in suffering. Be utterly confident that God is at work in this for your good (Romans 8:28). As you pray for the Lord to deliver you from the distress of this moment, remember to ask Him to accomplish His good in you. Be aware that your character is being built and that such work is essential. It will help you to represent Jesus more fully and powerfully. It will lead to greater fruit and more glory for Jesus. Submit to this process. Be intentional as you partner with the Holy Spirit in your own sanctification.

You are becoming more patient, loving, gracious, kind, and pure. This is good!

Thirdly, redirect your focus onto eternity during this trying moment. However intense and miserable your suffering is, you can be fully confident that it is temporary. You will one day be ushered into a place where there is no more suffering. This world does not have the answers for you. You will not receive all that is promised you in this fleeting life, but because of Jesus, you are eternal! You will outlive this trial. Remember Jesus, who "for the joy set before him endured the cross" (Hebrews 12:2). And you have this promise, "For our light and momentary troubles are achieving for us an eternal glory that far outweighs them all" (2 Corinthians 4:17).

Finally, remember that Jesus is worth it. Whatever you are passing through, walk through it in the love of Christ. Remember that He loves you, and you love Him. You can endure this hardship out of love for Him. You can rejoice in this suffering because it will lead to greater glory for Jesus. He went through so much for you. He is so good to you. He loves you with such depth and loyalty and passion. He is worth the suffering. His cause is worth the afflictions that come. You can endure this. He is with you.

Before we leave this discussion on the cup of Jesus, allow me one more exhortation. For all the reasons mentioned above, and probably more, as a leader in Christ's Kingdom, you are called to prepare others for suffering, just as Jesus did for His first followers. Floyd McClung suggests, "We are guilty of asking too little of each other. We are created to serve God with passion, and passion is impossible without sacrifice."[23]

In worldly leadership, a good leader will seek to protect his or her followers from suffering. If he is a very good leader indeed, he may take the suffering onto himself to spare others. This is certainly praiseworthy. However, we serve in a Kingdom in which our King willingly and wisely leads us into hardship and difficulty and suffering. Of course, He has demonstrated His love for us by suffering tremendously on our behalf, so we know that He is not being cruel or uncaring. As we follow Him, we will also be called to lead others into the joy and the privilege of suffering for the sake of His Name. We can do this because we want them, too, to become more like Christ, to be fruitful in His work, to know Him more deeply, and to glorify Him more profoundly. We cannot get them there apart from suffering,

---

[23] Floyd McClung, *You See Bones, I See An Army* (YWAM Publishing, Seattle, 2008), Kindle loc 3124.

so we must prepare them to drink the cup. Do not try to remove all the pain from the lives of those you serve. Do not take on the false responsibility of protecting them from everything bad. Do not quench the passion within them to take risks for the sake of Jesus. In leading others to this place of testing, while experiencing the same kind of sufferings ourselves, we honor them. We realize that side-by-side, we enter into the fray as fellow servants, joyfully giving our all for the glory of the One who loved us with His very life.

Prepared by My Father
(Matthew 20:20-23)

These places belong to those for whom they have been prepared by my Father.
— Matthew 20:23

After Jesus warned James and John about the cup, He told them that even though they would indeed drink from it, He could not promise them the positions they wanted. The cup is not the only obstacle in the path of their ambition. The other issue is Who makes that decision. It is the Father. In a moment, Jesus will give a clear, though shocking, bit of instruction for those who will fill those prize appointments. But first and foremost, the disciples must know that this is the Father's choice. There is no ladder to climb, no clearly laid-out steps to advancement. The Father will choose. This truth has several implications for us.

First, we are not to grasp for position. We are to not value it to the point that we crave it and strategize to get it. This is not a democratic process. Political savvy is not the way of the Kingdom. Again, it is noteworthy that Jesus did not rebuke James and John for this move. But He does cut short any attempt to maneuver for the higher places. These brothers and their doting mother would not receive advancement based on any worldly methods or schemes. The decision is firmly in the Father's hands, and He is not in the least bit influenced by any political scheming that you or I could devise.

Remember, Jesus had the ultimate position and power in the universe, but He "did not consider equality with God something to be used to his own advantage" (Philippians 2:6). Another version says He "did not regard equality with God something to be grasped" (NASB). As Nouwen writes

The way of the Christian leader is not the way of upward mobility in which our world has invested so much, but the way of downward mobility ending on the cross.[24]

It is an ingrained part of our nature to desire position and power. But this is not the nature of Christ. He had ultimate power, and He freely released His hold on it. Following Him means that we have the same attitude. Of course, because this is such a part of us, we can only hope to succeed here by receiving the free gifts of value and identity and belonging that the Father offers in the gospel. If you have not intentionally accepted these from the Father apart from position or effort on your part, you will not be able to release your grasp on, or craving for, power, position, or title. This is key.

Having received these amazing gifts from the Father, you are free to let go of your ambitions of worldly greatness. You do not need to increase your value by climbing the ladder of success because God Himself values you. You do not have to claim identity through an impressive title because the Father has given you the identity of a son or daughter of God. This is wonderful news! There is no need to strive to belong by earning your way to the top because God has openly welcomed you into His family already. You belong. Your identity is secure. You are more valuable than you imagine.

So do not grasp for position. Be content with the Father's choices. Allow Him to promote. Now, there is a caveat to this application in our current situation. There are times when it may be appropriate to apply for a leadership job or to let it be known to those in authority that you are interested in a particular role. Many of our systems in the Church and in other organizations are based on this type of understanding. There are processes in place for people who sense God calling them into a particular field or ministry, and so in that regard, you may have to actively seek the position. However, even so, it is essential that you keep a watch on your attitude. You must never sacrifice truth for the sake of impressing someone because ultimately you trust that promotion is in God's hands. Although you are interacting with human beings who have their own set of values and guidelines, you also trust that God is leading you and them. So, you can apply, but trust the Lord with the outcome. It may be that choices are made that make no sense to you. You are more qualified or more experienced or just a

---

[24] Henri Nouwen, *In the Name of Jesus* (Crossroad Publishing, New York, 2002), pg2 81-82.

better fit, but still the place is given to another. Trust God. He has something for you. He is working out something good. He is able to work through the person chosen ahead of you. And that leads to the next point.

Secondly, trust God when you are not promoted. When you do not get the recognition or the assignments you want, you can be comforted in knowing it was the Father's choice. And when you are given a position of leadership, you can trust that God is truly the One appointing you. Of course, rejection is painful. It hurts when others are chosen ahead of you. It is easy to see the biases and the mistakes made by those with the human authority to promote and appoint. They do not know all the relevant facts. They do not know you or your capabilities or character. Perhaps they did not pay attention to the right things. Still, trust in the Lord.

I have often not been given the recognition or position I desired or thought I deserved, and it has always been a humbling — even humiliating — experience. It has been painful and at times seemingly unfair. Rejection has a bitter sting that is not easily ignored or healed. However, the more I have been able to take my attention off of all the whys and simply trust God, the better it has been. Eventually, I have always had to come to the conviction that God is indeed in control. Looking back on certain disappointments in this regard, I am actually bursting with gratitude. In the moment I would never have believed that the day would come when I would be thankful that God did not put me in the coveted position, but that is exactly what has happened.

Trust is, of course, not easy; not when pain and insecurities are involved. But work for it. Labor to trust the Lord. It is the Father who appoints, and He always makes good decisions. He is working for your good. And He is working for the glory of Jesus in the nations. He is even working in the process and pain of disappointment and rejection to make you more like Jesus. Submit to His process.

Does this mean that every person who has ever been given a position of leadership was promoted by God's direct decision? No. People make wrong choices all the time. However, in His sovereignty, God is able to turn every choice, even the most ungodly ones, to His own good ends. He will not allow my life (or yours) to be ruined because of failing to get a certain job, promotion, or ministry opportunity. He is so much more powerful than that! I find that, on a personal level, it is better to accept leadership decisions as His will from the outset. I gain nothing by convincing myself or others that the choice was a poor one. I gain a lot by simply trusting in Jesus, the One who brings good out of bad choices.

Thirdly, qualifications for leadership position are those of the Kingdom, not of the world. If God Himself is the One making the choices, then it will be based on what He values, not what the world does. God may be less concerned with your experience, gifts, abilities, education, and Enneagram number than you would think. He is likely more interested in your heart and your character and your love for Him. What have you laid down for Him? What have you left behind? Remember the list from Matthew 19? Houses, brothers, sisters, father, mother, wife, children, fields. Maybe another way of looking at it would be to ask what are you grasping? Where do you draw the line with God? What are you withholding from Him? How is your obedience? Remember, Jesus claims that this is the mark of genuine love for Him: "Whoever has my commands and keeps them is the one who loves me"(John 14:21).

God is the giver of gifts, so He does not have to limit Himself to choosing the apparently gifted. He is able to gift you in the moment of need. He may have set yet undiscovered gifts within you already, waiting for the opportunity to be revealed. While taking them into account, do not be overly impressed by gifts, abilities, or education. These do not make good leaders. God makes good leaders out of people who love, sacrifice, obey, and faithfully endure.

Fourthly, there is no competition for Kingdom leadership. This is amazing! Think about it. You have no rivals in the family of God, only brothers and sisters that you want to succeed even more than you want yourself to. This realization brings amazing freedom. You do not have to put others down in order to elevate yourself. When you have rivals, you are tuned into their weaknesses and amplify their mistakes. You secretly rejoice when they fail and hope their faults are noticed by people in authority. Things are so different from this in the family of our Father! Having no competition frees you from needing to impress others or promote yourself. You can do good without caring if anyone notices. You are free to serve without worrying about being recognized for it. This is freedom! You do not have to compare yourself, evaluating your performance in the light of another's. And you do not need to evaluate theirs in the light of yours. You are free to be utterly *for* everyone else. You can rejoice when they do well and celebrate when they are rewarded without any worry about how their success impacts you personally.

You do not need to be concerned about whether or not your strengths are being noticed or if the person in authority sees the sacrifice you made. The place of leadership goes to the person chosen by God, and He has His own reasons. In the world, the position goes to the better candidate, the most impressive applicant, the one with the right connections. But not in the Kingdom!

When I was growing up, I played on the same basketball team as my older brother for a few years. As much as I always wanted to win the game, I had another goal every time we played. My ambition was to outscore my brother. It rarely happened, but when it did, I was on cloud nine. During the game, I would rather take a shot than feed him the ball. I was innately aware when I was coming close to scoring as much as him, and in those moments I became even more focused on getting my points. He, on the other hand, was confident in his value and leadership on the team. He would happily give up personal opportunities to get me a good shot and would rejoice when I scored a lot. He was able to have this attitude because of his own security and confidence. His passion was for us to be better as a team and to win more games. This is Kingdom leadership. There is no competition.

God has a place prepared for you. You do not have to scheme to get there. You do not have to be better than someone else for it to come to pass. You just need to be faithfully obedient and to trust your good Father, who sees all and will work for your good and the glory of Jesus.

5 - NOT SO WITH YOU
(Matthew 20:24-28)

Jesus called them together and said, "You know that the rulers of the Gentiles lord it over them, and their high officials exercise authority over them. Not so with you." — Matthew 20:25-26a

Jesus did not train His disciples in a vacuum. There were well-ingrained notions about what it meant to be great; about how rulers and high officials should behave towards their subordinates. Jesus calls attention to these worldly values before giving the twelve His own version. We, too, should be aware of the cultural values that surround leadership in our own time and place. Jesus' brief summary of how leadership looked in His time is strikingly familiar today. The world, perhaps, has not progressed much in this regard. The leaders known by James and John and crew "lorded it over" those they led and they "exercised authority." These were the defining traits of leadership.

In our time, we see the implications of this philosophy of leadership everywhere. It is evident in the world of business, politics, sports, education, and the service sectors. And yes, it is very present in the Church. We have dressed it up with scripture passages and character studies to the point we have come to believe that these are the very same leadership foundations taught by Jesus and the biblical authors, but the truth is that the world's leadership values are very different from those of the Kingdom of God. John Mallison makes this claim:

From my observations I argue that so much coaching of leaders has been driven by secular management know-how (helpful though it may be) rather than by primarily trying to learn how Jesus related to his Father and went about his ministry.[25]

With remarkable brevity, Jesus topples the most ingrained ideas about leadership. All the disciples' assumptions and convictions about greatness are rendered null and void. While acknowledging that these are the expected and accepted values and practices of leadership in the world, Jesus insists that things in His movement will be different. And this is the point that cannot be overstated. Things in the Kingdom are different. We cannot accept the leadership values of the world. We are not to tweak them or slap scriptures on them. We do not fix a few things here and there or make some minor adjustments. We reject wholesale the wisdom of the world, particularly regarding how we lead. Jesus has a radically different way.

Unfortunately, this is not so easily done. Jane Overstreet directs an international leadership development organization. Her experience with leaders all over the world has led her to this grim analysis, "Usually our leadership looks more like the culture in which we live than like the culture and values of the kingdom of God."[26]

From Hollywood to news outlets to podcasts and books and blogs and social media, the wisdom of the world is available at every turn. We find "helpful" advice from the "experts" on every imaginable topic or issue: finance, self-care, meaning, work, politics, health, time management, food, culture, and on and on. They spout their so-called expertise regarding relationships, marriage, parenting, mental health, emotional strength, what to think about so-and-so's speech and what to eat (or not eat) for breakfast and how to keep yourself regular. Has there ever been a time when pop psychology and pop philosophy so dominate our conversation and convictions?

What is even better(?) is that we can get all the above in whatever flavor we prefer: liberal or conservative; Christian or materialist; baby-boomer or

---

[25] John Mallison, <u>Mentoring to Develop Disciples and Leaders</u>, (Australian Church Resources, 2010), pg 24.

[26] Jane Overstreet, *Unleader* (Biblica, Colorado Springs, 2011), pg 3.

gen-z; capitalist or socialist. This ensures that we can easily find ammunition to prove that which we already "know" (want? feel?) to be true.

As devoted followers of Jesus, I would like to make a counter-proposal. Let's search the Scriptures and seek the wisdom of God's Word.

> See to it that no one takes you captive through hollow and deceptive philosophy, which depends on human tradition and the elemental spiritual forces of this world rather than on Christ. — Colossians 2:8

Listen as the Holy Spirit, through the Apostle Paul, warns the church of Colossae not to be captured by what the world teaches. Oh! How we need to take this to heart in our time! We are in grave danger of basing our lives on "hollow and deceptive philosophy" that originates in "human tradition" and "the spiritual forces of this world." Nouwen puts it succinctly: "The leadership about which Jesus speaks is of a radically different kind from the leadership offered by the world."[27] Neil Cole adds:

> God's kingdom is counterintuitive. It is the opposite of what we see as normative. The problem is that we try to lead right side up in an upside-down kingdom, and this leads to warped leadership.[28]

Where do your favorite teachings about leadership originate? In the academic towers of secular education? In the political or financial halls of power? Do not be fooled by the addition of a few Bible verses. What is the origin of the idea? Do not be taken by vague statements suggesting Jesus taught or modeled such and such. Cultivate a healthy skepticism. This is important because Jesus Himself commanded His first leaders-in-training to very intentionally not follow the prevailing wisdom of the day, telling them clearly, "Not so with you." I suspect He says the same to us. In spite of this, we see two phenomena happening that greatly impact Christian leadership today.

First, there is the classic but relentless movement of worldly leadership ideas into the Church. We are familiar with this because it happens not only with the ideas of leadership but in every area of life. Within the Church, we feel pressure to accept the world's way regarding family and

---

[27] Henri Nouwen, *In the Name of Jesus* (Crossroad Publishing, New York, 2002), pg 62.

[28] Neil Cole, *Organic Leadership* (Baker Books, Grand Rapids, 2009), pg 164.

morality and finance and so on. The surrounding culture infiltrates Christian thinking and, instead of us being salt that seasons and transforms the world, we end up taking on the poisonous philosophy of the world and calling it our own. This clearly happens with leadership.

I was in a southern Asian nation with a group of Christian leaders from various sectors of society, and I asked them to describe the cultural leadership values that are prevalent in their country. Their answers sounded a lot like "lord it over" and "exercise authority." Then I followed up by asking if these values are primarily seen in the world or if they are also accepted in the Church and Christian organizations. They readily confessed that leadership in the Church tended to follow the same assumptions and values as in the world. I have had similar conversations in other nations as well, and I would say it is certainly the same in the US. In fact, we as followers of Jesus seem to be mesmerized by the world's teaching on leadership.

We buy books, listen to podcasts, and read articles that people with no faith in God produce, and we eat them up. We assume that because they have a degree or experience or carry the rather vague credential of "expert," they must have the wisdom and answers we need. Even Christian authors are tempted to base much of their work on the conclusions of these secular gurus. We try to create a synthesis between the wisdom of the world and the wisdom of the Scriptures. After all, "all truth is God's truth." But what if what they are teaching is not actually true? What if Jesus looks it over carefully, finds it wanting, and concludes, "Not so with you?" Nouwen makes the strong statement that "The world in which we live... has no models to offer to those who want to be shepherds in the way Jesus was a shepherd."[29] No models. Neil Cole says it this way:

> The kingdom is opposite from the way we normally see things. Much of what the world sees as good is in fact bad. What the world sees as great is not. What the world thinks is wise is indeed foolish. Therefore, getting direction from the world system is a bad idea. Learning how to lead from successful businessmen, politicians, sports stars, or military leaders is not the best endeavor in God's kingdom. It can become a lethal direction, not only for the leader but for all who would follow. This, however, is what we have often done.[30]

---

[29] Henri Nouwen, *In the Name of Jesus* (Crossroad Publishing, New York, 2002), pg 62.

[30] Neil Cole, *Organic Leadership* (Baker Books, Grand Rapids, 2009), pg 169.

Secondly, we in the Church sometimes tend to think we are impacting leadership philosophy in the world, but often upon closer inspection, we see that we are doing so only on a very surface level (if at all). They have adopted some of our language and practices but remain unchanged on the level of values and worldview. And we have been foolishly satisfied, thinking we are transforming society when a politician or CEO talks about being a servant-leader.

Knowing we as Christian leaders have something significant to offer, we seek to develop content that will be received and practiced by secular people. (I am using the term secular simply to refer to people whose worldview is not centered on God). This can be noble. We know that Jesus' teaching on leadership (and everything else) is true and right and beneficial for all people. So, we attempt to teach about leadership based on biblical principles but without the outright Jesus stuff, thinking it will help a wider range of people, and perhaps ultimately lead them to Him.

To the extent that this draws people to consider Jesus and His ways, it is of course good. It is amazing. However, what often happens is that we in the Church end up being satisfied with these watered-down Jesus "principles" that do not truly capture the essence of His teaching. Jesus did not offer generic leadership principles that anyone could follow; that was not His intention. His purpose was not to help corporate bosses, politicians, and basketball coaches to be more successful in their various pursuits. His purpose was to build a movement and save the world. He was gathering followers who would in turn lead others in the great work of redemption. In doing so, He presented an impossible, unworkable way of leading (and living) that cannot succeed apart from Himself. His intent was never to give Christian principles of leadership that would make secular business people, politicians, and athletes great leaders. That is a myth. The only way a secular person can benefit from Jesus' true leadership teaching is to put their faith in Jesus, take up their cross, and follow Him.

It is impossible to lead in the way of Jesus apart from the presence and activity of Jesus. The gospels do not provide a five-step guide to amazing leadership that anyone can follow. They reveal Jesus to us. When Jesus speaks about greatness or authority, He is very specifically instructing leaders within His movement. He is creating a leadership culture that is in all ways counter to the prevailing one of the world. "The first shall be last and the last first" is not a leadership principle designed to make your venture more successful. It is simply the way of the Kingdom. It assumes obedience to the King. The cup of suffering is not necessarily a strategy to create a better business. It only "works" when we drink that cup *with Jesus*. Kingdom leadership is not a collection of great principles. It is the presence of a Great Person.

We know what the leadership gurus teach. Our society sustains a dizzying array of consultants and authors and conferences and schools and experts on the subject of leadership. None of these are telling us to be bad leaders. They nearly all give some kind of credence to a version of "servant leadership." They want us to be sympathetic, wise, disciplined, inclusive, and many other good things. But the whole foundation for their systems and philosophies comes from what Paul called "the elementary principles of the world" (Colossians 2:20, NASB).

What I want us to get at is the heart of leadership. Once we have our solid foundation in the gospel and Jesus' teachings, we can of course learn some helpful practices and techniques from many different sources. I love to study biographies and glean helpful ideas from those who have led successfully. But it is crucial that we build on Christ; that the heart and soul of our leadership is fully and exclusively Jesus. In this we must be resolute and uncompromising. Jesus draws a sharp distinction between His Kingdom and "the rulers of the Gentiles." So must we.

There is a way of leading that works in our culture. Intelligent and successful people have studied, drawn conclusions, and articulated these principles very skillfully. Jesus, aware of all this, turns to His followers and says, "Not so with you."

Rulers of the Gentiles
(Matthew 20:24-28)

The rulers of the Gentiles lord it over them. — Matthew 20:25b

This concept of "lording over" has several implications that are as true about modern cultural leadership values as they were at the time of Jesus. Firstly, rulers are over. That seems clear enough. There tends to be a clear pecking order, and everyone knows where they are in it. It is usually not difficult to discern who is the boss in a given context. Being a "natural leader" typically implies a person who stands out in a crowd and can easily sway others. They have the charisma and decisiveness to take charge in any situation. The boss wants everyone to know who he is, that he is over.

Not so with you.

There is a sense of pride in the phrase "lord it over." It implies that the person who is leading does so in an air of superiority. This perhaps originates from an underlying assumption that **leaders are better** than followers, or at least that they should be. They are smarter, more skilled, or more knowledgeable. In the way of the world, it is, at least in part, a person's better-ness that makes them fit to lead. This is evident in the Christian world as well. A leader must be more spiritual or more mature than those they lead. The leader is more gifted. The leader is better.

Leaders are better. This is one reason so many of us want to be leaders. Given the two categories of "better" and "not better," nearly all of us would desire to be in the "better" group. This also is why people have a difficult time leading their peers or being led by them. It is comparatively easy to believe and accept that the older and more experienced, the ones who have paid their dues, are better. But the guy who is mostly like me? That can be harder to accept.

Not so with you.

The good news is that you do not have to be better in order to lead. God appoints, and we do not always know His reasons. If scriptural examples are any indication, though, we can be sure that "betterness" is emphatically not the primary criterion. Our emphasis is not on anything that causes us to compare ourselves with others. "When they measure themselves by themselves and compare themselves with themselves, they are not wise" (2 Corinthians 10:12).

This works in Jesus' Kingdom because He Himself is with the one He chooses. His presence makes you the leader you need to be. He can supply the gifts and the wisdom. In the world, perhaps it is better to have the best lead. But Jesus has a record of choosing the unlikely to the point of absurdity. Consider Gideon, fearfully hiding from the enemy when the angel of God called him to lead out in battle. Moses the stutterer was in exile in the desert because of murder. David was not even called by his own father to appear before Samuel. And what about Peter the impulsive fisherman? Or Simon the zealot, Matthew the tax collector, Paul the persecutor? God does not necessarily call the best, but He chooses the ones through whom He can receive the greatest glory.

> Brothers and sisters, think of what you were when you were called. Not many of you were wise by human standards; not many were influential; not many were of noble birth. But God chose the foolish things of the world to shame the wise; God chose the weak things of the world to shame the strong. — 1 Corinthians 1:26-27

In Jesus' new order, leaders do not have to be better, because Jesus is better. He has that part covered. Under-leaders are content with being chosen. As a young man, I found myself in a position of leadership over a group of men and women who were mostly my age and older. In retrospect, I can see that the level of maturity required to follow my lead was much higher than the level of maturity needed to lead these genuine servants. In this case — and I have seen this repeated in other scenarios — the leader was the least in spiritual strength and giftedness. And yet I was the leader, and appropriately so, at least for a season.

Many people find it difficult to lead their peers unless they have a natural confidence (bordering on arrogance) that they are more deserving or better than others. Those who lack such convictions either feel unworthy and insecure in their position or they feel the need to strive to be better than others. They cannot be caught at being not better, lest their leadership be revealed as a sham. That pressure rarely brings about good results. They cannot rejoice from the heart in the accomplishments of others, because they feel threatened. They have to be better. They cannot empower and promote others because, in their minds, their whole justification for leadership is in being better. We know Hudson Taylor as a great missionary and leader. However, this is how he saw it:

> I sometimes think that God must have been looking for someone small enough and weak enough for Him to use, so that all the glory might be His, and that He found me.[31]

---

[31] <u>Hudson Taylor and the China Inland Mission</u>, by Howard Taylor and Mrs Howard Taylor, pg 265.

Leaders lording it over also points to the idea that attaining a leadership position is an end unto itself. It is seen as an admirable goal and something for which we should all strive. It is the motivation behind being a good employee or getting additional training or education. Position is proof of success. It also brings a higher pay grade. People are encouraged to work hard and be faithful so that they can climb to higher positions. Attaining a recognized leadership role is a reward to be sought. It validates the late hours and the hard work and all the effort to please. This is very common in Christian circles, too. There is pressure and motivation to lead because it seems to build value and success.

Not so with you.

In Jesus' movement, leadership is always a means to another, greater end, and that end is the glory of Jesus revealed in the whole world. It is not appropriate for followers of Jesus to claw and strive and compete for leadership positions, because that is not the ultimate goal. We are all working together for something so much more worthy and more noble. As a believer, I want the cause of Jesus to go forward and am willing to do whatever it takes to that glorious end. That may at times mean that I lead, and other times that I do not. It is all the same. I do not compete with my brothers and sisters for recognition, authority, or position. That is not our way.

Leaders of the world expect honor. Their position or their accomplishments should bring them respect. Sometimes such desires become very important indeed, and leaders attach personal value to position and the accompanying honor. They expect to reap the benefits of being boss. Leaders have perks: designated parking spots, the first choice of days off, the better office. In lording it over, they take advantage of the position they have gained. It is acceptable and even expected for them to do so. It is all part of the reward that comes with climbing the ladder.

Not so with you.

In a limited sense, it is perhaps appropriate for leaders to expect honor. The scriptures certainly teach that it is right for people to honor their leaders (for example, 1 Timothy 5:17, Hebrews 13:17). However, the focus of the biblical instruction is towards the people who are being led. These are exhorted to show proper respect to those in authority. To those who are in positions of leadership, on the other hand, it is different. They are not to "lord it over," demanding respect and shows of honor. Leaders in God's Kingdom are first and foremost followers of Jesus, and their desire is always for His honor and glory, not their own. Jesus alone is worthy of this. We rejoice not in receiving praise and adoration and acclaim from people, but from seeing the Lord receive His due. A key difference in the Kingdom is that leadership position is fully unrelated to identity, value, and belonging. We are given the honor of a place in His Kingdom and in His family, not because of any authority that we wield or position that we hold, but because of His grace. And this honor that is graciously bestowed on us is far greater than any prestige or respect we can earn from people. This cannot be over-emphasized.

If you as a leader concern yourself with whether or not people are appropriately honoring you, I want to suggest that you are missing the mark entirely. Your concern is for people to fully honor Jesus. True Kingdom leaders cannot feel slighted by others. They are utterly free from the sting of being snubbed, disrespected, or overlooked. This is easier said than done, but it is nonetheless true. The secret lies in focusing on Jesus and receiving the amazing gifts granted by His love. Whether or not those who follow you show you the respect you feel you deserve is simply not worth noticing. The only times Paul demanded respect for his authority was when the gospel itself was being threatened, and others who claimed greater authority and knowledge than Paul were leading people astray. To combat this, Paul reminded his hearers (such as in Galatians and Corinthians) of the authority he rightly held, so that they would have confidence in the gospel he proclaimed. The end was the glory of Jesus in the right understanding of the gospel, not Paul's need to feel appreciated or respected.

High Officials
(Matthew 20:24-28)

Their high officials exercise authority over them. — Matthew 20:25c

It seems redundant to say that leaders exercise authority. That is inherent in the very definition of the word, isn't it? One could say that leading is exercising authority over another. To lead is to control. Surely leadership comes with responsibility, and responsibility demands authority. In order to meet the demands of responsibility, there must be a measure of control. After all, how can a person be responsible for something they cannot control?

Some would argue that the degree of a person's ability to control others is the degree of leadership they wield. Leaders have the ability to get other people to do what they want them to do. Again, this often comes from a place of heavy responsibility. Leaders must be in control in order to accomplish their objectives and perform their job.

Leaders seek to control the actions of others. A strong leader can get a law passed, be elected to office, motivate their team to work harder, have more people show up to church services, or convince people to volunteer. They get things done through the agency of other people by their ability to lead; to control. They exercise authority.

On the other hand, not being in control is an anxiety-ridden experience. With the pressure of desired outcomes always looming, anything that cannot be controlled is a source of stress. A leader will be assessed based on the results, and when these results are dependent upon other people or circumstances beyond one's control, the anxiety is understandable.

Not only do leaders have authority, but they use it to the utmost. They exercise authority. They make things happen. They get people to do what needs to be done because they have the power to do so — and the responsibility even. A leader who does not utilize the power at their disposal is a poor leader.

Not so with you.

As backward as this seems, leaders who are followers of Jesus do not "exercise authority." In the Father's wonderful Kingdom, leadership is not synonymous with control. You can lead without being in control. Again, this may not be in the least bit feasible in the world. But in the Church, we do not have to be in control. In fact, we cannot be in control. Because Jesus is. Our leadership is based on the sovereignty of Jesus, our King. In the world, leaders motivate, manipulate, encourage, punish, and reward to get people to do what they need them to do. This is intrinsically tied up in what it means to lead. We have a radically different perspective. There are significant implications to the fact of Jesus being in control.

(1) Because Jesus is in control, my leadership is not ultimately tied to my ability to get others to do what I think they should. I do not primarily need followers to obey me. Rather, I am working to connect them to the true Leader, who is Jesus, that they might obey Him. This is a very different process. There is no chain of command *per se* in the Kingdom. We are used to a system in which the person on top makes his or her directives known to those immediately below him or her. These second-level leaders carry out their orders, at least in part, by giving instructions to their own subordinates. And so it continues down the line. We do not typically see the person at the top, be that CEO, president, general, owner, pastor, or whatever, give instructions to each person in the organization directly. There is a chain of command.

With Jesus, it is not exactly like this. We may set up organizations that have some similarities, but in the end, we know that Jesus the King can and does speak personally to every person in His Kingdom, from the least to the greatest. We also know that obeying Jesus is the prime responsibility of each individual person. Of course, Jesus does use human leadership and structures. However, for now, the point is that, because Jesus is in control, our job as leaders is to help everyone to hear and obey Jesus rather than to hear and obey us.

(2) Because Jesus is in control, leadership in God's Kingdom is a partnership, and we are the junior partners. We do not work solo. We do not receive orders from Jesus and then go carry them out in any way we see fit. We intentionally involve Him in every facet of our leadership, and in every step we take. We are very aware that Jesus is directly speaking to those we are also leading, and that He is the senior leader. We are constantly looking to His Word and listening for His voice. We are aware that He is just as likely to speak to us through the one we are leading as He is to speak to them through us.

(3) Because Jesus is in control, prayer is the primary job of leadership. Jesus is the One responsible to move others to appropriate action. As followers of Jesus who lead others, we place a lot of confidence in His ability to motivate — to stir up, convince, and convict. We will at times seek to wisely use motivation techniques, such as positive and negative feedback, but ultimately, we do not trust in those methods. We trust in the inner work of the Holy Spirit. We are convinced that He is at work in the hearts of those we lead, convincing them of what is right and convicting them when they are wrong. This means that the ability to motivate others to action is a useful gift to have and to employ with wise restraint, but it is not a requirement for Kingdom leadership. More importantly, it means that prayer is the great work of a leader. Instead of seeking to move other people to action through the natural means at our disposal, we learn to entreat God to do so. "How important to learn... to move man, through God, by prayer alone."[32]

It is an elemental fact of the Kingdom that prayer is the work of ministry. It is not the only work of ministry and leadership, but it is the foundational work, and it is essential. Prayer is not a last resort to get you out of difficult situations. It is not something you can choose to engage in or not based on your temperament, time, or capacity. It is your work. Jesus is in control. Prayer does not merely make a good leader a little bit better. The fact is that you cannot truly lead in Jesus' movement apart from a devotion to prayer. If you are leading even though your prayer life is anemic, you are not as successful as you may think you are.

Remember, this is a partnership, and you are the junior partner; the very junior partner. The degree of your belief in that truth will be reflected in your prayer life. If you give lip service only to the truth that you are a junior partner (very junior partner), you will not take prayer very seriously. If, on the other hand, you know to the very core of who you are that you are desperately dependent upon Jesus, your prayer life will also reflect that.

(4) The fact of Jesus being in control forces us to redefine success. As leaders, we want to see results. We want to see visible signs that validate our leadership. We want proof that we are doing it right. We assess leadership based on concrete outcomes: more people coming to church, more money in the offering, projects brought to a desired end, goals reached. This is all good, but only to a point. Measurable outcomes are usually not ultimate. The ultimate test of success for a Christian leader is obedience. Did you do what Jesus said to do in the way He said to do it? If so, you are successful, even though the outcomes may not have been what you hoped.

God sometimes told the prophets in advance that their message would not be received and the people would not repent, yet they were to go and speak anyway. Jeremiah was successful, not because Israel heeded his warnings and turned from sin (they did not), but because He spoke the messages given him by God. Stephen's ultimate success was not that many came to Jesus through his preaching (though they did), but that he was a faithful witness even unto death. On the other hand, you may have wonderful results but not be truly successful if you are not following Jesus' directions. It

---

[32] <u>Hudson Taylor's Spiritual Secret</u>, by Howard Taylor and Mrs Howard Taylor, pg 20

may look to everyone like you are a huge success, but in the eyes of the One who matters you are far from that.

Jesus being in control does not negate the need for us to obey human leaders, but it does put that need in proper perspective.

Remember, obeying Jesus is primary. As a leader, I bear fruit when those I lead obey Jesus. That is what I am working towards. Obeying me is never the end goal. Obeying me can be an early step along the discipleship journey, but it is not the destination. Obeying Jesus is the destination.

Obeying human leadership is a way of obeying Christ. This is the "why" of human obedience. It is not because of anything inherent in the person or position that calls for obedience, but because Jesus has commanded obedience to earthly leaders. This means to disobey them is to disobey Jesus (unless, of course, obeying them requires disobeying Jesus). Jesus has ordained that there be civil leaders, church leaders, family leaders, and perhaps other kinds of leaders as well. They are in place at His pleasure. Any authority they have flows from Him, even when they do not acknowledge or even believe in Him.

As a leader, I can rightfully expect obedience only when I am speaking the heart of Jesus. My authority comes from Him and His Word. Therefore, I am not to expect obedience for my personal desires. I expect people to obey me when I speak what Jesus is speaking. This does not cover me telling a subordinate to get my coffee, wash my car, or take care of my child. I can request someone to do that out of friendship. I can pay someone to do these things. But I cannot claim their obedience to such directives on the strengths of me being a pastor or apostle or some kind of Christian leader. I have authority in the lives of others to build up the Kingdom of God, and no more. There are limits. I am not to use leadership for personal ends but for Jesus' will. I will always primarily be a follower, and only secondarily a leader.

As mentioned above, worldly leadership focuses on impacting behaviors. Jesus leadership focuses on transforming the heart. In the world, a person is considered a leader largely based on their ability to influence outward behavior. In the Kingdom, behavior is also impacted, but it is secondary. Inward transformation brings about outward change. The heart rules speech and conduct. Worldly leadership typically bypasses the heart and deals directly with behavior. This is understandable, because, apart from Jesus, heart change poses a truly formidable obstacle.

Exercising authority is all about behavior; getting people to do what you need them to do. This is the realm of the world's "high officials," and Jesus says, "Not so with you." We are to lead apart from exercising authority. Sometimes the exercising of authority works against heart transformation. A person might obey while inwardly remaining rebellious, cynical, or selfish. This is the opposite of true leadership. Exercising authority relies on position, strength, or motivation. Leadership in the Kingdom seeks to help a person desire to do what is right and trains them in how to follow through. This is far beyond the scope of worldly leadership and authority.

Phariseeism is what happens when we attempt to bring this "high official" kind of leadership into the Church. It focuses on getting people to follow the law — or in our language: to do what is right — through whatever means necessary. We know that people should come to church and read their Bibles and not have sex outside of marriage and give tithes. These are good, Christian behaviors. However, we do not "exercise authority" to increase conformity to these standards. We have other more powerful methods. Exercising authority makes use of such unholy tools as guilt, shame, and pride to bring about what it sees to be holy ends: pure and upright behavior. It manipulates. It is (rightly) concerned with issues of sin and rebellion in the Christian community, but it fights these foes with carnal weapons. It is satisfied when behavior changes without considering the heart condition. It is the opponent of apathy and carelessness in the Church, but it prods people to action using anti-gospel techniques.

In contrast to this, as followers of Jesus, we recognize that deviant behavior or decadent lack of action comes from a person's heart not being aligned with the gospel. The answer is in the arena of belief and devotion, not dos and don'ts. Many of the epistles have a clear order to them: first, the author deals with issues of gospel understanding, and then from there moves to the outworking of these beliefs in lifestyle. This pattern is especially clear as you read through books such as Galatians, Colossians, Ephesians, and Romans. Faith leads to action. Believing leads to doing. What I believe about Jesus and about myself ultimately determines what I am to do; how I am to live. We do not have the luxury of skipping this step and going right to behavior. The work of a Christian leader is always the work of the heart.

We do not exercise authority.

6 - SERVANTS AND SLAVES
(Matthew 20:26-28)

Not so with you. Instead, whoever wants to become great among you must be your servant, and whoever wants to be first must be your slave— just as the Son of Man did not come to be served, but to serve, and to give his life as a ransom for many. — Matthew 20:26-28

But among you it will be different. Whoever wants to be a leader among you must be your servant, and whoever wants to be first among you must become your slave. For even the Son of Man came not to be served but to serve others and to give his life as a ransom for many. — Matthew 20:26-28 (NLT)

This is a jolting climax to our passage. To lead is to serve? To be first is to be a slave? As I mentioned in a previous chapter, you cannot even get close to hearing what Jesus is saying here without filling your heart with gospel thinking. You can choose to be slaves to other people because you are confident that God loves you, that God approves of you, that God affirms you, that God cares about you, that God values you, that God lifts you, that God thinks you are great. And He does all of that because of Jesus, not because of what you can attain in life. I hope this is sinking in. You can debase yourself because of your confidence in the Father's love for you. His love is the only force in heaven or on earth that has the power to move you to be a slave to other people and to keep you in this pursuit for a lifetime. Only in His love can you be a Kingdom leader. "Remain in my love," says Jesus.

Having settled that, or, I should say, having progressed in this pursuit, we get to the very heart of this book. Jesus did not merely reveal some good ways to lead, sharing heavenly techniques that will help us reach our goals. No. He turned the entire idea of leadership on its head and fully redefined the concept of what it is to be great. This is difficult for us to grasp because we are so immersed in a culture of leadership that is very different from what Jesus taught and demonstrated. Even in the church, we cannot use the word "lead" without being pulled into connotations that are wholly contrary to the teachings of Jesus.

> Leslie Newbigin goes so far as to question whether the church ought to encourage the concept of leadership, so difficult it is to use without being confused with its non-Christian counterpart. The church needs saints and servants, not "leaders."[33]

We give lip service to the servanthood model but do not allow it to truly shape how we influence others. We talk of being "servant-leaders," but the emphasis always seems to be on the second part of that phrase. Jesus seemed content with the word "servant," apparently not feeling a need to qualify it by attaching "leader." Unfortunately, serving tends to become a method or a technique in the all-important function of leading.

> Many leaders get this backwards. They teach that if you have a position in the kingdom of God, it is important to lead as a servant. But Jesus meant us to see that those who serve are indeed the leaders in his kingdom. Position and title are useless in such an arrangement.[34]

"People who serve are indeed the leaders." Servanthood is not a path to gaining leadership, nor is it merely a good way of leading. It is in itself leadership. It is greatness. It is influence. Jesus is painfully clear and direct in this passage. When you choose to serve, you are leading. When you submit, you are influencing. When you try to lead in any other way than by serving, you are not leading people towards Jesus.

------

[33] J. Oswald Sanders, <u>Spiritual Leadership</u> (Moody Publishers, Chicago, 2007), pg 150.

[34] Floyd McClung, *You See Bones, I See An Army* (YWAM Publishing, Seattle, 2008), Kindle location 1184.

Remember, this is not a technique or a philosophy that is meant to work in the world. We must be clear on this point. We are talking about Kingdom leadership, and the most important fact about the Kingdom is that there is a King. Jesus is the Leader. When He calls you to a specific role that may or may not include what we consider a position of leadership, He is calling you to be a servant in that role. The primary difference between Kingdom leadership and worldly leadership is the presence and rule of the King. When the King is present, we are all servants. Mike Patz and Brian Sanders issue this crucial distinction:

> If we are leaders who serve, then it is only a tool or a tactic that we think will help us lead. But if we are servants who lead, then we lead because we are told to. We are leaders who are always conscious that we are under another. When we are servants first, the goal is not leadership, it is obedience and pleasing the one we serve.[35]

In the Kingdom, leading itself is an act of service, because it is simply obedience to the King. We lead because we are given the mandate to do so by the One Leader we all follow. Thus, it would be better to be in the habit of thinking of ourselves as servants rather than as leaders.

> We tend to think we need leaders who serve, but really we need servants who lead. Servanthood is not an adjective to describe a good leader, as if it is one of many qualities of a good leader. Servanthood is what we need, even more than leadership... We don't first find leaders and hope they take on the qualities of a servant. We need to find servants and let them be just that. Servanthood is not the path to leadership; it is the leadership that the kingdom requires.[36]

To speak of being a "servant who leads" rather than a "leader who serves" may seem to be splitting hairs, but I assure you this is not mere semantics. Not at all. Here we begin to get to the root of many of our leadership issues and outright failures. Because we have not fully immersed ourselves in gospel thinking regarding our own identities and purpose, we insist on elevating the

---

[35] Mike Patz and Brian Sanders, *Different: Reimagining Holiness for a Wandering Church in a Watching World* (Underground Media, 2014), Kindle location 1405.

[36] Neil Cole, *Organic Leadership* (Baker Books, Grand Rapids, 2009), pg 204.

concept of being a leader and downplaying the divine call to lower ourselves into servanthood. This is no insignificant oversight on our part. It is detrimental to the work of the Kingdom. It blocks us from truly glorifying and revealing Jesus as we are commissioned to do.

What does it mean to truly be a servant rather than simply a leader who (sometimes) serves? In this chapter, I will attempt to lay out three core traits of servants: humility, diligence, and invisibility. Before getting to that, though, I will offer several thoughts regarding what it means to make servanthood primary as opposed to making leadership primary.

(1) Jesus calls you to be a servant, not just to do servant-like things. Honestly, it is easy to serve people. Sometimes. In the way I choose. To a certain degree. According to my schedule. Under the right conditions. The difference is control. As a leader who serves, you can do servant-like things when and how it seems best or convenient or beneficial for you to do so. But as a servant who may sometimes lead, you lay down the luxury of dictating the details of your acts of service. You lift others above yourself. You put them and their needs before your own. You submit to those you are called to lead. When you think of yourself first as a leader, you inevitably make a show of servanthood. But when you think of yourself primarily as a slave, you surrender control.

The servanthood that Jesus calls you to is a mindset that produces a certain kind of action and behavior. It begins with an attitude of the heart. You have to choose to identify yourself as a servant. Remember, because of the gospel and all that Jesus has done for you, this is not belittling. You can do it because you know who you are in the Father. Paul, Peter, James, and Jude all introduced themselves in various letters as servants. Jesus Himself took on "the very nature of a servant" (Philippians 2:7). To take on the nature of a servant is more than working at a soup kitchen once a month or occasionally doing some task that you deem to be menial. It is an intentional state of mind. It produces actions every day that are in keeping with being a servant. It accepts the inconvenience and the fatigue and the degradation of becoming a slave. To take on the nature of a servant is to be a servant 24-7.

(2) To be a servant is to be vulnerable. It requires taking a great risk. "Whoever wants to be first must be your slave." These are the actual words of Jesus. To make yourself a slave is to put yourself in the most vulnerable position imaginable. You could be mistreated, taken advantage of, used, and abused. It could happen. In truth, it probably will.

It might be disturbing to you that Jesus offers no comforting caveats about healthy boundaries or not allowing another to walk over you. You may feel the need to offer "balance" to Jesus' rather extreme language. But I exhort you: don't. Let's listen to Him without adding to or subtracting from His message. Jesus simply says, "Must be your slave." How is this possible? The key, of course, is faith. You must trust Him. You may not have complete confidence in the one you are serving, but you can fully trust Jesus who is present with you in your servanthood. You can afford to give the gift of trust to flawed people because Jesus has your back. It is true that you may still get hurt, worn out, or betrayed. Jesus experienced all of that. But when it happens to you, you can take it as part of that cup you agreed to drink with Him. You will be walking in deep fellowship with Jesus Himself. What glory! What a privilege! He is so good and full of grace. He is trustworthy, and He loves you with great affection. Because of that, you can do this.

(3) Choose to value the qualities of servanthood more than the so-called gifts of leadership. When choosing others for positions of authority, search out the person who has taken on the nature of a servant; who has made himself a slave to all. This will bring much better results than choosing the person with the most obvious abilities to sway people and get others to follow them and make decisions quickly and firmly. We tend to notice people who possess what we consider to be "leadership gifts" and promote those people into positions that give them authority. This is how things are done in the world, and it just makes sense. However, Jesus has forged a different way for us. The servants are the leaders. It is the character qualities of a servant rather than the skills or personality of a leader that are in higher demand in the Kingdom. Greatness does not come by bending others to your will. It comes by lifting others that they might connect with the King of kings and learn to follow and obey Him.

(4) To be a servant who leads means that you are wholly free from the need for position or title. This is nothing short of amazing. Servanthood — greatness — does not require any kind of designated role or recognition or bestowed authority. You are free to serve others right now, in whatever setting you currently exist. There are no limits. You can make yourself a slave at work, at home, at school, in the neighborhood, with your friends, at church, everywhere. And in so doing, in the power and anointing of Jesus Himself, you will be great. You will influence. You will lead.

(5) The kind of servanthood we are discussing gives purpose to leadership outside of position. For many, the purpose of leading is simply to be a leader. That is the end goal. For others, the goals are only those that relate to their particular enterprise: Winning more games, making more money, getting more people to church. In contrast, true Kingdom leadership always has the same ultimate purpose: to help others to know and follow Jesus; to reveal Jesus to the world; to bring redemption and reconciliation. Servanthood is the only path that will get us there.

Humble Servants
(Matthew 20:26-27)

> Not so with you. Instead, whoever wants to become great among you must be your servant, and whoever wants to be first must be your slave. — Matthew 20:26-27

The key to us making ourselves slaves of other people is, in a word, humility. As Jesus followers, we all give a nod to humility. We readily admit that it is important and should be cultivated, but in practice, we tend to consider other traits much more important when it comes to leadership. The fact of the matter is that humility is the essential virtue for Christian leadership. *The* essential virtue. All leadership in Jesus' Kingdom is built on it. The presence of true humility is sufficient to make up for any number of other deficiencies. Similarly, there are no gifts or virtues that can overcome the lack of humility. Andrew Murray, in his classic work on the subject, says this:

> Humility is the only soil in which the graces root; the lack of humility is the sufficient explanation of every defect and failure. Humility is not so much a grace or virtue along with others; it is the root of all, because it alone takes the right attitude before God, and allows Him as God to do all.[37]

Following are a few thoughts about the kind of humility that will allow us to be slaves of others, and thus the leaders God calls for His Kingdom work.

---

[37] Andrew Murray, *Humility* (Fig Books, 2012), pg 4

(1) Humility is not having too high of a view of yourself.

> Because of the privilege and authority God has given me, I give each of you this warning: Don't think you are better than you really are. Be honest in your evaluation of yourselves, measuring yourselves by the faith God has given us. — Romans 12:3 (NLT)

Be careful to not miss the emphasis. He is not writing to make sure you think highly enough of yourself, but is combating the propensity to think rather too much of yourself. It is a warning. "Don't think you are better than you really are." Be willing to admit that you naturally think you are better than you are. Maybe that is tough to accept, but I know it is true for me. It is Paul's inspired intent to bring attention to this tendency.

We are prone to think that, to protect our fragile emotional well-being, we need to rehearse positive things about ourselves. We need to glory in our strengths and focus on our gifts and our good qualities. This is not so. The danger we are called upon to beware of is thinking too highly of ourselves. Clearly, this is not achieved by putting ourselves down all the time either. The best course is probably to simply think about ourselves less (a very difficult sell in our age of self-awareness, personality tests, social media, etc). But when we do indulge in a little introspection, we must avoid the danger of thinking too highly.

(2) Humility is valuing others.

> Don't be selfish; don't try to impress others. Be humble, thinking of others as better than yourselves. Don't look out only for your own interests, but take an interest in others, too. — Philippians 2:3-4 (NLT)

Again, please note that the emphasis is far from something like this: "Paul says 'don't look out **only** for your own interests.' So he is teaching me to be sure to look out for my interests too, as well as those of others." If that is where your mind goes, I suggest that you are (perhaps unconsciously) shielding yourself from the intent and the true weight of the apostle's words. Paul is taking it as an accepted truth that you are already proficient at looking out for your own interests. Now, he says, turn that same devotion to the interests of others.

Consider this more deeply. Think about how devoted you are to your own interests. You are fully committed to getting what you want, to avoiding getting hurt, to eating when you are hungry, to being with who you want, to watching that movie or going to that concert. You are all in for your morning cup of coffee, for getting well when you are sick, for sleeping when you are tired. Now, be as serious about the interests of others as you are about these things.

Of course, the real issue we have with this verse is how Paul associates humility with thinking of others as better than ourselves. This does not sound like the self-help, self-esteem Jesus we have come to know and love. Yes, Paul uses the word "better." He purposefully does not say "as good as." He says "better." Some translations interpret the phrase as meaning "more important." So we have to think of others as being more important than us. This sounds wrong to our cultural (worldly) sensibilities, but truly you cannot understand humility without learning to consider others as better.

Now, it does not say that others *are* better than you. Nor does it say that God sees others as better than you. However, it does say to "consider" others or to "think of" others as better than you, as more important than you. This is an intentional training of the mind to view others in a certain way. It includes two parts: First, esteeming others more highly than you are prone to; and second, not thinking too highly of yourself (as discussed before). This is a mental and emotional discipline. It is a practice, and you can become better at it.

Before getting into this more, allow me to offer a word of comfort. Going down this path will not lead you into insecurity or low self-esteem or depression. It will not make you a wimp. It will not even usually cause you to be less honored and respected by others, though that is the least of our concerns. In truth, it will lead to freedom and peace, and, in all probability, you will find that people respect and honor you more, not less. It is one of those beautiful and profound paradoxes of the Christian life, similar to "If you try to hang on to your life, you will lose it. But if you give up your life for my sake, you will save it" (Luke 9:24).

Esteem others more highly than you are accustomed to doing. There are some people on whom you readily bestow great honor. We all have our heroes. Let us remove those people from this exercise. Think rather of all the others: the very normal people with whom you do life; the too-worldly people you worship with every week, the outright sinners you work with, the awkward or annoying people in your family. Consider them more important. Better. Does that seem hard? Impossible? I hope so. We need Jesus to help us do this!

Our default mode is to consider others as less so that we can see ourselves as more. When I criticize you, I feel better about myself. I like being better than. When I notice your sin, I feel less badly about my own. But we need to — we desperately need to — turn this around. I must see you as better. It is imperative for me to train my gaze to not lock in on the things about you that annoy me, the things that you do not do well, the outright sinful actions, wrong attitudes, foolish choices, and immature behaviors. Amy Carmichael said,

> If I can easily discuss the shortcomings and the sins of any; if I can speak in a casual way even of a child's misdoings, then I know nothing of Calvary love.[38]

Instead, I need to look at your heart, giving you more credit for right motives and intentions than my critical mind wants to do. I need to intentionally see your strengths and successes and gifts and to focus on the beauty and value and glory of who you are. You are better. You are better than me.

As mentioned in a previous chapter, we are sometimes called upon to lead people who are in a similar stage of spiritual growth and even to lead those who are more mature than us. It should go without saying that the key to this kind of leadership is humility. Serve them. Honor them. Consider them as better than you. And what will the results be? You will grow. Your ministry will prosper together. You will gain the respect of those you lead. You will ensure that their gifts and experience and all that they have to offer are used in a valuable way.

The importance of this attitude cannot be overstated. The work of the Kingdom depends on humble leaders who do not set themselves above others. Consider this:

> All religions tend to create a class of people who are above others so 1) they can revel in that and 2) the rest of us can say it's their job. Christianity was started without any of those structures, and ended up like so many false religions do

---

[38] *If*, Amy Carmichael, CLC Publications: Fort Smith, PA, 1938.

when they create a ministry caste structure. When we see real movements of God take off, they happen when people are free. [39]

(3) Humility is an awareness of your desperate need for God.

Apart from me you can do nothing. — John 15:5.

Each time he said, "My grace is all you need. My power works best in weakness." So now I am glad to boast about my weaknesses, so that the power of Christ can work through me. That's why I take pleasure in my weaknesses, and in the insults, hardships, persecutions, and troubles that I suffer for Christ. For when I am weak, then I am strong. — 2 Corinthians 12:9-10

Charles Spurgeon said it like this:

I must confess that I never realize Christ's preciousness so much as when I feel myself still to be, apart from Him, an undeserving, hell-deserving sinner.[40]

So, are we to beat ourselves up? To morosely stare at our sin, our shame, our wretchedness? Are we to weigh ourselves down with the burden of our guilt? Clearly not. We are forgiven. We have received grace. We are the righteousness of Christ. We are clean. We are a new creation. Yes! The help comes, though, when we also intentionally keep in our consciousness the clear fact that we are so only because of the grace of Jesus and that it takes nothing less than His death and resurrection to make us so.

My depravity is so deep and profound that it requires the most precious and powerful substance of the blood of God Himself to make me okay. That is a sobering thought, but a helpful one. Humility is the only right grid through which I see myself and the world.

"How can such meditations possibly help me?" you ask. "I am insecure enough as it is." The issue, perhaps, is that you are basing your security on false and unreliable sources. To feel secure and significant, you are trusting in your goodness, your gifts, your position, your appearance, your influence, your

---

[39] Ed Stetzer, from an article at a website no longer functioning: http://www.rev.org/article.asp?ID=3113

[40] Charles Spurgeon, <u>The Complete Works of Charles Spurgeion</u>, Volume 55, Delmarva Publication, 2013.

success, your popularity, your cleverness, your standing in comparison with others, your spirituality, your devotion, your faith. These things will fail you. Your security can only be in Jesus.

Remember Paul's beautiful rant in Philippians 3. After listing all the things that at one time gave him a sense of self-worth and importance, he says, "I once thought these things were valuable, but now I consider them worthless because of what Christ has done" (Philippians 3:7, NLT). Are you willing to face the utter worthlessness of all the things that give you a sense of value outside of Jesus? Do not skip over that. This includes your leadership, your position, your achievements, your influence, your ministry, and the respect that others have for you. Again, hear what Andrew Murray says:

Humility, the place of entire dependence on God, is, from the very nature of things, the first duty and the highest virtue of the creature, and the root of every virtue. And so pride, or the loss of this humility, is the root of every sin and evil.[41]

Servants Work
(Matthew 20:26-27)

Not so with you. Instead, whoever wants to become great among you must be your servant, and whoever wants to be first must be your slave. — Matthew 20:26-27

In the last section, I wrote about the key to becoming a servant, humility: not thinking too highly of yourself, considering others as more important than you, and always remembering your desperate need for God.

Now I want to highlight another self-evident element of servanthood: Servants work. Servants serve. It is what they do.

If our calling as leaders is truly to be servants, part of that must mean that true Kingdom leaders work hard. In appointing you to lead, Jesus is calling you to a new level of diligence. This is extremely important. Oswald

---

[41] Andrew Murray, *Humility* (Fig Books, 2012), pg 3.

Sanders writes, "The young man of leadership caliber will work while others waste time, study while others snooze, pray while others daydream."[42]

When I was a young, newly married man setting off to change the world, I learned a tough lesson. More accurately, I was taught a hard lesson, but I am still working on truly learning it. My wife and I had joined a missions-sending organization and were participating in three months of pre-field training. All of us in the program lived together, and we all were required to put in a certain number of hours of labor on the property every week. Each week, I completed my required hours. At least, I was able to convince myself that I did. I put the time in — within a few minutes per day. I did not necessarily finish the jobs I was assigned, but the agreement was a certain amount of time. I kept the letter of the law (if you rounded up). I grumbled. I was slow. I was lazy. There you have it. Even now it hurts to admit it. The director called me out on it. I was furious. I had my hours recorded. How dare he?

My wife, on the other hand, was a servant. She consistently worked more hours each week than were required, and she never complained. She worked hard and went beyond fulfilling every responsibility given to her. She has always been like that. Fortunately, over the years, I began to pick up on it, and have grown in this area. I am still tempted to laziness, but years of life and the steady example of my wife help me more and more to overcome.

If you want to change the world, it is going to be a lot of work. Yes, Jesus carries the lion's share of the burden. Compared to Him, your part is truly lightweight. But it will not feel that way. No vocation in the world will require more of you than partnering with Jesus to bring redemption. And remember, this is your calling, no matter what your job. Your primary work is to serve Jesus in His great work.

Leaders serve. They find what needs to be done, and they do it. They show up early to set up and stay late to clean up. They do not do so in a half-hearted way. Leaders put in long hours, willingly staying up late or getting up early, or both, to faithfully fulfill their responsibilities. They sacrifice "me time" without a thought in order to do the work of the Kingdom. They take initiative, not waiting for someone else. They do not complain about their disappearing free time. They are not stopped by obstacles but instead find

---

[42] J. Oswald Sanders, Spiritual Leadership (Moody Publishers, Chicago, 2007), pg 53.

ways to overcome challenges, though it costs them dearly in time and energy. They are reliable. You can count on them. Leaders serve.

The church in the West must take care to not embrace the narcissistic, "take care of me first" values of our culture. Otherwise, we will be in danger of growing a crop of lazy, complacent leaders. We will produce leaders who know all about self-care, but little about sacrifice. We will raise leaders who are so steeped in the worldly wisdom of saying "no" that they forget they belong to a Master with the right to make demands of them. Friends, leaders are slaves. We can (and should) often feel tired because of the Kingdom work in which we engage.

> If a Christian is not willing to rise early and work late, to expend greater effort in diligent study and faithful work, that person will not change a generation. Fatigue is the price of leadership. Mediocrity is the result of never getting tired.[43]

Does this sound like a recipe for burnout? That is an important concern. Yes, it is possible for us to overdo it and to push ourselves too much. It happens fairly often. That is not what I am advocating. We can, however, work very hard consistently and still not burn out. I am convinced that a misunderstanding of the following factors is at least as significant in causing burn-out as the amount of work we do:

Expectations. Many of us, especially in the West perhaps, expect to have significant free time each week. We have been led to believe that it is our right and even our responsibility. We are told that it is important for our physical and emotional health and we have bought that line wholesale. But we must consider: is this in fact true, or is it merely the attitude of an affluent and self-absorbed society? We have created expectations for ourselves that make it all but impossible to give significant time in service to others and to the church. The idea of ownership of time is at the root of this false expectation.

We embrace the idea that our time, or at least the time when we are not occupied at work or with other life responsibilities, belongs to us. We, maybe begrudgingly, offer some of that time to God and congratulate ourselves on our generosity in so doing. It is the same way that some people treat the tithe, as a kind of God-tax that belongs to Him, leaving us the rest to do with as we please. This is as false with time as it is with money. God owns all of us,

---

[43] J. Oswald Sanders, <u>Spiritual Leadership</u> (Moody Publishers, Chicago, 2007), pg 119.

including our time and our money. It is all His. The wonderful news is that He loves us and wants good for us. He gives us gifts of leisure, entertainment, and fun. He blesses us with meaningful social interactions and special moments: hikes and movies and games and conversations and books and museums and coffee shops and bikes and sports and concerts and on and on. But, instead of responding in simple gratitude, we often take the gift as our right. The result is that when He withholds the gift — when our time becomes full and we begin to lose opportunities for free time — we feel disappointed and even ill-used. We, perhaps unconsciously, think that "our" time has been stolen. We manage this either by continuing to "do it all," thus pushing our bodies and minds further than their capacity allows, or we remove other things from our schedule so that we can remain with our "rightful" free time. The other things we remove too often are our spiritual practices and acts of service to others.

Priorities. You choose how to spend your time. If Jesus is your Master and the Church His instrument on earth, you can expect that He wants you significantly invested in a local fellowship. This is doubly true for those with the aspiration to lead. You may need to ask some significant lifestyle questions: Does the career you have chosen allow you the space to serve the Lord and His people? If not, are you choosing a certain level of affluence, security, and prestige over Christ? In many cases, perhaps, the space is there, but you simply choose to fill it in other ways. Do you give lesser activities, such as personal hobbies, entertainment, and leisure, the same weight of priority as others-focused service and Christ-centered spiritual exercises? Please note that I am not saying that those things are wrong or that they have no legitimate place in our lives. That is not at all what I am getting at. However, I am suggesting that some of us tend to give them more weight than they deserve. We end up feeling pressed for time and overwhelmed with life because we are unwilling to give up or cut back on lesser things.

Some of the most common conversations among Christians that I hear revolve around two things: (1) how incredibly busy, tired, stressed, and burned out they are; and (2) the details of show after show that they faithfully follow on Netflix (or the detailed exploits of their favorite sports team). The church tends to get what is left over, and sometimes that is not much.

Refreshment. True refreshment comes from time devoted to the Lord. Prayer, Bible meditation, gathering with God's family, worship. These concepts are included in the biblical idea of Sabbath. Our culture, however, is convinced that refreshment comes from tv, movies, video games, shopping, eating, lounging on our couch. The truth is that often we burn out because we are not filling up. We pull into a gas station, put a dollar's worth of gas in our car, spend $19 on junk food for ourselves, and then wonder why our car is stranded on the side of the road later in the day.

To be clear, burnout is often much more complicated than what I have made it out to be in this short discussion, and the causes are complex and myriad. It is a very real and difficult circumstance, and I by no means intend to put the blame on those who experience it or to belittle its effects. Most people who experience burnout are devoted, hard-working servants who are trying to make it all work. I do, however, want to insist that we can avoid burnout while at the same time engaging in long-term, sacrificial service. Servants are hard workers.

Servants also work without regard for what the task is. It does not have to be something they enjoy or feel confident in. It does not have to be in alignment with their gifts or passions. It is just work. It has been said that "nothing is really work unless you would rather be doing something else." That may be overstated, but there is a grain of truth in it. Of course, we can enjoy our work, and the Father likes it when we do. But please hear this: We do not have to enjoy it for it to be God's will. Servants do not have the luxury of choosing their service. Sometimes you serve somewhere not because a gift analysis points you in that direction, but simply because the Lord asks you to. You do not have to be a natural fit for everything you are called to do. You do it because He chooses.

Sometimes you do things simply because someone has to do them. In fact, much of the time you do things for this reason. Slaves do not get to choose.

But what about serving according to my gifts, abilities, and passions? Yes, there is a place for that. Yes, we all are different members of the body, each with different graces. Yes, it is good to focus on those areas. Yes, yes, yes! But be careful.

We have become overly enamored with examining ourselves to determine just what we should be doing. Although this often comes from a genuine desire to be fruitful for the glory of Jesus, it very naturally denigrates into a self-focused attitude toward ministry. People join churches or go on mission trips so that they can use their gifts and thus feel good about themselves, rather than for the glory of Jesus. The difference is perhaps a subtle one, but very important. We end up making our service about ourselves rather than about Jesus.

Do not use the latest gift or motivation tool to avoid doing things you simply do not want to do. When they were younger, my kids emphatically did not like to wash dishes. They were convinced it was not their gift, and frankly, I was inclined to agree. They were certainly not passionate about it. But, because I was an abusive father, I made them do the dishes all the same. No, I did this because I am a loving father. I did this because they had to learn that their lives will always be full of such tasks and they will never be mature servants of Jesus if they do not learn to embrace work. And, more than that, they had to do the dishes because the dishes tended to get dirty. You do not outgrow working on tasks you do not like. In the world, you can graduate to having others do that stuff. Not so in the Kingdom. You remain a servant. The more you "lead," the more you serve. Or, more accurately still, the more you serve, the more you lead.

> The heights by great men reached and kept
> Were not attained by sudden flight;
> But they, while their companions slept,
> Were toiling upward in the night.[44]

Invisible Servants
(Matthew 20:26-27)

Not so with you. Instead, whoever wants to become great among you must be your servant, and whoever wants to be first must be your slave. — Matthew 20:26-27

A third essential element of servanthood is that servants do their work unseen. Servants do not insist on being in the limelight. They do their work in the background. The better they do their job, the less they are noticed. They can work quite apart from the hope of appreciation. Jesus said:

---

[44] Unknown poet, quoted in J. Oswald Sanders, Spiritual Leadership (Moody Publishers, Chicago, 2007), pg 55.

Suppose one of you has a servant plowing or looking after the sheep. Will he say to the servant when he comes in from the field, "Come along now and sit down to eat?" Won't he rather say, "Prepare my supper, get yourself ready and wait on me while I eat and drink; after that you may eat and drink?" Will he thank the servant because he did what he was told to do? So you also, when you have done everything you were told to do, should say, "We are unworthy servants; we have only done our duty." -- Luke 17:7-10

Slaves of the Kingdom resist recognition. Instead of positioning themselves to be noticed and rewarded, they scheme to be invisible. This is no easy task in our social media world, but it is all the more needed because of that. Their ambition is for Jesus to be recognized, for Him to be more and more visible.

Many people with the worldly ambition of leadership can serve. They can and do work extremely hard. They can even do lowly tasks. But try taking away all hope of recognition and appreciation, and you will see the zeal of their diligence melt away. Yet Jesus calls us to serve in this way because we have volunteered to be slaves, not to be top dog or to be praised and honored. That is for Jesus, the Master. Ours is the joy of seeing Him glorified.

Does this arrangement seem unfair? Are you "triggered" at the thought of being an inconsequential, under-appreciated servant? Remember the gospel! Remember what He has done for you! What He has rescued you from! Remember that He loved you and died for you when you had done nothing to earn His favor. Talk about not fair! Jesus is so good! His glory motivates us. Not being noticed or appreciated by people is nothing. Our service is truly an act of love for Jesus. Love, in its very essence, focuses on the other. We do not serve for personal gain or glory, but in love for the One who has given all for us.

Examine yourself. How do you work when nobody will know? How will you work when, though people know, they will not appreciate? Until you come to grips with this, you will experience much frustration and angst as you attempt to lead. You need to accept this simple fact: As a servant in God's Kingdom, you will not be appreciated in this life for all you do. This is true not only because people are mean or insensitive. It is true because you are not meant to be appreciated for all you do. This may be difficult to receive at first, but think about it. Jesus is the One to be appreciated. If you are doing your work right, in the power of the Holy Spirit, Jesus will receive the praise. Is that not awesome? You can work in such a way that Jesus is more known and more loved and more obeyed.

If all of this makes you think that Jesus is a harsh and selfish Master, take heart. As you serve and give and sacrifice out of love for Him, remember that He does the same for you! Jesus is so good! Hear what the master says to the faithful servant in the parable of the talents:

> Well done, good and faithful servant! You have been faithful with a few things; I will put you in charge of many things. Come and share your master's happiness! — Matthew 25:21

He will invite you and me to share in His happiness. He does not need to do this. There is no scenario whatsoever in which we deserve it. We are His servants and do not deserve to be even that, yet He insists on making us sons and daughters. So do not fear. He will share His joy with you and even His appreciation. But do not grasp for it. Do not begin to think you deserve it. That is the key. He does more than reward your faithful service. He makes you sons and daughters and heirs. He does so not because you have a right to it, but because He is good. In the end, your "reward" will far outweigh your sacrifice, and you will know that what He offers you is a gift disguised as a reward.

> For our light and momentary troubles are achieving for us an eternal glory that far outweighs them all. — 2 Corinthians 4:17

> I consider that our present sufferings are not worth comparing with the glory that will be revealed in us. — Romans 8:18

The slave is in the background, in the periphery. He is the one furthest from the center of attention, and this is our special privilege as leaders. The Kingdom is not about you being fulfilled, or you being great, or you being recognized. We must dispense with the petty competitions and excruciating insecurities and offenses. Jesus is bringing redemption to the world! People are dying — literally dying — for His cause, His glory, and His love for the lost and the hurting and the confused. So, we must stop thinking the Kingdom is about how we feel or what we get out of it. Jesus is calling us to something so much greater.

Servants not only seek to glorify Jesus rather than themselves but they also are called to lift other people. In fact, herein lies one of the greatest works of Christian leaders, and one of the things that most sets them apart as different from the world. Instead of grasping and climbing to get to the top, they use their influence, gifts, and position to push others up and ahead. Their joy is to see those they lead surpass them. They labor to make others look good and to give recognition rather than seek it for themselves.

As a father, I do not worry that my children will surpass me, receive more acclaim or respect than me, or be more successful than me. In fact, that is my desire. I long for it and work for it. I want them to do better than I have done. I rejoice in their every accomplishment, no matter how modest or how magnificent. I relish being known as "Rebekah's dad" more than as pastor or author or any other position. My heart leaps when one of my children receives recognition for work well done. I feel proud of them. And so it is meant to be in all Kingdom relationships.

Many Christian leaders around the world fear the success of those they lead. They refuse to give them too much responsibility or to recognize them with public acclaim because they themselves do not want to be surpassed. They want to remain in control. They are jealous for the honor and the adoration and the respect of those they lead. They are afraid that if their "subordinates" become too popular they will "steal" members. They worry that their own glory will be diminished or their financial resources diverted to another, so they set up their disciples as opponents in the competition for applause, power, and greatness. They put down when they should be lifting up. They micro-manage instead of empowering.

Not so with you!

As slaves of Christ, we have the great privilege of making ourselves slaves of all.

Though I am free and belong to no one, I have made myself a slave to everyone, to win as many as possible. —1 Corinthians 9:19

Whoever wants to become great among you must be your servant, and whoever wants to be first *must be slave of all.* — Mark 10:43-44 (emphasis added).

As a Christian leader, your glory is to see those you disciple do greater things than you. This was even true for Jesus.

Very truly I tell you, whoever believes in me will do the works I have been doing, and they will do even greater things than these, because I am going to the Father.
— John 14:12

Let us attempt to make this practical. I hope you are convinced that Kingdom leaders are servants and that an important quality of servants is that they serve in anonymity. They do not seek fame or glory or even simple appreciation. Their motives spring from love and are rooted in gratitude for all Jesus has done for them. They seek the glory of Jesus in all things, and their work is largely to see others lifted beyond themselves. How do we do this in real life?

It all begins in the heart. To be a true servant you must begin by cultivating trust, gratitude, and love. You can serve Christ and others because ultimately, you trust Jesus. You know that He will not call you to anything bad or wrong. You know that He wants good for you. You trust that even if it feels like He is calling you into something painful and even demeaning, it is ultimately for good. He will reward you in the end far more than you deserve. You can trust Him.

As you trust Him, you also need to be intentionally grateful all the time. No matter how difficult a thing you are going through, you can recognize that He has been good to you. He has given you so much. He has set you free, made you a son or daughter of the Father, granted you everlasting life and eternal rewards. Be thankful.

Gratitude leads you to love. The more you realize and think about what He has done for you, the more you will love Him. Love is the ultimate and only force that can compel you to choose to truly be a servant. No other motivation will do. Only love for Jesus empowers you to lay down your ambitions and pride and selfishness to become a slave.

Move your heart into alignment with the powerful forces of trust, gratitude, and love. As your heart is softening to the great influence of Jesus through these pursuits, you can begin to do things intentionally as a servant.

Begin by trying to do small acts of kindness or love anonymously. Build an appreciation in your own soul for doing good things that only God sees. Do these acts without social media posts and without sharing the testimony of how God used you. Let them just be little sacrifices in the Name of Jesus and for His eyes alone. Learn to revel in the joy of His notice and appreciation. Receive His "well done," and be satisfied. I am not saying to never share what God has done through you as a way of encouraging others, but I am suggesting that, in order to build the "muscle" of servanthood, intentionally do some things without others knowing. And from there, move on to bigger and more costly deeds. Enjoy your secrets with Jesus.

> Be careful not to practice your righteousness in front of others to be seen by them. If you do, you will have no reward from your Father in heaven. So when you give to the needy, do not announce it with trumpets, as the hypocrites do in the synagogues and on the streets, to be honored by others. Truly I tell you, they have received their reward in full. But when you give to the needy, do not let your left hand know what your right hand is doing, so that your giving may be in secret. Then your Father, who sees what is done in secret, will reward you. — Matthew 6:1-4

Another way of growing in your invisibility as a servant is to actively seek to lift others. Give younger leaders opportunities to lead even when you are not fully sure they will succeed, and be ready to take the blame when they fail and give them credit when they do well. Practice the beautiful art of giving honor to others, both privately and publicly. Force yourself to do this until you begin to experience the joy of watching others receive appreciation while you stand back in the shadows with a gratified smile on your face.

Leaders serve because leaders are servants. Work hard. Go unnoticed. Change the world. Glorify Jesus.

Ransom for Many
(Matthew 20:28)

> Just as the Son of Man did not come to be served, but to serve, and to give his life as a ransom for many. — Matthew 20:28

Jesus concludes this astonishing teaching by drawing the disciples' attention to Himself. He is the supreme example, and He summarizes His own leadership in three powerful statements.

First, He did not come to be served. The King of Everything, who has legions of angels at His beck and call, did not come to earth to be served.

He did not come to conquer by force or to overpower mankind so that they would serve Him. Of course, He could have done so, and it would have been well within His rights. It would seemingly have been appropriate and even good. He could have brought order to the chaos and extinguished evil. But would He have inspired love? Would He have transformed hearts?

He is our example. He did not come to be served. What about you? Do you carry an expectation that others should serve you? Perhaps you have paid your dues and now it is time to reap the benefits? Maybe you have given and given and given, and now you have a natural expectation that it is your time to receive. Are there people from whom you expect service? Do the people in your church or ministry or circle of influence exist to serve your vision and make it come about? Do you see yourself as the man of God who rules in His stead, issuing decrees and telling people what to do? Do you come to be served? That was not the example set for us by Jesus. What if your role as leader is not to convince people to follow your vision and make it come to pass, but rather to help discover what their vision is and do all you can to see that happen?

Secondly, He came to serve. Even beyond not having the expectation of being served, Jesus came with the proactive intent of serving others. Again, this is our King. This is the greatest Being that exists, and He came to serve, to act for the benefit of others. Whom did He come to serve? He did not come to serve only great people — the powerful and wise and rich. He came to serve ordinary people such as fishermen and tax collectors and prostitutes and businessmen and political activists and losers and average Joes. The startling fact that cannot be ignored is that Jesus came to serve you.

Now, if Jesus came to serve you, what does that do to your own ideas about leading others? As I wrestle with this impossible thought, my mind spins in a confusing swirl. Jesus coming to serve me? It is so unexpected. Even after more than thirty-five years of following Him, it feels so wrong. I know on one level that my entire faith rests on this proposition, and yet my humanity rebels. How could He come to serve me? I know I do not deserve that kind of treatment. I am aware of how ludicrous it would be for me to be served by Him. And then there is the troubling question of implications. How does this fact apply to my life? What does it mean in the way I see others and treat others and lead others? Can I, too, come to serve?

Thirdly, He gave His life as a ransom. Jesus gives a parallel picture to further clarify what He is trying to teach. To the figure of servant, He adds the concept of a ransom. Jesus' servanthood is nothing less than laying down His life for those He serves. He does not merely do some nice things for them or give them wonderful gifts. He gives Himself. He surrenders everything. You and I were held hostage by the murderous power of sin, and Jesus secured our release by giving Himself up to that power. His life was the price paid for our freedom. Furthermore, Jesus is very clear that He did this willingly. This was not something done to Him. He was the initiator. He gave His life.

Jesus is saying all of this to His disciples in order to point to Himself as their example. He is the perfect leader and this is what His leadership is: not being served, but serving; giving His life as a ransom. Jesus is not requiring anything of us that He has not demonstrated in His own life to a greater extent than we will ever be able to replicate. We can make ourselves servants because that is what He did. The very essence of Jesus' example is that He laid down His life for us. He gave His life as a ransom. He refused to use His authority, power, knowledge, wisdom, or connections for His own good. He gave Himself to be rejected, tortured, and killed.

What might be the implications of Jesus' example for leadership today? Let's consider a few ideas.

(1) Leadership is about giving, not grasping. We have considered this idea previously, but it is worth taking another look. Leadership in the world is a grasping for power, prestige, position, and preeminence. Unfortunately, this mentality has taken firm root in the Church as well. As good Christian people, we of course disguise our grasping with religious language, but the reality is easy to see. We talk of serving when we mean manipulating. We crave the honor brought by titles and crowds and affirmations of all kinds. We use position to get our own way. We seek to consolidate and strengthen our position so that we can remain in charge. This is not the way of Jesus.

Jesus' leadership is all about giving. Leaders in the movement of Jesus give and give and give. We are to give our time and our finances and our reputations and our influence. We give honor and acclaim and gratitude. We do not seek these for ourselves, but continually deflect them to others. What do you have to give? Are you more prone to grasp?

(2) Leadership is for the benefit of others, not my own. This is one of the most foundational differences between worldly and Kingdom leadership. In our culture, people climb the ladder of leadership as an end in itself. It is good to reach higher levels, and so they do what is necessary to get there. In Jesus' movement, we think of leadership very differently. We lead only to the degree that in doing so we benefit other people and bring glory to Jesus. Are those you lead receiving good things or are you using those people to fulfill your own ambitions? Are you a pastor because that is fulfilling to you and a dream you have cherished? Or are you a pastor (leader, director, etc) because God has given you people to shepherd into greater fullness and life and maturity? Is Jesus Himself benefitting from your leadership? Is He being glorified?

(3) Leadership does not subjugate others but lifts them. Are other people gaining more power because of your leadership or are they there to add to your prestige and influence? Are they being stretched into wider vistas, growing in their gifts and abilities? Or must they be content to labor in your shadow? Do you relish doing everything for them so that you can be the hero? Do they rely on you? Still? Or are they growing into confident and powerful leaders themselves? Our aim is not to amass followers for ourselves, but more servants for Jesus and for the world. Kingdom leadership is empowering.

> Christian leadership is not about having a more compelling vision and larger-than-life goals. It is a race to empower and exalt as many people above yourself that you can in your short lifetime. That is upside-down leadership, and that is the example Jesus showed us.[45]

I often hear from young leaders about their frustrations in trying to step out in obedience to God's call. Many feel trapped by the paternalism and control of their own leaders. They have been taught that their role is to serve those in positions of authority until those people either climb to a higher position, retire, or are otherwise out of the picture. To do otherwise would be arrogant and rebellious. There are of course two sides to this issue. Older leaders often feel betrayed and used by youngsters who have ignored their solid counsel and done their own thing, causing division and destruction as they selfishly push their way forward.

This does not have to happen. If leaders would learn to lift rather than subjugate, many of these problems would disappear. If those we lead are confident that we are laboring to equip and support and resource them to

---

[45] Neil Cole, *Organic Leadership* (Baker Books, Grand Rapids, 2009), pg 195.

fulfill all that God puts in their hearts, they will be much less likely to go their own way. Power is not given to Christian leaders as their right. It is given to be used for others. When we use authority to keep others below us, we are not doing the work of Jesus. D.E. Hoste says it like this:

> When a person in authority demands obedience of another, irrespective of the latter's reason and conscience, this is tyranny. On the other hand, when, by the exercise of tact and sympathy, prayer, spiritual power and sound wisdom, one is able to influence and enlighten another, so that a life course is changed, that is spiritual leadership.[46]

Jesus laid down His life for you and me, and this is the essence of His leadership example. A central question we are forced to consider, then, is whether or not we are willing to do this for others. If we can honestly answer in the affirmative, then we must consider how we are to do so in our own context. How can dads and moms lay their lives down for their kids? How can business owners lay down their lives for their employees? How can pastors lay down their lives for their congregations? How can politicians lay down their lives for their constituents? This is the question you have to consider. There is no doubt at all that Jesus is calling you to this.

---

[46] Quoted in J. Oswald Sanders, <u>Spiritual Leadership</u> (Moody Publishers, Chicago, 2007), pg 59.

7 - WASHING FEET
(John 13:1-17)

Now that you know these things, you will be blessed if you do them. — John 13:17

Part One of this book is rooted in Jesus' teaching to His first apostles concerning greatness. As we conclude this part of our study, let us consider Jesus' final example and instruction to these ambitious followers as told by one who was present. As we look at this passage, we will have the opportunity to strengthen various themes that have come up already. John gives an incredible look into Jesus' last evening with the twelve in chapters 13-17 of his gospel account. The evening is kicked off in an extraordinary manner, as Jesus seeks to get His message across one last time.

Jesus knew that the hour had come for him to leave this world and go to the Father. Having loved his own who were in the world, he loved them to the end. — John 13:1

John makes it clear that what Jesus is about to both do and teach flows out of His love. Jesus loves the twelve, and indeed the entire world. He washes their feet because He loves them. He tells them to do the same because He loves them. And He goes to the cross and suffers a horrendous death, all because of love. As we seek to lead as Jesus did, we must also seek to do all that we do out of sacrificial love for others.

> Jesus knew that the Father had put all things under his power, and that he had come from God and was returning to God... — John 13:3

What Jesus is about to do will come across as self-demeaning. It will seem as though He is becoming less. A King who lowers Himself to serve in such a humble way is not necessarily inspiring. It is awkward. John makes it clear why Jesus is able to do this. First, He knows His power. He has nothing to prove in that regard. All things have been put under His authority. He can choose the posture of weakness because He is fully confident in His strength. He knows that the source of His power is the Father, not people, so He is profoundly unconcerned with trying to grasp or fight for more. Serving His disciples cannot make Him less. That is an impossibility. The message to us is clear. We too can, and indeed must, clothe ourselves with weakness and humility. We can afford to appear weak and inconsequential because we know the truth: we are powerful in Christ. The Spirit that raised Christ from the dead dwells also in us! (Romans 8:11). When we are aware that our power and greatness come from God, we can make ourselves weak and small in the eyes of others with no fear of actually being diminished in any meaningful way.

Secondly, He "came from God and was returning to God." Jesus did the work of the very least because He knew who He was and Whose He was. He was secure in His identity. He was fully aware that He was God's unique Son, and nothing would rob Him of that. The idea that menial work could lessen His worth or His status was impossible. Again, the application is obvious. Because you are a son or daughter of the Father, you too can take on the role of the very least servant without worrying that you are becoming less. The more you humble yourself, the more God wants to exalt you. Let everyone think you are nothing. God knows otherwise, and that is all that matters.

> After that, he poured water into a basin and began to wash his disciples' feet, drying them with the towel that was wrapped around him. — John 13:5

Jesus did not just talk about serving. He did not advocate some kind of internal attitude that had no bearing on actual behavior. Jesus' humility was clothed in concrete action. He waded through the awkward and humiliating moment. Slowly working His way around the room, He took time with each of these twelve men, the silence thick with discomfort and confusion. *What was He doing? Why was He doing it? I thought Matthew would wash our feet. Or John?*

This is not right! What should I do? Should I say something? But what? Should I allow Him to wash me?

They had seen Jesus stand up to the rulers of the land without fear. They were there when He fed five thousand men with a few loaves and fish. They saw Him raise the dead. And now, here in Jerusalem — at the very center of the nation's power and prestige — He does this. Unthinkable. Even as I write, so far removed from that evening of tension and weight, I also feel uncomfortable. When was the last time I humiliated myself (intentionally) to such a degree that it shocked others and made them fidget? When have I refused my "rightful place" to take the lowest position on purpose? Can I bow before Jesus and worship Him without allowing Him to serve me, too? To wash me? For me to serve like Jesus, I, too, will need to upset the natural order of things. I, too, will have to risk people thinking poorly of me.

> "No," said Peter, "you shall never wash my feet." Jesus answered, "Unless I wash you, you have no part with me." — John 13:8

Although he is undoubtedly in the wrong, I love that Peter says something. This is too much for him, and even if all the others are too afraid to speak up, he certainly will. There are a couple of significant things happening here. Jesus is making the point that only those cleansed by Him are truly clean. Only He can remove the stain of our sin. And on another level, He is saying that we have to allow the King to be a servant. To us. Is that too much to take in? Remember, He said something like that in our Matthew passage already, "The Son of Man did not come to be served, but to serve, and to give his life as a ransom for many." — Matthew 20:28

The idea of a Servant-King is not peripheral to the gospel story. The concept that the greatest are the ones who serve is at the heart of the Kingdom. Jesus is the exalted King because He was also the humble servant (see Philippians 2:8-9). Like Peter, when we are confronted face-to-face with this reality, it makes us very uncomfortable.

> "For he knew who was going to betray him, and that was why he said not every one was clean." —John 13:11

Jesus washed Judas' feet. He did so even though he knew the betrayal this "friend" was even then plotting. When Jesus bent down before Judas, all the arrangements had already been made. The price had been set — 30 pieces of silver. Jesus knew this. And He washed Judas' feet. Who can you not serve? Who is too beneath you? Who not worthy?

> You call me "Teacher" and "Lord," and rightly so, for that is what I am. Now that I, your Lord and Teacher, have washed your feet, you also should wash one another's feet. I have set you an example that you should do as I have done for you. Very truly I tell you, no servant is greater than his master, nor is a messenger greater than the one who sent him. Now that you know these things, you will be blessed if you do them. — John 13:13-17

Now we get to where the rubber meets the road. Jesus' example is not meant to be an extraordinary one. He fully expects that His followers would act in the same way. "Wash one another's feet." Peter looks across the room to John. *Wash his feet? Me?* The eyes of Simon the Zealot unintentionally meet those of Matthew the Tax Collector. *Are you serious?* And there it is. The gauntlet has been laid down. Will you take it up? Can you wash their feet as well? This is the way to greatness. This is the example of Jesus. It cannot be sidestepped. But how?

The secret, of course, is in observing Jesus Himself. There is no way that you could lower yourself as far as He did. For Him to wash your feet is far more scandalous than for you to serve *her*. Obviously, none of the twelve men sitting at the table with Jesus deserved to be served by Him in such a way. It is not based on that. Indeed, it says nothing at all about those who were washed — except of course that they were loved with a profound and powerful affection. But it says nothing of their character or their worthiness or their giftedness. No, this is not a story that is meant to convey anything special about the disciples. Jesus is at the center. It is Jesus who has the power and the security to lower Himself. It is He who is the worthy One, the remarkable One.

I hope that you have been challenged in many ways as we have looked at the teaching and example of Jesus. I also hope you have been convinced that the ways of Jesus are not the ways of the world, no matter how sophisticated or wise these worldly philosophies seem. You cannot be great in the Kingdom apart from Jesus. You cannot be a Jesus kind of leader without the Spirit of Jesus living within you. You cannot truly be a servant to all without being a redeemed son or daughter of the Father. You cannot lower yourself without Him lifting you. You cannot exalt in weakness without His strength.

PART TWO
MAKING DISCIPLES

8 - MAKING DISCIPLES

In Part One, we tried to get at the heart of the leadership values and philosophy that Jesus passed on to His first apostles. I made the argument that the leadership to which Jesus calls His disciples is radically different from that of the world and that only people filled with the Spirit of Jesus can indeed follow His instructions and example. To truly be servants and lay down our lives for those we lead, we must engage in "gospel leadership;" meaning that we lead out of the good news of all that Jesus has done for us. We do not use position or power to gain that which Jesus has freely given: identity, value, belonging, honor, purpose, and more. This frees us to lower ourselves to the kind of greatness God envisions for our lives as we lead others.

The first part of the book was devotional in nature. We walked through a section of scripture, attempting to align our hearts and practices with those of Jesus. This must be the foundation of all leadership study and development. Techniques and "practical" suggestions are worthless without this foundation firmly in place. Now, having done our best to root ourselves in the leadership of Jesus, we will endeavor to build on the foundation and consider key facets of what it means to lead in Christ's Kingdom. However, at this point I feel the need to plead with you: Do not simply move on from the first section and forget it. Everything I will discuss in the following chapters must be seen through the lens of this gospel leadership. The lessons and teachings of Matthew 18-20 must flavor all that we are about to discuss.

The next chapters will focus on making disciples. I will attempt to convince you that all Kingdom leadership is disciple-making and I will endeavor to offer a basic framework for this task. Finally, I will conclude with several chapters on the work of developing other leaders and wrap it all up with the biggest lesson of all.

Leadership and Making Disciples

All authority in heaven and on earth has been given to me. Therefore go and make disciples of all nations, baptizing them in the name of the Father and of the Son and of the Holy Spirit, and teaching them to obey everything I have commanded you. And surely I am with you always, to the very end of the age. — Matthew 28:18-20

The purpose of the Jesus kind of leadership is always to make disciples. As a Kingdom leader, that is your job description. It matters not in what sphere you lead: "secular" or religious; business, government, education, the arts, science, or non-profit. You may serve in a home, church, business, or school. Your primary objective as a follower of Jesus with influence in the lives of others is to make disciples. Perhaps you are a mid-level manager in a business that is not owned by believers. Maybe you are a principal in a public school or a volunteer for a non-profit that feeds the homeless. You could be a mom, coach, engineer, teacher, youth pastor, or small business owner. Wherever you have leadership, and that could be with or without official recognition or position, you are there to make disciples of Jesus.

Of course, there are other objectives as well, depending on your context: to provide a good education for your students, to make money for the business, to pass good laws, to care for those in need, to win the championship. The organization of which you are a part has a purpose and there are desired outcomes they are working to achieve. They have hired you or appointed you to that end, and integrity demands that you work hard in the pursuit of success for your organization. However, as you are doing so, you have a higher purpose. Jesus said that all authority has been given to Him, and based on that He tells you to go make disciples. Jesus has the authority in your place of work or influence to send you to make disciples there. He is truly the highest authority in that place. He reigns over your boss, the president, the CEO, the owner, everyone. It is the same in your family, sports team, church, school, neighborhood association, gym, etc. You have been sent to make disciples. Leadership is always about discipleship.

All of the things we discussed about Jesus' leadership in Part One of this book are focused in this direction: making disciples. When Jesus tells His apostles to be slaves, He is thinking about the great purpose of making disciples. When we consider the humility and diligence of servants, it is with the goal of discipling people. Following the way of Jesus in leadership is not a guarantee that your business will make lots of money, that your team will have a winning season, that you will be elected to office, or that you will climb the corporate ladder all the way to the top. However, it does lay out God's way for you to lead people as you seek to do those things, and it gives you an eternal purpose that far surpasses these temporal (though legitimate) ambitions.

I was a young leader, struggling to begin a new ministry in a new place. God provided an amazing team of Ugandan pastors to join with me, and they propelled the work forward wonderfully. One day, I was approached by one of these pastors with a request. He asked me to disciple him. He said he was a "Timothy" seeking a "Paul," and he wanted me to at least be part of the answer to that search. I was first embarrassed and then confused. I was embarrassed because we were peers and I felt uncomfortable at the idea of discipling someone my own age. I was confused because this request revealed something very startling about myself: I did not know how to make disciples. Though I had initially blanched at the idea because he was the same age as me, the truth is that it would not have mattered how old or what his position. I simply did not know how to do the thing. So I ignored him. I changed the subject quickly, and we moved on.

It was a couple of years later when the same pastor came to me again with the same request. Amazingly, I still had no answer for him. I still did not know how to do it and did not want to admit the sad truth. I was a missionary, training pastors to do the work of ministry. But I did not know how to make disciples. In a sense, I was discipling my students, but I knew my friend was asking for something more, and I did not have it. After another year or two, I was back in the States, and a young man came to me with the same request. "Will you disciple me?" This time I tried. We met for coffee. But our meeting was awkward and did not seem to get anywhere. We did not meet again, and that was the end of that.

By this time I was deeply troubled. I had served as a missionary for years and was at this point in my life feeling God's direction to plant a church. But I did not know how to make disciples. Maybe it sounds like I am exaggerating this, but it is true. God was of course doing things through me and there was some degree of fruitfulness. I could teach and share the gospel and I had significant relationships with people who could look into my life, my family, my work. So I was to a degree making disciples. But when someone asked me to very intentionally disciple them, I did not know what to do. Also, I had never discipled a seeker or new believer into obedience to Christ. So I became determined to learn.

I began an intense study of how to make disciples. I read the Bible, looking for principles, practices, and attitudes I needed to embrace. I questioned people who were doing it. I read books, attended conferences, took classes. I thought about it and prayed about it and journaled and discussed and immersed myself in the topic. The more I learned, the more excited I became and the more hungry to put it into practice and to learn more. I have been at this pursuit for twenty years now, and it continues with the same passion as when I started. I have so much more to learn, and I certainly need to better apply the truths that I have discovered so far, but by the grace of God, I've made some progress. What I am sharing in this book is by no means the result of satisfaction with how far I have come. It is rather an in-the-process picture of some things I have learned and am learning. Even more, perhaps, it is an attempt to go further. As I study and write and think and pray, I am learning more and developing more. Learning how to disciple for the glory of Jesus has become a great focus of my life, and my passion for it is only intensifying.

To disciple someone is to help them to know Jesus more deeply and to follow Him more closely. It is to lead them in knowing Jesus, becoming like Jesus, and making Jesus known to others. It is teaching them to obey all the commands of Jesus. If you are doing this, you are bearing good fruit as a leader. If this is not happening, regardless of the success you may be seeing in other areas, your leadership is not being fruitful. However, the good news is that we can all do better. We can learn how to make disciples. God has provided instruction and patterns for us, and He has promised to be with us every step of the way, empowering us by His Holy Spirit.

Since, then, leadership is essentially about making disciples, how does one do that? How do we make disciples? This is, of course, no small topic, and I will not seek to offer anything near an exhaustive teaching about it. However, I will attempt to provide a few biblical ideas that should be sufficient to help all of us, whether you are a complete novice in disciple-making or a seasoned pro. There is much, much more to learn than what I will attempt to cover here, and I am obviously still very much a student myself. At the end of the book, I will point you to some resources that are helping me to grow in these skills and principles, and I believe you will also find them valuable.

As I look through the New Testament with an eye for what it teaches about making disciples, I find several elements that stand out. I cannot suggest strongly enough that you try the same exercise. Do not fully trust me or any other author, speaker, or person who claims to know things. Look to God's Word. Read through the gospels, Acts, and the epistles and seek out recurring themes on the subject of disciple-making. How can you apply these to your particular context? In the following chapters, I will share some of my conclusions, but these are necessarily incomplete and imperfect. Still, my prayer is that they will be helpful to you as you seek the Lord in developing your own convictions and practices.

As we look to the examples and instructions of Jesus and the early apostles, I see four ingredients that are absolutely essential in making disciples. Other people may express them in different terms or organize them differently, but I think the ideas themselves are evident.

The first element is prayer. Disciple-making is a supernatural work from first to last, and it requires supernatural power. Just as Kingdom leadership is impossible apart from the presence of the King, so making disciples is unthinkable without the ongoing activity of the Spirit of God. As Bill Hull puts it, "The main goal of discipleship is to be Christlike. Only the Spirit can make a disciple; only the Spirit can create Christlikeness in any person."[47] In order to actively rely on this power, we pray.

The second element is the Bible. God has given us the scriptures for this very reason: to help us to know Him and to live the way He calls us to live. We must learn to wield God's Word with skill for its intended purpose. The third essential element is spiritual family. Discipleship does not typically happen alone, nor does it occur only through a series of one-on-one

---

47 Bill Hull, *Jesus Christ Disciplemaker* (Baker Books, Grand Rapids, 2004), pg 58.

appointments or impersonal classes. It certainly does not get far solely on the back of podcasts or books. People grow in Jesus in the crucible of relationships. Finally, the fourth needed piece is outward mission. Jesus and the apostles discipled others in the context of actual ministry to the lost and hurting. It is always on-the-job training.

Once again, all that we have discussed so far provides an absolutely critical foundation for the coming sections. These chapters are meant to provide some practical handles within an overall biblical framework for making disciples.

9 - PRAYER

In all my prayers for all of you, I always pray with joy. — Philippians 1:4

For this reason, since the day we heard about you, we have not stopped praying for you. We continually ask God to fill you with the knowledge of his will through all the wisdom and understanding that the Spirit gives. — Colossians 1:9

Epaphras, who is one of you and a servant of Christ Jesus, sends greetings. He is always wrestling in prayer for you, that you may stand firm in all the will of God, mature and fully assured. — Colossians 4:12

We always thank God for all of you and continually mention you in our prayers. — 1 Thessalonians 1:2

In making disciples, we tend to give lip service to the practice of prayer but apparently are not truly convinced that this is the essential work. The. Essential. Work. Our practice just does not reflect the reality of our desperate need for help from the Lord. We pray because we need. We cannot — no matter how right our principles and practices may be — make disciples apart from the power of Christ. And this power is released and made available through prayer. Jon Petersen claims that "Few leadership lessons are as pervasive and lifelong as learning to pray."[48] David Watson suggests, "You

---

[48] Jon Petersen, Unveiled: What a Pirate, a Pot Farmer, and a Gaggle of Prostitutes Taught Me About Being the Church (City Force Media, Castle Rock, CO, 2019), Kindle location 2328.

cannot have a Disciple-Making Movement without a prayer movement,"[49] and Samuel Kebreab joins the chorus, adding that "Every DMM [Disciple-Making-Movement] we have the privilege of witnessing traces its origin to intense intercessory prayer and fasting."[50] John Mallison similarly states,

> Prayer is the greatest need today in Christian service and unfortunately the most neglected. The most important thing I can teach a Christian mentor is to undergird their ministry with prayer. Unless they do this, regardless of how skilled a mentor they are, there will seldom be any lasting value in what they achieve for the kingdom of God and the glory of Christ's name.[51]

The transformation that is necessary in true discipleship begins from within. An obvious corollary to this truth is that we humans are powerless to effect such transformation in others. Indeed, we are not even capable of doing so in ourselves. We cannot change hearts. The best we can do is manipulate behavior change, and I have already made the point that this is not enough. Thus, Christian discipleship is a blatant impossibility apart from the actual activity of the Spirit of God. Of course, God can and perhaps does do His work on human hearts apart from prayer. However, this does not seem to be His usual practice. Normally, He works in response to prayer. He has intentionally molded the task of making disciples into a divine-human partnership. We cannot do it without Him. He will not do it without us.

When I was growing up, I had what seemed like a natural leaning toward spiritual things. I was convinced that God was real and had revealed Himself in Jesus coming to die for our sins. It took time for these beliefs to develop into actual trust in Jesus, repentance, and the new life of the Spirit, but from an early age, I had a desire to know who God is and to follow Him. I did not truly love Him, but I was open to Him and somehow knew that there was more and that I wanted it. To be sure, I have no fool-proof evidence of this, but I attribute this God-ward inclination to prayer. I have an uncle who

---

[49] David Watson and Paul Watson, Contagious Disciple Making (Thomas Nelson, Nashville, 2014), pg 90.

[50] Samuel Kebreab, "Observations over Fifteen Years of Disciple Making Movements" in *Motus Dei*, Edited by Warrick Farah (William Carey Publishing, Littleton, CO, 2021), pg 75.

[51] John Mallison, Mentoring to Develop Disciples and Leaders (Australian Church Resources, 2010), pg 99.

prayed for me to know God. His habit was to awaken very early in the morning and spend time in prayer each day before heading to work. He prayed faithfully for me for years. His desire was that I would be saved, that I would know and follow and love Jesus. And to this end, he labored in prayer. When I heard the gospel, I was gripped by it. I wanted to respond and to go all the way with Jesus. I attribute this readiness to the work of God's Spirit, preparing my heart to hear and receive His truth. And I attribute this work of God, at least in part, to the prayers of my uncle. Again, I cannot prove this cause and effect, but I am convinced of it myself. I have known others who, like me, readily responded to the gospel message after being prayed for consistently and passionately.

Friends, we need to pray for the people God has given us to lead. We need to do more than mention their names in a simple "God bless Mary and Joe and Frank and Cathy." We need help, and in order to obtain it we must get on our knees and call out to our God.

My guess is that we all agree with this in theory. My guess is also that we do not engage in prayer for our disciples nearly to the degree we say we must. Why this disparity? And, more to the point, how can we overcome it?

Perhaps our prayerlessness is a reflection of our lack of faith. Maybe we secretly doubt the efficacy of it. Or, it could be simply a matter of laziness or busyness. It is possible that we prefer doing tangible things over the more contemplative and abstract work of prayer. Some, no doubt, have good intentions but cannot seem to follow through as they would like.

"He is always wrestling in prayer for you" (Colossians 4:12). That is a gripping image, isn't it? It evokes thoughts of work, sweat, strenuous exertion, and pain.

How often do you wrestle in prayer for the people you lead? Of course, feeling guilty about this is not going to produce more or better praying, but through the Spirit's conviction and empowerment, we can change. This brings us back to our question: How can we improve? How can we partner with the Holy Spirit in leading His people? What is required of us? I want to suggest that you take some time to consider this for yourself.

This is a very personal and supremely important topic. I struggled for years with an anemic prayer life. I trudged through guilt and disappointment and despair. Would I ever get better? Could I become an Epaphras? Why could I not seem to pray with any kind of consistency or passion or expectant faith? The good news is that God is at work within me. Over time, He has breathed new life into my praying. I cannot tell you how grateful I am. By His grace, I enjoy a life of prayer now like I never have before. I have so far to go, but I am moving, however slowly, in the right direction. Prayer has become a joy in my life. The tendency to lower it into the realm of a mere duty or religious task still threatens to overtake me. The natural laziness of my sinful nature sometimes gains the upper hand again. But all in all, I am being led by the Spirit of God into regions I never before experienced. Prayer, though still requiring discipline and work, is mostly a delight. And it is fruitful. Through prayer, God is maturing me and transforming me from the inside out. He is also training me day by day to trust Him as I lift others to His throne and ask for help in the various situations that arise in life for which I need His help. I tell you this, my reader, with the hope that it brings encouragement. You can become stronger in prayer.

Of course, I cannot offer four easy steps to a greater prayer life. You need to ask the Lord and take some intentional time to make plans and create habits. Having said that, I will timidly offer a few thoughts.

(1) Grow in faith. We know that the scriptures teach us that "without faith it is impossible to please God" (Hebrews 11:6), along with many other similar exhortations. God wants you to pray and believe that what you ask will be done. Prayer is dependent upon faith. Trust God and believe that He answers prayer. Of course, there is much to say on this point alone, but this is just an overview. We do have to deal with disappointment in prayer and with many other real issues, but none of those changes the fact that prayer requires faith.

The encouraging news is that you can grow in faith. Saturate yourself in God's Word. Get to know Him. This will give you greater confidence in His will, which in turn will help you to be confident that He will do what you ask because you will ask according to what He wants. As you read the pages of scripture, you can also take note of the many prayers that are answered, often with dramatic results. God is the same and He encourages you to expect similar responses.

> The prayer of a righteous person is powerful and effective. Elijah was a human being, even as we are. He prayed earnestly that it would not rain, and it did not rain on the land for three and a half years. Again he prayed, and the heavens gave rain, and the earth produced its crops. — James 5:16-18

Notice the emphasis on Elijah being a human like us. James is making the point that if Elijah could pray with such power, so can we.

In addition to growing in faith through the scriptures, notice and celebrate answers to prayer in your own life. When you pray and the thing happens, note it and give thanks to God. Encourage conversations with your friends that highlight answers to prayer. Read contemporary stories or biographies.

(2) Cultivate humility. Grow in the awareness and conviction that you need God in this endeavor of discipling people. The more you entangle yourself with the brokenness of people, the easier this should be. Give up all attempts to do it alone. As you study about discipleship and learn methods and grow in skills, do not ultimately trust in any of that. Remind yourself that it is God who changes hearts. The more you rely on your experience or techniques or training, the more you will have to compensate for the lack of the one thing you need above all: the power of God. To disciple even one person into Christlikeness is infinitely beyond you or me. And yet He has sent us to make disciples of all peoples! The sheer magnitude of the task is overwhelming. Still, our good Father has commissioned us to this work. And in so doing He has made His power and love and grace available to us. But we must seek it. We must seek *Him*.

(3) Create habits. Prayer needs to be the most intentional part of your life. Bill Hull notes that "The battle for spending meaningful time with God is fought on three fronts: priorities, scheduling, and discipline."[52] Nothing will evaporate more easily than time to spend on your knees. Almost every time I begin to pray, a host of thoughts fill my mind about all the things I need to be doing. There are so many tasks to accomplish, people to contact, responsibilities to fulfill. I already struggle with the seeming insufficient time each day to do all I need to do. To block off an hour or two or three simply for prayer seems inefficient. It feels unwise and unrealistic. These thoughts become increasingly strong and convincing as I turn my attention to prayer. And yet the biblical exhortation is to be faithful in prayer, to be devoted to prayer, to be continually in prayer (Romans 12:2, Acts 2:42, 1 Thessalonians 5:17, Colossians 4:2).

Because of all this, you need to secure a place for prayer on your daily calendar. If you truly value prayer, it must be evident by the time you devote to it. And you cannot devote time to prayer with what is left over after all of

---

[52] Bill Hull, *Jesus Christ Disciplemaker* (Baker Books, Grand Rapids, 2004), pg 217.

your important activities are completed. I urge you to ruthlessly guard that time of prayer. Be willing to sacrifice other good things to make this happen. I want to emphasize this last remark. Be willing to sacrifice other good things to make time for prayer. You do not have time to pray, so you must make time to pray by eliminating or limiting other activities. Demonstrate your commitment to prayer by your willingness to give up the things that seem to make it impractical. If you are finding that you simply do not have enough time to pray, you must ruthlessly search your calendar and get rid of other things.

Once you have consistent built-in times of prayer established, maybe you can add other activities in again, but very carefully. I had this experience even recently. By God's grace, I eliminated multiple, regular activities from my routine, and in so doing was able to create more time for prayer. Now, after some time has passed, I have seen the benefits. However, there is a continual clamor to fill these newfound open spaces with other very good pursuits, and I am trying my best to guard them for prayer.

I feel compelled to drill into this further. Busyness is the great enemy of prayer in our day. I suspect that you feel it would be impossible to follow through on my suggestion of cutting out other things. But I have to insist that God is calling you to pray and that He is calling you to pray as a significant part of your day and week. You cannot lead others in His Kingdom apart from it. You have so many irons in the fire: work, family, friends, church and ministry responsibilities, perhaps other volunteer commitments. It is certainly overwhelming. Your business is demanding more time. Your kids are. Your spouse is. Your friends and your church and your aging parents are. And now God is too? Well, yes. But the difference is this: Of all the people and organizations and responsibilities that are pulling on you, God has the greatest right to make demands, not only on your time but on all of your life. In addition to this, He is the only One who can rightly order all the other parts of your life through time spent with Him. Time spent in prayer is not wasted. It enables you to face all the other responsibilities and demands of life in grace, love, and power.

Be creative as you seek to grow in prayer. And, after the challenge I just issued, I will also add this: be patient. You will probably not grow into a powerhouse of prayer in one day. Be willing to push on with slow and steady progress.

(4) Get help. You definitely need to tenaciously hold to that time of prayer alone with God, but you also need to pray with others. This is essential for your team. Again, it is a real challenge to spend significant time in prayer with your co-workers in the Kingdom, especially when there is much else that you need to do together. Who has time for another meeting, another responsibility? Who wants to fight the battle of scheduling something that everyone will be able to make happen on a regular basis? And yet it remains true that the benefits far outweigh the cost.

Before we move on from this admonition, I want to offer a word about intercession. There are of course different types of prayer, and you probably have your favorites. Maybe you love giving praise and thanks to God, or praying in response to the scriptures, or honoring God for who He is, or simply relating to Him as a loving Father about the ups and downs of your day. These are all wonderful and needed. However, as a leader, you must also be committed specifically to the work of intercession. You are called to spend time in prayer for those God has given you to serve. Pray for them by name. Pray for them regularly (continually, as Paul says). Pray for them specifically according to what is happening in their lives and ministries. Pray for them biblically (consider such wonderful prayers as Ephesians 3:14-21). Pray for them zealously (wrestle in prayer). Pray for them in faith, trusting the work of the Holy Spirit in their lives. Pray for fruitfulness in their Kingdom endeavors. Pray for their own spiritual formation and growth in maturity. Pray for victory in the spiritual battles they fight and for discernment in the decisions they face. Pray for wholeness in body and soul, for provision, for their relationships.

If you lead people, you are called to the work of intercession. You cannot leave that to those who seem better suited for such spiritual work. The brokenness and the need you encounter in others should lead you in desperation to your knees, just as your prayers of intercession must inevitably lead you to engagement with the world and love for the lost.

God's acquaintance is not made by pop calls. God does not bestow his gifts on the casual or hasty comers and goers. Much with God alone is the secret of knowing him and of influence with him. He yields to the persistency of a faith that knows him. He bestows his richest gifts upon those who declare their desire for and appreciation of those gifts by the constancy as well as earnestness of their importunity. Christ, who in this as well as other things is our Example, spent many whole nights in prayer. His custom was to pray much.[53]

Prayer Tools

At this point, I will endeavor to give some practical hope to the challenge of the previous section. As a busy leader, how can you follow through on that desire to pray more or better? To that end, I will offer a few ideas. Of course, you will develop many more beyond what I offer here, and there are fantastic resources available that can help us as well.

When it comes to finding (making) time for prayer, allow me to engage the problem-solving part of your brain with some suggestions. You may not use any of these, but perhaps as you consider them, other better ideas will surface.

My first suggestion is to re-state what I said earlier: If you do not have enough time to pray as you know you should, you absolutely must **remove other things from your schedule.** Of course, this is an extremely difficult step but, nonetheless, an essential one. Not only will it free up time for this most needed of all pursuits, but it will demonstrate your dependence upon God and devotion to Him above all else. If Jesus is the center of everything in your life, if He is in fact your very life, you should be able to demonstrate this by the way you spend your time. If you need His presence and wisdom and power in order to fulfill your greatest purpose and ambition, this will be evident in the regular structure of your days, weeks, months, and years.

Secondly, **write prayer into your daily/weekly calendar.** Do not just operate with the understanding that you will pray at such and such a time. Write it in. If this time is first thing in the morning (highly recommended), then be sure to get up when you need to in order to fulfill the engagement. If you find that you are oversleeping and thus missing prayer, change something. Go to bed earlier. Schedule prayer for a different time. Do not keep failing day after day simply because you cannot get out of bed. Or, if you do get out of bed, but become immediately distracted by to-do lists or kids or whatever,

---

53 Edward M. Bounds, *Essentials of Prayer and Power Through Prayer* (Brighton Publishing, Chandler AZ), kindle location 5620.

make a change. The point is, do not keep trying the same thing that does not work.

This seems like a good time to tackle the specific and very real challenge of small children. If you are a parent with babies or toddlers in your care, it does indeed seem like "quiet times" are a thing of the past, or perhaps of that wonderful, hazy thing called the future. Your issue is not only busyness. It is a lack of opportunities to be alone. As with every facet of parenting and managing your life with small children, there are no easy solutions. This is a season of life that is rife with special issues and challenges. However, it, too, is part of God's plan and is of course filled with beauty and wonder and delight and opportunity for those who have eyes to see. As you parent these little cherubs, nothing happens in the ideal: not cleaning the house or going to work or shopping or church or time with friends or dates with your spouse. And certainly, that is true of prayer. You will rarely have an hour of kneeling or sitting in your "prayer closet," with inspiring worship music gently playing in the background, the lighting just right, and your thoughts focused and clear.

However, you can still pray. Maybe your times will come in ten-to-fifteen-minute intervals throughout the day rather than all at once. Perhaps you and your spouse will have to work out a schedule that provides protected time of prayer for each of you during the week. Of course, make use of those precious moments when your child is napping or in bed for the night, giving a portion of that time to the Lord in prayer. Another thought is that some of your prayer time can and should be with your child. Again, I understand that this will not be the ideal as far as your desires for prayer, but it can be powerful all the same. Pray as you sit holding the sleeping newborn or as you pace the floor seeking sleep for the little one. Take a little time each day to train your energetic toddler to slow down for five (and then ten and then fifteen) minutes to pray with you, being sure to focus on things that are important to them as well as stretching them to be concerned for others. Obviously, as more kids come along, the challenge only increases. However, the point is that for the highly motivated person, there are ways to pray. You can do it!

Thirdly, **pray where you can**. This may be an actual closet, your bedroom, or some other designated spot in your house. It may be your back porch, garage, or shed. Or, you may prefer to pray on the move. I like to walk as I pray; in my neighborhood or a park or downtown in my city or on the hills that stretch upward from my home. I also make use of designated spaces that have been set aside for prayer. Many cities have houses of prayer or prayer rooms that are open at specific hours each day for people to come in and pray. Some churches have open spaces as well. Every once in a while I put in prayer time at my favorite coffee shop, enjoying an Americano as I read the Bible and write prayers in my journal. I have friends who pray on the treadmill or driving their car or pulling weeds in the garden. The point is to designate time and find your spot for intentional time with Jesus.

As I plan my calendar each week, I write in the time and place that will be set aside for prayer each day. When I do not do this, I simply do not pray nearly as much. Today I prayed as I walked a trail alongside the river that runs through the city. Yesterday I was at home in my room (my family was out of the house). The day before that I was in a house of prayer. And the day before that, well... I did not have a designated plan. I prayed a little in the car on my way to an engagement, and a little more as I went about my business. Not what I would have wanted, but it does happen that way more often than I'd like. I'm still learning.

For some, getting to that place of prayer would be more feasible if you just had some better ideas of what to do once you've gotten there. Once again, there have been so many good resources produced to help with just this need, and I will not spend much time here on that. However, I will try to point to a few practices that have been very helpful to me.

I think my most basic, "go-to" method of prayer is to simply go through the Lord's Prayer, statement by statement, using it as a kind of prayer outline. You can pray like this for ten minutes or fill a full hour or more.

Our Father in heaven, hallowed be your name. Approach God as your Father and let Him know from the beginning that your desire is for His glory; for His Name to be honored. Some days I linger a lot on the "Father" part, allowing myself to be in awe again at the gift of sonship. I fill my heart with gratitude for His adoption and for His calling me into His presence as a beloved child.

Your kingdom come, your will be done, on earth as it is in heaven. This is the place where I tend to take a deep dive into intercession, praying the Father's will and rule into the lives and situations that come to mind. I make sure to lift up by name those the Lord has given me to serve and to also remember those who do not know Jesus. I have written out a weekly schedule, designating specific people and groups of people to pray for each day. I try to be consistent with this. In addition to that, I trust the Holy Spirit to bring to mind others for whom I should intercede. And I pray almost daily for my wife and children.

Give us today our daily bread. I ask the Father, who loves to give good gifts to His children, to provide for my material needs. I also ask for the daily bread of His Word, that I might hear Him clearly and follow His voice.

And forgive us our debts, as we also have forgiven our debtors. This reminds me to repent of sin. It is better to do this in specifics rather than generalities. I acknowledge concrete ways that I have offended God, through words, deeds, or thoughts, and I ask for forgiveness. I also must remember those who have offended me and intentionally forgive them by name.

And lead us not into temptation, but deliver us from the evil one. I take time to ask the Lord to help me overcome the battles I will fight in the coming day, especially the attacks of temptation and sin. I know where I am most likely to stumble, and I ask for God's help.

For yours is the kingdom and the power and the glory. I end with declaring the awesomeness of God and giving myself to Him in reverent worship.

Pete Greig has developed a very simple prayer outline that is based on the various elements of the Lord's Prayer. I have also found this to be extremely helpful in my personal life and in equipping others. In his book, How to Pray: A Simple Guide for Normal People, Greig suggests an outline based on the acronym P.R.A.Y.[54]

Pause: Take a moment to reflect on the presence of God. You may read some scripture, recite a phrase, or simply turn your mind towards Jesus, acknowledging and welcoming His presence.

---

54 Pete Greig, *How to Pray* (NavPress, Colorado Springs), 2019.

Rejoice. Give thanks. Express gratitude and joy and delight in your loving Father. Tell Him specific things you are thankful for that He has done for you today or this week, and also remember the big things: His death, resurrection, and promised return to make all things right. Rejoice in the face of trials, thanking God for His presence and help in the midst of them.

Ask. Obviously, this is where we present needs to God, both our personal ones (petition) and those of others (intercession). Ask in faith. Ask in compassion. Remind yourself of the wonderful promises He has made and engage fully. Among others, read Matthew 21:22, Luke 11:9-13, John 14:13-14, 15:7, 15:16, 16:23-24.

Yield. This is a wonderful place to end because it brings us to the point of submitting our will to God's. It is the prayer of Jesus in the garden, when He declared, "Not my will, but yours be done." (Luke 22:42). It is a re-surrendering of our entire lives to the One who loves us and gave Himself for us.

There are many other tools available to help with the content of prayer. Some focus on praying the prayers of the Bible, or prayerfully reading and responding to scripture passages. Others bring us into silence, emphasizing the role of listening to God in prayer. Still others lead us to worship, using music or other helps. I like to journal my prayers from time to time, putting the longings and the cries of my heart onto paper as I offer them to the Lord. There are many ways to pray, and the more you experiment the more you will find methods that are helpful and full of meaning for you.

As I mentioned before, in addition to praying much alone, we need to learn to prioritize corporate prayer in our ministry life. Praying with others, especially those with whom we serve in Kingdom pursuits, is incredibly important. Here are a few ideas:

* Read a scripture to begin each meeting, and take several minutes of silence to meditate on the Word. Then encourage people to pray out in response to what God has said.

* Pray for one another. Listen to needs, and take time ministering to one another.

* Focus prayer on one person every time you get together.

* Pray together by name for the people you lead.

* Create multiple opportunities to gather for prayer: early morning, late night, etc.
* Several times during the year, devote full (or half) days to gathering for prayer.
* Utilize resources that teach about prayer. I recommend those available through 24-7 Prayer, especially the Prayer Course (https://prayercourse.org).

Finally, before leaving this topic, remember to not only pray *for* those you serve but also make it a point to pray *with* them as well. One of the most crucial things you have to pass on to those you disciple surely must be related to prayer. You can probably give fantastic teachings on prayer, and you can perhaps inspire with challenging words and uplifting stories. But nothing takes the place of doing the thing together. In Luke 11:1 it states that "One day Jesus was praying in a certain place. When he finished, one of his disciples said to him, 'Lord, teach us to pray, just as John taught his disciples.'" Observing Jesus at prayer made His disciples want to learn more. Jesus' habit of prayer was well known by His closest followers because they were there. Find ways to include those you lead in your own prayer disciplines, and they too will want to prioritize prayer and grow in their practice of it.

10 - THE BIBLE

But as for you, continue in what you have learned and have become convinced of, because you know those from whom you learned it, and how from infancy you have known the Holy Scriptures, which are able to make you wise for salvation through faith in Christ Jesus. All Scripture is God-breathed and is useful for teaching, rebuking, correcting and training in righteousness, so that the servant of God may be thoroughly equipped for every good work. In the presence of God and of Christ Jesus, who will judge the living and the dead, and in view of his appearing and his kingdom, I give you this charge: Preach the word; be prepared in season and out of season; correct, rebuke and encourage—with great patience and careful instruction. — 2 Timothy 3:14 - 4:2

Although discipleship is more than knowledge, the passing on of knowledge is a necessary foundation for discipling people. To obey the commands of Jesus, we have to know what they are. We also need to know Him Himself; His nature and character, what He likes and dislikes. This is enhanced through teaching and it is right and good for us to take advantage of all the resources we have to that end. More than anything, though, we need to connect with God Himself, and we need to help those we are discipling to do the same.

God speaks to us in various ways. He speaks through His Spirit directly to our hearts, through other people, through dreams and visions, through circumstances, through the Bible, and probably a host of other methods. However, we must be firm that without the written Word of God — the Bible

— as the focus of our teaching and discipleship, we will end up relying on the flawed wisdom of our times.

> Don't let anyone capture you with empty philosophies and high-sounding nonsense that come from human thinking and from the spiritual powers of this world, rather than from Christ. For in Christ lives all the fullness of God in a human body. So you also are complete through your union with Christ, who is the head over every ruler and authority. — Colossians 2:8-10 (NLT)

Friends, we have available to us the very wisdom of God. Why would we settle for human thinking? Perhaps because it is easier to access a podcast than to dig into God's Word. Maybe because we so much prefer to find "high-sounding nonsense" that strengthens our own opinions than to allow ourselves to be challenged by God Himself. Perhaps we simply do not believe that the wisdom we need is accessible in the Bible, at least not to ordinary folk like you and me.

The truth is that the Bible does reveal God's wisdom regarding money and relationships and parenting and work. It may not answer every question we have in all the details and specifics, but it does provide a framework for how God intends us to think about and live in these various arenas. What does the Bible teach about raising kids and spending money and overcoming life-controlling habits and conquering anxiety? Before turning to the experts of human thinking, shouldn't we at least put some work into discovering what God has always said about these things? And then we can begin to filter all the other information and opinions and "wisdom" through Him. There is good advice out there — and lots of the other kind. The problem is that we are so immersed in our culture that we do not naturally have what it takes to determine the difference. We trust too much in our own instincts and experience even though it should be clear to us that those are no match for the devil and his lies. But, as we intentionally fill ourselves with the Word of God, we develop the ability to see what is gold and what is garbage.

> You have been believers so long now that you ought to be teaching others. Instead, you need someone to teach you again the basic things about God's word. You are like babies who need milk and cannot eat solid food. For someone who lives on milk is still an infant and doesn't know how to do what is right. Solid food is for those who are mature, who through training

have the skill to recognize the difference between right and wrong. —
Hebrews 5:12-14

As I mentioned before, there are many ways that God speaks to us, and I do not intend to go deeply into that subject here. However, I do find it necessary to emphasize the Bible as our primary source of direct, specific, and clear revelation of who God is and how we relate to Him. I am not discounting other means that the Holy Spirit employs to speak and reveal Himself to human beings. Not only are these other methods of communication valid, but they are also essential. However, first and foremost it is imperative that we commit ourselves to the Bible as God's standard. Dennis McCallum and Jessica Lowery make the simple but disturbing observation that "many disciplers put too little emphasis on Bible study with their disciples."[55] Pastoral author John Mark Comer makes the frightening admission that

> In my teaching, I increasingly have to appeal to research from the social sciences because fewer and fewer people view the writings of the New Testament as trustworthy and true.[56]

This should not be so! We need to feed on the eternal truths of God's Word found in the scriptures. Comer goes on to say, "If [the devil] can get us to doubt God and instead trust in our own inner intuition as an accurate compass to the good life, he has us."[57]

When a pastor claims that God told him to divorce his wife and marry his secretary, we know he was not hearing God *because of the Bible*. When a (so-called) evangelist begins to tell people that he is God's mouthpiece on earth and all communication between people and God must pass through him, we unequivocally know and agree that he is wrong *because of the Bible*. When two men who profess Christ request a pastor to bless their marriage, he can with confidence say that this is not God's will, and so refuse the request, *because of the Bible*. These are all actual scenarios that have happened and do happen

---

55 Dennis McCallum and Jessica Lowery, *Organic Dicsipleship: Mentoring Others into Spiritual Maturity and Leadership* (New Paradigm Publishing, 2006), Kindle location 1930.

56 John Mark Comer, *Live No Lies* (Waterbrook), pg 42.

57 John Mark Comer, *Live No Lies* (Waterbrook), pgs 60-61.

repeatedly, and there are thousands of similar cases happening all the time. In each situation, the people involved claimed to have heard from God that what they desired to do was in fact His will. When they try to make the case that other people cannot know what God says to them personally, we can respond that God has spoken an objective Word on those subjects which is for all people of all times, and we have access to that Word in the scriptures.

The Bible serves us as an objective standard by which we can measure all the other divine encounters. This is not because God is unable to speak clearly in other ways. However, the Bible serves as a safety net and boundary to help us discern what He is actually saying through other means. Having said all that, the Bible is much more than a way to judge other forms of divine communication, as significant as that is. The Bible is an essential positive tool for growing in Christ, and I urge you to place it at the very center of your discipling efforts.

Perhaps you have fallen prey to the assault on the validity of the Bible for us today. After all, it is so... old. We have made so many advances since that time. Things are just different now. The Bible is good for things like affirming that Jesus loves us and died for us and rose again, but in the nitty-gritty of life, we need... We need experts. Brothers and sisters, do not be taken in by that lie! The Creator of heaven and earth and of you and me knows best, and He has revealed Himself.

In him [Jesus] lie hidden all the treasures of wisdom and knowledge. — Colossians 2:3

Maybe you have been frustrated in your efforts at Bible study and have come to believe that you do not have the ability to rightly interpret the message of the scriptures. You have become confused by the way different scholars interpret various passages, and you wonder what the hope is for an average person who has not been to seminary. I want to assure you that you can read and understand God's Word. There are indeed confusing and difficult-to-decipher passages. However, most of the teachings of the scriptures are quite clear, especially in the New Testament. These contain all the essential truths about who Jesus is and how we are to follow Him. Rather than focus on the parts that are legitimately difficult to interpret, if we put our attention into trusting and obeying the clear parts, we would have plenty to keep us occupied in our pursuit of becoming more Christlike. With that as our primary focus, we can then enter into study, using various tools, to dig more deeply into the parts that tend to confuse us. God wants you to understand His Word. He has made it accessible. It does require effort, but the rewards are well worth it.

In addition to diving into the scriptures for personal growth in Jesus, we need to learn to think, teach, and mentor biblically. We must get beyond "That sounds good" and "I've never seen that verse like that before" and "I need to post that quote." Instead, we must move on to "Is that what the Bible intends to teach on that subject?" and "What does the Bible have to say about...?"

Discovery Bible Study

We need good, solid, Bible teaching, and it is possible to access that in various ways. In discipling other people, I also want to submit to you the power of a discovery process. Ultimately, our goal is to help our disciples to connect with and obey God directly. One way to facilitate this process is a "Discovery Bible Study." In this method, you gather together with several people for the purpose of discipleship, and the focus is on learning to obey God's Word. It can go something like this:

(1) Read a pre-selected passage of scripture out loud multiple times.
(2) Have someone recount what was read in their own words. I like to emphasize that this step is not for preaching a sermon, sharing "what you got out of" the passage, or highlighting what "stood out" to you. You ask the person to simply summarize the passage in their own words as if they were telling someone who had not read this before what it said as accurately and clearly as possible.
(3) Ask two questions: (a) "What does this reveal about God?" (b) "What does this reveal about people?" Allow for good discussion and encourage as many as possible to participate. Try not to dominate as a leader. This is a discovery process, and people are learning how to read the Bible for themselves. If things get off-subject or if people begin to conclude things that are contrary to God's Word, you can gently re-direct and share your insights as well.
(4) Ask everyone to share how specifically they will obey the passage in the coming week, and with whom they can share the truth of the scripture.

That is a very simple but powerful tool. We will add more to it as we go, but this in itself can be a fruitful way of meeting with believers for discipleship.

I am praying that God's people rediscover His written Word as the powerful discipleship tool that it is meant to be.

Obedience

Teaching them to obey everything I have commanded you. — Matthew 28:20a

"Jesus replied, 'Anyone who loves me will obey my teaching...'" — John 14:23a

Our home was filled with chatter and laughter as we gathered with a group of eleven people. We ranged in age from 13 to 50. Our number included four students, two public school teachers, a convenience store worker, a homemaker, a lab technician, a missions director, and someone hunting for work. We read together a passage of scripture: 2 Timothy 3:1 - 4:5. In this section of the Bible, Paul warns Timothy about ungodliness in the last days and encourages him to stand firm in the midst of false teaching and perversion. Paul further warns his young co-worker that a time was coming when people would not listen to solid teaching but would demand to hear only what made them feel good. Paul exhorts Timothy to continue to hold onto the scriptures and to be ready to proclaim God's Word at any time.

Our group found this to be a challenging and powerful portion of the Bible, and we enjoyed a lively discussion. We worked together to get at the intent of the passage and to hear what God was saying to us. Before wrapping up our time together, the leader asked us to consider what Jesus was calling us to obey from His Word in the coming week and to share that with the group. One person shared that as we read about God's Word being useful to correct and rebuke, she thought about a friend who is making sinful decisions. Jesus put it on her heart to lovingly confront this friend with the truth. Another shared that she was convicted to be "ready in season and out of season" to share God's Word with people. She felt Jesus nudge her to actively look for opportunities to do this. Another was struck by the description of wicked people who are disrespectful to their parents, and confessed his guilt in this area, along with a concrete action to take in the coming days.

I myself was impressed by the statement that Timothy had known the scriptures "from infancy," and that he had learned it from reliable people (apparently his mother and grandmother). I had the thought to take time this week to consider what I need to do in the coming year to provide similar instruction for my own children. And so, we went around, each person sharing some specific way they were committing to respond to God's Word. The following week would find us together again, and our first point of discussion would be to recount what we said we would do in obedience to Jesus and share with our friends in the group how it went. If our past history is any indication, it will be a mixed bag. At least one person will have forgotten all about it during the week. Others maybe will have had it in mind but will have not followed through as they felt they should. Others, by God's grace, will report success in their obedience commitment. For those who failed to follow through, we will offer grace and perhaps an admonition to push on. We will rejoice with those who experienced the joy of intentional obedience and encourage them to continue in that path.

When Jesus issued the Great Commission to those eleven amazed men on a mountain in Israel, He placed obedience to His commands at the center of making disciples. Disciple-making, put succinctly, is obedience training. Yes, there is more involved, but discipleship is never less than that. "Teaching them to obey everything I have commanded you."

We have accepted a discipleship that is far less demanding, designing programs around the transfer of knowledge rather than the transformation of character. This philosophy has produced some amazing teachers and we all have access to them like never before in history. We can listen to their podcasts, watch their livestreams, and maybe even read their books. We have also developed some fantastic curriculum. There are Bible studies and topical studies and a glittering array of "How to" material for our small group delight. Regular Joes are accessing deep theological material through online seminary classes, well-produced video instruction, and apps on their phones. Never before has the church known more. But knowledge is not discipleship. Obedience is. Paul warns us that "Knowledge puffs up while love builds up" (1 Corinthians 8:1). As I mentioned before, passing on knowledge is an essential element in discipling people, but it is hardly the end goal. We are called to lead people into obedience. Paul succinctly described his calling like this:

> Through him we received grace and apostleship to call all the Gentiles to the obedience that comes from faith for his name's sake. — Romans 1:5

Jerry Trousdale has studied numerous discipleship movements in some very difficult contexts. When it comes to following the Great Commission, he says,

> Jesus didn't tell us to teach all the things that He has commanded us; He commanded us to teach others to obey these things. There is a big difference between teaching knowledge and teaching obedience. A disciple is taught to obey what Jesus commanded.[58]

The question before us, then, is how to move from a knowledge-centered approach to one of growing in obedience? To that end, I will offer a few suggestions, but I also encourage you to prayerfully, biblically, and creatively think through this dilemma yourself.

(1) Shift the focus of teaching from impersonal to personal. By impersonal, I mean any teaching context in which the one learning has no, or very limited, contact with the one teaching. Impersonal teachings are books, podcasts, blogs, and often Sunday sermons and conferences. These are very useful and helpful in discipleship, but we have perhaps over-emphasized those contexts to the detriment of the more relational kind. Personal teachings are more interactive. There is, ideally, a relationship between teacher and student. These are ongoing, regular times of learning together. Small groups, simple (small) churches, and even one-on-one opportunities can be great times of personal teaching. This is significant for centering on obedience because there is some degree of shared life and accountability. There is an opportunity for the people involved to actually speak about direct applications of the Word in their real, everyday lives. The teacher can be less concerned with eloquence and producing something novel and be more attuned to the

---

[58] Jerry Trousdale, *Miraculous Movements* (Thomas Nelson Nashville, 2012), pg 100.

specific needs of those in his group. This can lead to a greater emphasis on obedience.

(2) Ensure that the Bible is the center of our teaching. It should be clear that the obedience we are striving for is obedience to Jesus, not to man. Thus, our teaching needs to be ruthlessly biblical. Many people today are drawn to "How to" teachings or sermons rather than more purely biblical ones: How to have a great relationship with your wife; How to be financially successful; How to win souls. How to lead (yes, I feel the irony in writing that line in my book about leadership). These self-help, how-to kinds of sermons are often a blend of Bible and us. There is nothing wrong with that per se, and I use this type of teaching myself. However, since the core of discipleship is obedience to Jesus, I need to eventually bring people to a point of hearing what Jesus is commanding and giving them the encouragement they need to follow that.

(3) Challenge people to make obedience commitments. In order for people to grow in obedience, they need to have concrete things to obey. The interesting thing about the scriptures, though, is that although any given passage can logically have but one meaning, it can have many applications. We can take a simple, direct command as an example. In Matthew 5:44, Jesus tells us to love our enemies. This is straightforward and simple. We know what it means. However, each of us may apply it in different ways at different times.

One person, perhaps, has a co-worker who consistently makes fun of his faith. When this person hears Jesus say to love his enemy, he immediately thinks of a way he can offer an act of service to this antagonizing peer. Another thinks about a prominent political figure from an opposing political party. He immediately feels conviction, knowing that he has harbored hatred for this person and has slandered and spoken badly about him or her. In this situation, obedience requires that he pray for the political leader and speak respectfully. Another, sadly, thinks about a parent who consistently belittles and nitpicks and argues and finds fault. To love this "enemy," perhaps, is to lovingly confront and to go out of the way to serve and speak words of kindness.

Steve Smith and Ying Kai have equipped disciplers who are bearing abundant fruit all around the world. They remind us that it is not enough to be moved or inspired by a Bible teaching.

"Remember: conviction does not equal obedience! You don't know who is obedient until you give them something to commit to."[59]

The point is, people are far more likely to obey if they have something definite in mind that they can and must do. Knowledge must find its way to specific application.

(4) Provide loving accountability. Of course, saying we will do something is one thing, but following through is something else entirely. Loving accountability can be the difference-maker. When you know that you are going to report to your friends next week on how you did with your obedience commitment, you are more likely to follow through. You are more likely to remember what you said and more likely to actually do it. This is loving accountability, because you know that you are not going to be condemned or shamed if you fail this week. In fact, you can expect the kind of encouragement and grace that will make you all the more determined to obey next time.

(5) Begin training in obedience at the outset of your discipleship relationships. I have seen groups in which not even a majority of the participants are believers yet, but they are nonetheless being shown that to be a Christian means to learn to obey Jesus. These seekers take the obedience part seriously because that is what the group is about. It is unfortunate that we often wait months after a person comes to faith before we begin to talk to them about obedience — if we ever do. By this time, they have developed the all-too-common tendency to think that knowing Jesus can be unrelated to how one lives one's life.

(6) Model hearing and obeying God's Word. This part cannot be over-emphasized. As a discipler, you too are being discipled and growing more like Jesus. You, too, are learning to obey. The best way for you to help others in this endeavor is to let them see you in all your glory and all your failures. Share what you intend to do in obedience to God's Word and then report vulnerably and honestly how it went. Demonstrate repentance. Model how a person receives forgiveness and grace. And, even better, follow through in obedience! Obey the Word, and report your successes to the group. Allow Jesus to challenge you to do difficult things and walk through that with your friends that you are discipling.

---

59 Steve Smith and Ying Kai, *T4T: A Discipleship* Re-*Revolution* (WIGTake Resources, Monument, CO, 2011), pg 170.

(7) Develop a culture of growth and grace. As I mentioned before, even those who are not yet committed to following Jesus will try to obey if that is the culture of the group. Find ways to enjoy and to celebrate the reports of obedience. Imagine a group of friends meeting together regularly in the context of a culture that is actively pursuing growth in Jesus through obedience to His commands. This is powerful! It is also important to remember that we are desperately in need of God's grace. This is obvious for the times that we fail, but we acknowledge that the same is true in our successes. We cannot truly obey Jesus part from His grace actively at work in our lives.

> For the grace of God has appeared that offers salvation to all people. It teaches us to say "No" to ungodliness and worldly passions, and to live self-controlled, upright and godly lives in this present age. — Titus 2:11-12

Teaching people to obey is not easy. It requires a vulnerable and humble heart. It demands a diligence to study and hear from God and a tenacious commitment to obey Him in all things. You must be full of grace and patience and compassion, for there will be many failures along the way. You will be stretched in your ability to believe in people and to champion them, but you must. Jesus has given you the authority and power to do this.

11 - SPIRITUAL FAMILY

Pointing to his disciples, he said, "Here are my mother and my brothers. For whoever does the will of my Father in heaven is my brother and sister and mother." — Matthew 12:49-50

If I am delayed, you will know how people ought to conduct themselves in God's household, which is the church of the living God, the pillar and foundation of the truth. — 1 Timothy 3:15

Do not rebuke an older man harshly, but exhort him as if he were your father. Treat younger men as brothers, older women as mothers, and younger women as sisters, with absolute purity. — 1 Timothy 5:1-2

A group of twelve of us were in our house for a family game night. We are not all related biologically but are part of an intentional spiritual family (church). We had a lot of fun competing, eating snacks, and talking smack. There were a couple of tense moments when a few of us were a little too zealous in our pursuit of victory, but we got over it. An argument broke out at one point. Maybe more than one. Everyone stayed a little later than I would have wanted, and I became slightly vexed thinking about how early I needed to wake up the next morning. All in all, there was something unmistakably familial about the whole thing: fun, annoyances, inconsequential bickering, food, laughter. And some deeper elements were also wonderfully at play: belonging, acceptance, affection, love. We all gathered again a few days later, along with a number of others, for worship, Bible study, and the Lord's

Supper, including more food. And there was more food. Some of us made plans to get together at a coffee shop one day. Most of the crew came together to help two of our number move into an apartment the following week. There were many texts and other communication back and forth in the ensuing days: memes, jokes, prayer requests, encouragement, testimonies, logistics.

Leadership in the Kingdom of Jesus is about making disciples. Disciples are made in the context of spiritual family. Leadership in the Kingdom of Jesus is carried out in the context of spiritual family.

Family is a potent word. For some, it brings feelings of pain, bitterness, or remorse. For others, it comes with positive emotions of security, care, and love. We all have some degree of longing for the reality of family. In fact, marketers play on that when they invite you to be part of the "family" of people who borrow money from their bank or work out at their gym or buy cars from their lot. Employers try to build camaraderie and a positive work environment by claiming to be a family. But we all know that these uses of the word only cheapen the concept. Family is a real thing for which we have a deep longing in our soul. The Father offers us true family that is even beyond what we experience in the best of home circles. He offers us belonging and security and intimacy with Himself and with other people. God's gift of family fulfills these basic yearnings of the human heart, but it also serves the purpose of helping us to grow in discipleship. In fact, it is essential to that process.

God uses spiritual family in many ways to form us into the image of His Son. He uses the "iron-sharpens-iron" nature of relationships (Proverbs 27:17) in which we experience conflict and anger and intimacy and forgiveness and frustration and camaraderie and affection and sacrifice and on and on. In family we have to learn how to get along. We develop skills of working together and living together. We learn how to not get our own way and to strive for the good of the family over the self. We learn that we cannot make it without forgiving quickly and often. We become aware that people are different than us and that this is a good thing. We learn obedience and submission and humility. We experience grace and acceptance; belonging and being wanted; affection and intimacy. We endure pain and sorrow and frustration and rejection and anger and fear, and we learn how to respond in grace and maturity to those realities, not allowing them the final say. We learn how to stick it out even when we are offended or annoyed or even deeply hurt.

Spiritual family is a work of the Spirit. It is not created by man. In that sense, it is a divine mystery. Only God can gather people from different backgrounds and races and beliefs and parents and make them into a household of faith; a family, a local church. Only God can do that, and in truth He does do it all the time. We have to overcome our tendency to trust in formulas or models, our own cleverness and abilities. Anyone who has truly made the attempt at spiritual family knows that no matter how good it looks on paper, the process is fraught with difficulty and danger. Humans are not easy to work with, let alone love, forgive, defer to, and honor. The creation of family is the prerogative of God. He is the author of family, both the big idea of it and each particular manifestation.

> For this reason I kneel before the Father, from whom every family in heaven and on earth derives its name. — Ephesians 3:14-15

It is God who puts you in family, who creates spiritual family for you, who does the mysterious work of joining individuals together into something beyond any of them. No matter how hard you labor at it, you must know that you will fall short of your dream apart from the miraculous and definite work of the Spirit of God. From the outset, it is important to realize your desperation for Him. You must zealously seek Him for this great purpose.

> God sets the lonely in families. — Psalms 68:6

Just as God is the only legitimate originator of family, so is He also the central reason for it. Families of all kinds exist for the glory of Jesus and the accomplishment of His purposes. There are, of course, many other wonderful benefits that the Father lovingly imparts to us through the gift of family. Through family we experience acceptance, safety, and love. We know that we belong. We have people to lift us when we are discouraged, to help us when we are out of money, to forgive us when we have been selfish. Our family members are there to play games with us, help fix our car, and babysit our kids. But none of that is primary. The Father is the center of His family, and we are not a true spiritual family without the foundation of that unified conviction fixed in our hearts.

One of the Father's primary purposes for putting people in family is to help them become more like Jesus. He has other reasons to be sure, but this is one of them. He does this work in the furnace of family in powerful and beautiful ways. As a leader or aspiring leader in the family of the Father, you are called to cultivate family and to leverage it for God's good purposes.

Spiritual family is not a bonus that a few fortunate disciples have the privilege of experiencing. It is a central part of the Father's plan. You simply cannot grow to maturity and strength alone. You cannot lead others into the fullness intended by God without spiritual family. As a Kingdom leader, you need to learn how to cultivate this spirit of family. This is important. As I have said, building spiritual family is a work of the Spirit, and Jesus is the central reason for it. Even so, there is an essential part for you to play. As a leader in any sphere of life seeking to make disciples for the glory of Jesus, part of your responsibilities is to cultivate the reality of family among those you are discipling. In this chapter, we will study four qualities of spiritual family that can lead to genuine discipleship: trusting commitment, availability, vulnerability, and grace. Before getting to that, let us briefly consider a leader's role in developing spiritual family.

First, as a leader in the Family of God, you are called to take on the role of a spiritual father or mother. You are called to lead not as CEO or president or boss, but as a loving mom or dad. This has profound implications. Take time to consider what this will mean to you in your context.

Secondly, in order to cultivate the spirit of family in whatever context you lead, you must be an example. You yourself need to begin to treat others in the group as family. Be available to them. Show them grace. Grow in your affection for them. Give them the gift of trust. Be vulnerable with them. Do not hope that they will do this without seeing it in you. In many ways, family begins with the leader. This is a powerful way for you to be a servant. Lay your life down consistently for those you lead; your desires, ways of doing things, ambitions, comfort, etc.

Thirdly, work hard at creating a culture of family among those you lead. Labor to see your group grow into a true family of the Spirit. Make it a priority to pray into this. Do small things that add up. Celebrate birthdays. Encourage volunteers to help a member move. Challenge the group to meet a financial need that arises. Pray together. Provide meals for the couple with a newborn. Of course, your example will be a big part of doing this, but do all you can to gently draw others in as well.

Fourthly, continually share the vision of spiritual family.   To be honest, this point poses problems.   To speak too grandly about family and what you as a group aspire to is to ensure that some will be disappointed and hurt by unmet expectations.   Therefore, be sure that in expressing the lofty vision you also paint a picture of reality.   Let everyone know that you as a group will surely fall short — badly and often.   Some will not feel like they belong. Others will continue with unmet needs. One will feel he has not been forgiven for a failure.   Another will be convinced she has nothing to contribute.   One will think his gifts are not being appropriately used.   There will be many ways that the group falls short, in reality and in perception, of the ideal of family.   However, I want to encourage you that it is still worth it to strive towards this end, and to strive together.   It is right and necessary to articulate the great vision while at the same time preparing everyone to walk through disappointments with great grace and understanding.   For this, too, is family.

Spiritual Fathers and Mothers

Even if you had ten thousand guardians in Christ, you do not have many fathers, for in Christ Jesus I became your father through the gospel. Therefore I urge you to imitate me. For this reason I have sent to you Timothy, my son whom I love, who is faithful in the Lord. — 1 Corinthians 4:15-17

"Just as a nursing mother cares for her children, so we cared for you. Because we loved you so much, we were delighted to share with you not only the gospel of God but our lives as well. — 1 Thessalonians 2:7-8

For you know that we dealt with each of you as a father deals with his own children, encouraging, comforting and urging you to live lives worthy of God, who calls you into his kingdom and glory. — 1 Thessalonians 2:11-12

To Titus, my true son in our common faith: Grace and peace from God the Father and Christ Jesus our Savior. — Titus 1:4

Paul saw himself as a spiritual father to many, especially his young co-workers and apprentices such as Timothy and Titus. Of course, God is our true Father, and we do not give that honor to another (Matthew 23:9). We do not need any person to stand between our Heavenly Father and us. However, He does use people in our lives as fathers and mothers in miniature. This is a powerful concept when it comes to leading and discipling people, and I want to point out a few implications of this mindset.

Leading as a spiritual father or mother means:

(1) Responsibility. We all know that parenting is a huge responsibility, and that is certainly one reason the biblical writers use the image of spiritual parenting. In our natural families, we have a responsibility before God to raise our children well. In the early years of their growth, we are constantly aware of where they are and what they are doing. We protect them and provide for them and ensure that they are secure and healthy. We feed, clothe, and hold them. As they grow, we continue to be concerned for their welfare and for their maturity. We instruct and listen to and watch over them with diligence and constant care.

> My dear children, for whom I am again in the pains of childbirth until Christ is formed in you, how I wish I could be with you now and change my tone, because I am perplexed about you! — Galatians 4:19-20

You can sense Paul's passion to see his disciples grow into the maturity of Jesus. He feels the weight of it. His job is far more than running programs or preaching to crowds or leading committees. He is caring for the souls of the saints, and he carries the burden to see them grow strong in the Lord.

> Besides everything else, I face daily the pressure of my concern for all the churches. Who is weak, and I do not feel weak? Who is led into sin, and I do not inwardly burn? — 2 Corinthians 11:28-29

(2) Devotion to their good. For years I have attended basketball games and soccer matches, choir concerts, talent shows, and school plays. Every time I am there it is because at least one of my children is performing in some way and I want to encourage them. I take joy in watching them. My heart's desire is for them to do well. I want to see them play better than I ever did and achieve more distinction for their exploits on field and stage. (Not that this provided a very high bar for them, but that's beside the point). I wanted them to do well, to succeed, to do better.

In ministry, I have observed a diabolical reversal of this natural order. Fathers and mothers in the faith work to hold their spiritual children back so that they will not surpass the parent. I have seen pastors who are more concerned with holding their position and keeping "their sheep" than in seeing the ones they have raised in the faith go beyond their own achievements and fruitfulness. They feel threatened. They cling to control and to the addictive power of spiritual leadership. They arrogantly believe that only they can be trusted with God's work and so they fail to launch others into successful ministry. They put more energy into protecting their little kingdoms than in advancing the Kingdom of God.

Obviously, this should not be. The antidote to this aberration is learning to see disciples as beloved sons and daughters. When we adopt this perspective, we naturally begin to seek the good of those we lead, and even to hope to see them surpass us in maturity, spiritual power, and fruitfulness.

(3) Sacrificial. Parenthood is nothing if not a sacrifice. It costs a lot to raise kids to adulthood. We lose sleep. We lay down deeply held personal desires and ambitions. We offer all we have to give of our time and energy and money. We face pain, sorrow, anxiety, and loss. And we do all this knowing that it is just part of the job description. We do not expect it to be otherwise. Spiritual parenting is the same.

> Now I rejoice in what I am suffering for you, and I fill up in my flesh what is still lacking in regard to Christ's afflictions, for the sake of his body, which is the church. — Colossians 1:24

Until you are prepared to lay down your life for that of another, you are not ready for spiritual leadership. Parenthood teaches us that. You cannot make disciples without experiencing loss. You cannot achieve Jesus' dreams for your life until you lay down your own ambitions and seek to steward those of others.

Parenthood teaches us that discipleship is a long-term proposition. We do not raise kids from infants to adulthood in a few weeks. Nor do we guide disciples into spiritual maturity in so short a period. It takes time. We may not have as significant a role in their lives a decade in the future as we do now, but we are committed for the long term. We remain available. We do not give up or become discouraged because of temporary setbacks. We stay the course.

(4) Affection. Perhaps the greatest attribute of spiritual fathers and mothers is the affection they feel for their sons and daughters in the faith. We are more than directors and mentors and coaches. We are dads and moms. We love. Our hearts are touched by those we serve. We feel strongly. It is this affection which fuels our ability to sacrifice and give and protect and provide for and cheer and bear that burden of responsibility. Kingdom leadership is not simply a transaction in which I give you something in return for what you can do for me. We work in the soil of actual relationships, with all their complexity and pain and beauty. We work through disappointment and offense. We resist jealousy and competition. We cultivate kindness and warmth. We love.

> Just as a nursing mother cares for her children, so we cared for you. Because we loved you so much, we were delighted to share with you not only the gospel of God but our lives as well. — 1 Thessalonians 2:7-8

It would be impossible for me to describe the tender affection I feel for each of my children. As I ponder this, and bring their beloved faces to my mind's eye, I feel something. Even as I search for the words to write, I am aware of a deep well of emotion in connection with my kids. The feeling I have towards those I have discipled and led is akin to that. It is not exactly the same nor does it quite bring the same depth of emotion, but it is of the same kind and it does have a potency to it. Again, as I sit and think about different people who have been to me as sons and daughters in the faith, I feel. I experience the emotions of affection and tenderness. I feel joy. I feel pain. I feel gratitude. I feel wonder. I feel tenderness. Paul experienced something like this when he thought about Timothy and Titus and all the Thessalonians and Corinthians in the churches he planted. Without that secret ingredient of affection, discipleship becomes cold and hard; a duty, a program, a profession. But with the tender affection that the Spirit works in us, the whole endeavor of leadership takes on a different texture, a different feel. Sacrifice and devotion and responsibility do not need to be excruciatingly worked for. They become natural.

It is important at this juncture to issue a warning: Spiritual parenting is not paternalistic. It is not condescending and it is not about control. This should perhaps be obvious by this point in our study, but it needs to be mentioned all the same. Do not think of those you lead as helpless, completely vulnerable newborn babies. Most of the time the image of adult children learning to make their own way in the world is more appropriate.

In the book of Exodus, we see Moses climbing the mountain to meet with God. The people of Israel are left to await the outcome and receive the instructions from on high. In fact, when given the opportunity to be more active participants in the divine encounter, they politely demur.

> When the people saw the thunder and lightning and heard the trumpet and saw the mountain in smoke, they trembled with fear. They stayed at a distance and said to Moses, "Speak to us yourself and we will listen. But do not have God speak to us or we will die." — Exodus 20:18-19.

This paradigm of divine guidance and leadership is one many leaders continue to follow. The leader figuratively goes to the mountain to hear from God and then delivers His Word to the people, who are expected to receive and obey the word. However, this is not New Covenant leadership! Each follower of Christ is filled with the Holy Spirit, who speaks, guides, empowers, and leads. True leadership seeks to connect people to the One true Leader and King, Jesus Himself. It does not presume to be the authoritative voice of God in the lives of those they lead. They trust the Spirit to play that role in conjunction with the scriptures.

One final thought: Spiritual parenting does not always need to be explicitly stated in some awkward exchange of fabricated intimacy. I do not use this vocabulary with the ministry team I currently lead. It is not our style, nor would it naturally fit with the relationships we enjoy. However, I do seek to serve these co-laborers with a sense of responsibility and sacrifice, being devoted to their good, and always in the context of deep affection. I respect them as I do my adult children, not trying to make decisions for them or manipulate them into doing what I deem to be right. In my heart I value them as beloved sons and daughters, and I seek to demonstrate that in appropriate ways.

Trusting Commitment

Therefore if you have any encouragement from being united with Christ, if any comfort from his love, if any common sharing in the Spirit, if any tenderness and compassion, then make my joy complete by being like-minded, having the same love, being one in spirit and of one mind. Do nothing out of selfish ambition or vain conceit. Rather, in humility value others above yourselves, not looking to your own interests but each of you to the interests of the others. — Philippians 2:1-4

God is the creator of spiritual family, and without Him it is flat impossible. At the same time, we clearly have a part to play, and you as a leader have an important role indeed. I am not trying to provide a "how-to" for being spiritual family, but I will offer some basic qualities that are essential to cultivate. None of these are easy. In fact, apart from the sanctifying and empowering work of the Holy Spirit, they will not develop. At the same time, apart from an intentional and determined effort on your part, they also will not develop.

On a pleasant, early summer day in Tulsa, Oklahoma, I sat outside on the patio of our family home. My wife Jill and I were in earnest conversation with two other couples, elders together with us in our local church — our spiritual family. We were just finishing a nice meal and enjoying one another's company. Over the years we had developed an ease and pleasantness in just being together. I trust these men and women. Still, my insides began to slightly churn as I broached the subject with these long-time friends. Jill and I sensed the Lord leading us into a significant life change. We had discussed it with our children and we were all excited, but also apprehensive. As we shared with a mix of trepidation and enthusiasm, we came to the point. For years I had been promising this group that I would make no major life-changing decisions without their input and approval. Yes, approval. We had committed to seek the Lord's will together in a discernment process before making significant changes in our lives. At this crucial juncture, with our future on the line, my wife and I reaffirmed this pledge. We submitted to God's will for us as discerned by our co-workers and co-leaders in spiritual family.

In all honesty, the affirmation of this commitment and the actual submission of my family to a group of leaders did not feel particularly risky to me in this moment. I was not worried about the outcome, because I believed God would lead us as we sought Him together. I was confident that my friends wanted good for me, and especially that they wanted me to follow God's path for my life. If, as we prayed and talked together, our proposal would be rejected or significantly altered, I would be fine, trusting in God's ability to lead us. If, on the other hand, we were to receive affirmation in our plans, we would move forward in greater confidence, knowing the Lord was leading us. In the ensuing months and years when doubts assail us (I know they will), we will be encouraged and strengthened by having gone through this process of group discernment and submission. However, getting to this place of peace and confidence had been a slow process.

Although by this time I was at ease regarding our commitment to submit to this group, it had not always been so. When first making the solemn promise years ago that we would make no significant life change apart from their approval, it felt risky indeed. My wife and I were the founders and senior leaders of this church. Others on our team were younger and less experienced than we were. I was acutely aware of their faults and weaknesses (as they were of mine), and there have been moments when the temptation to not trust had been strong. Was it truly wise to allow this crew of flawed and broken people such power in my life? What if they got it wrong? Why make this commitment? It is not what pastors normally do. Nobody was demanding it of me.

Family is built on trusting commitment to one another. If I want my spiritual family to be strong, I will take the risk to trust again and again. I will empower those in my family to speak into my life, even if I am the senior leader. I will practice the sacred art of submission. I am not a hired hand. I am not shepherding this family just until some better opportunity arises. I am climbing no ladder of success. I am committed to these people.

Trusting commitment is an essential part of family and it must be modeled by those who claim to lead. In training leaders around the world, I often hear pastors and others complain about the lack of commitment they see in the people that make up their churches or organizations. As leaders with a vision and plan, we highly value strong commitment in those we lead. That is, we value commitment to us and to our vision. I suggest we turn this on its head. Instead of craving the commitment of others to me, what can I do to radically bind myself to them? How can I expect them to commit to me wholeheartedly when I am not committed to them?

Commitment does not come easy, and knowing where to put your commitment can be a big challenge as well. Some people tend to over-commit. You cannot say no. You take on every task and position offered to you, and you always seem to be hunting for more. There are probably many reasons why a person would tend to over-commit, but one common culprit is a performance mentality. If you have so many commitments in your life that you are not fulfilling any of them well, this is something you need to consider. Perhaps you are still striving for the Father's (and people's) affirmation, love, belonging, and honor. You have not been able to receive God's grace and value as a free gift. Instead, you are struggling to earn it. And one good way of earning it is by doing more. And more. And more. Saying "no" makes you feel guilty. You feel like you can never quite give enough or be good enough or do enough. If this is you, do the necessary work of releasing your striving to God and receiving the gift of His acceptance and love, and then prayerfully look over your commitments with a view to eliminate the ones God is not calling you to shoulder.

Others under-commit. Again, there are surely a lot of reasons why this may be the case. Perhaps you are just lazy and prefer to fill your time with fluff. If that is the case, repent. For most, though, I suspect something more subtle. You under-commit because you do not like to surrender control. Every commitment you make snatches some of your personal autonomy. If you commit to being at a certain place at a particular time, you automatically have ruled out every other place to be at that time. And what if a better opportunity arises between the time you made the commitment and the moment of fulfillment? You have surrendered control of that piece of your time, and you either have to swallow the pill or break your commitment. Even more to the point, when you commit to a group of people, especially a group of people with some kind of structure (such as spiritual family), you eliminate many other options. You will have to say no to things you would prefer to do because you have committed to serve and support these people, this family. Committing to people is an intentional act of giving up personal control and independence and giving it to others, trusting that in so doing you are in fact placing your life under the control of the sovereignty of God.

Availability

They devoted themselves to the apostles' teaching and to fellowship, to the breaking of bread and to prayer. Everyone was filled with awe at the many wonders and signs performed by the apostles. All the believers were together and had everything in common. They sold property and possessions to give to anyone who had need. Every day they continued to meet together in the temple courts. They broke bread in their homes and ate together with glad and sincere hearts, praising God and enjoying the favor of all the people. And the Lord added to their number daily those who were being saved. — Acts 2:42-47

In a world of boundaries and "me-time" and self-care, the Father is building His family with a radically available people. Obviously, we are available to the direction and leading of Jesus, but we are also available to the people He has given us. When I read the stories of Jesus in the gospels, one of the things that grips and challenges me time and time again is the amazing availability of Jesus, both to His disciples and to the crowds. Yes, He does seek time away, and He does pull His disciples aside for solitude and refreshing. And yet He also allows people to disrupt and trample on His plans.

Consider Matthew's account of Jesus feeding the five thousand in chapter 14 of his gospel. Jesus has just heard the painful news that John the Baptist has been murdered. His initial response is what you might expect, but what follows is striking:

When Jesus heard what had happened, he withdrew by boat privately to a solitary place. Hearing of this, the crowds followed him on foot from the towns. — Matthew 14:13

Jesus immediately seeks to be alone, probably to allow His Father to bring comfort and strength to His troubled soul. We would all agree this is a reasonable and healthy response. However, a whole crowd of people, in blatant insensitivity, seek Him out that He might continue to minister to them. And the shocking thing is that He complies. In fact, it is in this context that He performs one of His most well-known and powerful miracles. He actually feeds thousands of the very people who broke into His well-earned and deeply needed private retreat. Jesus was radically available.

I can see that concerned look in your eyes. You are seeing red flags all over the place. You have been trained to militantly protect your boundaries and be sure to take care of yourself first so that you can be strong enough to help others. There is some wisdom in that. But please remember that our standard is not found in worldly experts, but in Jesus our King. Also remember that He is the One who gives you capacity. If you are determined to be obedient to Him, He will provide strength every time. That does not mean you will not be tired or forced to miss out on things you enjoy or that you will not be required to make a myriad of other sacrifices. Of course you will. But that is part of the real joy of serving with Jesus.

Yes, there will be plenty of times you do need to say "no" to people in need. Sometimes you will find, in the wisdom God gives you, that it will be better for the person to not get from you what they desire, or to not get it according to their timetable. You will work through issues of enabling and creating dependence and a host of other complexities that arise as you seek to help people. Yet in all of it there will be a thread of availability that will cause your therapist to throw a fit.

It may also be important to note that your availability is not the same for everyone. As a minister of Christ, you are available to help the poor and needy whoever they may be. But as a member of spiritual family, you are even more available to your brothers and sisters with whom you are journeying in Christ.

> Therefore, as we have opportunity, let us do good to all people, especially to those who belong to the family of believers. — Galatians 6:10

Radical availability goes beyond even your time, which is significant enough. It intrudes into your physical space and into your money and into all your resources. Like we see in the early church (such as Acts 2:42-47 quoted at the head of this section), maybe availability means that every need within your fellowship can be met by the sacrificial generosity of each member. We are available to meet needs. We are available to lay down our time and money. We also make our space available, violating that most sacred of western values: personal privacy. Many introverts such as myself cringe at such a thought. We make excuses and cling tightly to our rights and to our cozy little corners of this earth. But in the end, we are called to surrender to the loving demands of the Father as He sends needy people our way.

What does this radical availability look like in your life? I obviously cannot answer that with any degree of definition or detail. I just know that it will be costly, and it will be rewarding, and that it is an essential element of family. When my daughter calls me late at night because she has a flat tire on the other side of town, I go to her without thinking about it. When my young child wakes up crying in the night because of a bad dream, I run to bring comfort and security. When my brother in Christ needs help packing up his house or working through emotional pain or putting food on the table, I know without having to deliberate that I have to help in some way. Availability will intrude on my time and on my space and on my possessions and on my energy and even on my emotional comfort and "wellness." But it is the way of family. It is the way of Christ.

Vulnerability

All the believers were one in heart and mind. No one claimed that any of their possessions was their own, but they shared everything they had. With great power the apostles continued to testify to the resurrection of the Lord Jesus. And God's grace was so powerfully at work in them all that there were no needy persons among them. For from time to time those who owned land or houses sold them, brought the money from the sales and put it at the apostles' feet, and it was distributed to anyone who had need. — Acts 4:32-35

We sit together in a space familiar to all of us. Our leader team is gathering to make decisions and plans for our community. As we spend a few preliminary minutes checking in and sharing a little about life, one person simply states that she is not doing well. She begins to tell us about some intense situations that she is navigating. She communicates that she honestly feels like she is not going to make it. It is not going to be okay, and she is not okay. I am in awe. In the power of Christ through the courageous vulnerability of a beloved sister, a business meeting becomes a family gathering. We encourage. We pray. We listen. We probably do not do any of these particularly well, but we do try. There is simply no other possible response. Jesus binds us more closely together in unity and in love.

In order for a group of friends to become family, they will need to learn to walk in vulnerability with one another. They will put away masks and false selves. They will be open with their messes and their victories. They will not hide the things that make them feel small or weak or unworthy. There is a unique and mysterious power in vulnerability. Henri Nouwen asserts that

> The Christian leader of the future is called to be completely irrelevant and to stand in this world with nothing to offer but his or her own vulnerable self.[60]

As stated before, one of the obstacles we, particularly those in the West, must overcome in order to be vulnerable is our obsession with privacy. We have to welcome others into our space and into our lives. Our family knows when the house is a mess and we fail to make our bed and our closet is a disaster. It is aware of the dishes in the sink, the toys on the floor, and the heap of dirty laundry overflowing its basket. It is also aware of the metaphorical messes in the non-public parts of our lives and hearts. Vulnerability means being known. It means trusting that others will accept and love and even respect me in my imperfection and weakness. It means being genuine, authentic, honest.

Another obstacle that must be overcome in vulnerability is the extreme individualism that mars many of our relationships and communities. We often look at the beautiful description of the first church in Acts 2 and 4 with puzzled admiration, wondering how it happened that "there were no needy persons among them" (Acts 4:34). Obviously, part of this was that there was an amazing generosity that clearly permeated this incredible fellowship. But there was of necessity something else: a vulnerability to let needs be known. In order for lack to have been so fully vanquished, there must have been an abnormal awareness of one another's need. I have found that our communities are often full of people with a willingness to give, but what we lack is a willingness to ask and to receive. In pride, we so value our own ability to provide for ourselves and not be dependent on others that we are ashamed to communicate that we need help. We can admit it in general terms, but hesitate when it comes to specifics: paying rent this month, getting my child to the doctor, providing food for my guests. Radical generosity can be made impotent without radical vulnerability.

---

[60] Henri Nouwen, *In the Name of Jesus* (Crossroad Publishing, New York, 2002), pg 30.

Grace

May the grace of the Lord Jesus Christ, and the love of God, and the fellowship of the Holy Spirit be with you all. — 2 Corinthians 13:14

We are recipients of amazing grace. Jesus died for the cleansing of our sins. We are free and holy and accepted because of His grace. We are members of His family, heirs of eternal life, filled with the Spirit of God, all because of grace. We have received wonderful things that we could never deserve or earn. We know that our selfishness and impurity and pride disqualify us from all of the above, but we have received them, nonetheless. The grace of Jesus is truly amazing.

Incredibly, we can also give grace to others. Because we have received so much from the Father, we have much to pass on. We too can make a place for people to belong and be accepted and loved. We can cover sins and touch uncleanness and receive broken people. Jesus-centered families are communities of grace. Instead of accusing, we cover. Instead of competing, we champion. Instead of condemning, we defend.

If our spiritual family is to be a true discipling community, we must grasp the principle that grace is not only the thing that brings forgiveness and salvation, but it also is the agent of transformation. This sounds right, but it is almost always counterintuitive in real life situations. When facing a sin issue in my life or the life of my friend, grace is the means by which Jesus will sanctify us. Our natural instinct is to use other, unholy, methods: fear, shame, manipulation. We see something that needs to change, and we utilize the tools with which we are so familiar. The reasoning, such as it is, goes something like this: If I can make myself (or make you) feel badly enough about the sin, I will be motivated to stop engaging in it. Or, if I can create or discover a consequence that is particularly odious, I will have the strength to stop sinning. What I am doing is looking for external forces that will help me to stop a particular behavior or pattern of behaviors. We can call this behavior modification, and many of our Christian communities are quite happy with that, as long as it "works;" as long as it brings about an outward change of behavior.

Woe to you, teachers of the law and Pharisees, you hypocrites! You clean the outside of the cup and dish, but inside they are full of greed and self-indulgence.

160

Blind Pharisee! First clean the inside of the cup and dish, and then the outside also will be clean. — Matthew 23:25-26

"First clean the inside." At best, we tend to go about this backwards. At worst, we never do get to the heart, which is the central thing in Jesus' program. We satisfy ourselves that so and so no longer cusses or gets drunk or is mean to people or steals. We are happy that they attend church, give in the offering, and finally got a job. These are good things, but they are not necessarily fool-proof evidence of salvation or discipleship. We take little notice of the true condition of the heart.

Grace brings true transformation that moves from the inside out. It is not satisfied with any kind of change that does not issue from a transformed heart. There are no easy steps to this kind of discipling.

Grace-based discipleship offers acceptance apart from performance. We do not require a disciple to live up to all the standards of mature Jesus people right away. We offer the beautiful gift of acceptance, allowing the person to be part of our fellowship and family even when they get it wrong, when they make us feel awkward, when they offend, when they embarrass.

Grace-based discipleship loves unconditionally. We are with people for the long haul. We let it be known that we are not going anywhere; that we will be a consistent presence and a faithful friend. We do not withhold our love or affection when the person disappoints us. We are tenacious.

Grace-based discipleship seeks to cover rather than expose. We recognize shame as the weapon of the enemy and we do not try to use it, even for good purposes. The end does not justify the means. We do not talk flippantly about the sin of another, and we do not seek to make anyone do good by feeling bad.

Grace-based discipleship forgives again and again.

Then Peter came to Jesus and asked, "Lord, how many times shall I forgive my brother or sister who sins against me? Up to seven times?" Jesus answered, "I tell you, not seven times, but seventy-seven times." — Matthew 18:21-22

We have been offered endless forgiveness by Jesus, and in His strength, we are able to offer the same to others. When this is difficult and even seems to be impossible, it is helpful to meditate on the grace that we have received and continue to receive. Remember that the ways you have been offended by your friend are nothing in comparison with how you have offended God, and yet you are forgiven freely and completely.

Grace-based discipleship focuses on obedience. All of this talk of grace can make it seem that what a person does has no significance at all. This is not so. A person who is being transformed from within will begin to demonstrate this through outward actions. If there is no progress in obedience to God's Word, that is a sign that there is no change within. We can see this, of course, at work perfectly in the earthly ministry of Jesus. He offered grace so freely that it became a scandal (He "eats with tax collectors and sinners!" — Matthew 9:11). Yet He consistently called His followers to obedience ("Anyone who loves me will obey my teaching" — John 14:23).

The crux of the matter is this: the transformation to which Jesus calls His followers begins with the gift of a new heart which leads to a steady growth in obedience to Him. All this is accomplished by grace. We receive the gospel by grace through faith, and we live the gospel life by grace through faith. In practice, this looks like an ongoing dance with mercy and truth. We affirm the disciple's place in God's family by faith. We serve in the new identity given as a free gift. And we teach the commands of Jesus with an expectation of obedience.

It is important to add that we also lovingly correct as needed. Our examples in the New Testament certainly did not shy away from speaking about sin or confronting people who were doing wrong. It is important that we do this in grace and love rather than out of annoyance, anger, or self-righteousness. We always have in mind the good of the person and of the community at large. We encourage, exhort, and instruct. Paul describes this beautifully in reminding the young Thessalonian church how he had discipled them:

> Just as a nursing mother cares for her children, so we cared for you. Because we loved you so much, we were delighted to share with you not only the gospel of God but our lives as well... For you know that we dealt with each of you as a father deals with his own children, encouraging, comforting and urging you to live lives worthy of God, who calls you into his kingdom and glory. — 1 Thessalonians 2:7-8, 11-12

12 - MISSION

When Jesus had called the Twelve together, he gave them power and authority to drive out all demons and to cure diseases, and he sent them out to proclaim the kingdom of God and to heal the sick. — Luke 9:1-2

When Jesus made disciples, He did not cloister them away from the world until they should become strong or mature or "ready." Instead, He sent them out into it. How things have changed. Mission is both a primary purpose of discipleship and a primary means of discipleship. It is, at least in part, both the "why" and the "how." Jesus' mission of saving the world is the reason He called the first disciples. "Come, follow me," Jesus said, "and I will send you out to fish for people." (Matthew 4:19). The vision from the very beginning was that those called by Jesus would go out and do the works of Jesus. "He appointed twelve that they might be with him and that he might send them out to preach and to have authority to drive out demons." (Mark 3:14-15). Discipleship that does not lead to mission is not true Christian discipleship.

Not only is mission the goal, or certainly a goal, of discipleship (and thus of all legitimate Christian leadership), but it is also one of the primary methods used by Jesus to actually do discipleship. It is how He made disciples. The first disciples grew in maturity through being given missional responsibility. This is an often overlooked practice in Jesus' disciple-making. Jesus' first followers were fully immersed in His work of redemption from the very beginning. They were proclaiming the Kingdom and driving out demons before they even really knew who Jesus was. Engagement in the work of mission is absolutely critical in the making of disciples.

Where does discipleship mostly happen in your context? Perhaps you typically think of the church building, a classroom, and maybe a coffee shop. These are all good, safe places. They highlight some of our discipleship values, too. We tend to see discipleship largely as a transfer of knowledge (classroom). We also rightly value the authoritative proclamation of God's Word in the context of worship and encounter (church building). And of course, there is the one-on-one relational element that is demonstrated in the coffee shop sphere. All of these are good and necessary and very powerful. Do them. However, there are significant omissions that need to be addressed. I suggest we desperately need to add two more settings, and perhaps even make them primary. The first is the living room. I attempted to make this point clearly in the chapter about spiritual family. Disciples are made in the real stuff of life and relationships. Unfortunately, in today's common style of discipleship, we often lack the opportunity to observe our disciples in real-life situations. So, we need living rooms.

In the same way, we need to add whatever place that you "do mission." This could be on the streets of your city, with international students at a local university, welcoming refugees with a service agency, or perhaps most needed of all, at your place of work or in your neighborhood. All of these represent you engaging the world with the love and truth of Jesus. Your primary sphere of ministry is probably not within the four walls of your local church building. The places where you interact with the lost and hurting and broken are the places of mission for you.

Disciples are made in the context of mission. As we consider the example of Jesus, we see that He made disciples in the mix and the mess of intense missional activity. Jesus came to "seek and save the lost" (Luke 19:10), and this is what He spent His time doing. What is significant to the current discussion is that He did it with His disciples. He brought the disciples with Him as He preached to the crowds, healed the sick, drove out demons, confronted the Pharisees, and declared the Kingdom. They were there when He fed the 5,000 and actually participated in that great miracle by distributing the food. These encounters often led to conversations which Jesus used to teach His followers.

Jesus always brought disciples with Him when He did mission. He did not gather the twelve together in a secluded place for two years to teach them in a ministry school or seminary. He invited them along into His work of redemption, took advantage of opportunities to train and empower, provided additional focused teaching as they went, and sent them out to do the work He had been equipping them to do all along. I suggest that this provides a helpful pattern for us as well.

Invite into. It should go without saying that you do not make disciples unless you are doing something worth reproducing. If you are not proclaiming the gospel or caring for the poor or being a witness at work or raising godly kids or living a godly life in the midst of an ungodly culture or overcoming the works of darkness in your neighborhood or interceding for your city, there is not much point in duplicating yourself. However, if you are a leader in Christ's Kingdom, you are engaging in at least some aspect of His mission. Discipleship begins right there. Consider how you can invite those you are called to disciple into that. Your disciple may be a co-worker or employee. If so, the place of work is the natural focal point of discipleship. This of course feels like a lot of pressure, and to some degree that is okay. Feel the weight of your need for the power of the Holy Spirit. Invite your disciple into your struggles, but also your successes and fruitfulness. If your mission is more of a "going out," invite others into that as well. Ask them to accompany you as you feed the homeless or teach English to refugees or pray with people on the streets. Certainly one of the most powerful discipleship tools you have is your example. Use it.

Seek Opportunities to Train. As you do the work of mission together, there will be many opportunities for conversations that provide important equipping. Matthew tells the story of a man who brought his son to the disciples, who were unable to help him. Jesus eventually came on the scene and saved the day, and later the disciples sought to find out why they failed.

> Then the disciples came to Jesus in private and asked, "Why couldn't we drive it out?" He replied, "Because you have so little faith. Truly I tell you, if you have faith as small as a mustard seed, you can say to this mountain, 'Move from here to there,' and it will move. Nothing will be impossible for you." — Matthew 17:19-20

Jesus used the opportunity to teach them a key lesson. In driving out demons you need to have faith. This teaching came about because of the circumstances of mission. It was not a lesson that Jesus had prepared with a power point and good stories. It was happening right before them. In the same way, you will find many openings to teach important lessons as you do mission together with those you are discipling.

For years, I have been part of a ministry that befriends the homeless and shares the gospel with them through a weekly meal. We have had many volunteers join us in this outreach over time. Some have been active participants for years, while others serve for a few months. I have found that regular interaction with the poor provides unparalleled opportunities for training disciples. We do very little in the way of orientation before people come to serve. However, we have many equipping conversations that come up because of things that happen each week. We talk about the nature of poverty and how we should respond. We discuss the power of the gospel to bring transformation and how to best proclaim it. We have discussions about helping people who are addicted to drugs or who suffer from mental illness. We have many "what should I have said to...." and "how could I have better helped..." conversations. Training that is in response to actual situations can be some of the most effective discipling that happens, because the application is immediate, and the motivation is strong.

Provide Ordered Teaching. Of course, Jesus did not only wait for circumstances to provide ideal opportunities to pass on necessary instructions. There were truths that He needed to deliver to those He was training, and so He took time aside for intentional teaching. A good example of this is found in Matthew 10, when Jesus gathered the twelve together for some needed instructions as He prepared to send them out with a missional task. We will discuss this concept more when we get to the sections about raising up other leaders. For now, I will just mention that Jesus was both opportunistic (taking advantage of teachable moments) and intentional in His training of the disciples.

Send Them Out. At the top of this chapter, I quoted the famous part in Luke's gospel where Jesus sends out His twelve disciples to do the work of mission. In the next chapter, He sends out seventy-two in a similar way. These followers had been watching Jesus up close for some time. They had seen Him do all the things He was now sending them to replicate (drive out demons, heal the sick, and proclaim the Kingdom of God). He had taught them what they needed to know and given them power and authority. Now it was time for them to go and do what Jesus had been equipping them to do. They could not truly have been considered disciples if they never went out and did what Jesus had been doing. This is the point. There is no discipleship apart from mission. Again, mission is what you are training people for, and it is also an essential part of that training. Obviously, those first disciples grew immensely in their faith through the experiences of proclaiming the Kingdom and healing the sick themselves. Later, after the seventy-two returned, they reported to Jesus what had happened, and He gave them further insights (Luke 10:17-24).

In a similar way, you must at some point — and sooner rather than later — entrust your disciples with legitimate, significant ministry responsibilities. Experience is a great teacher if you can leverage it well. Although it can feel risky, this is part of what it means to make disciples. Take the risk. Give those you are training permission to try and fail, while all the time doing what you can to ensure their success.

If we are going to disciple people in the pattern given us by Jesus, we must involve them in mission as we provide ongoing guidance and support. There is no substitute for this.

Leading Others into God's Purposes

I have been arguing that it is impossible to truly make disciples of Jesus apart from engagement in the mission of Jesus. If this is indeed so, we must consider what the missional context is in our own lives. Or, putting it another way, we need to understand, or at least to be seeking to understand, what God is calling us to do in regard to reaching people for Jesus and being agents of His redemption. What is your calling? Your specific commission from the King?

You may be wondering at this point how a book supposedly about leadership has come to all this talk about mission. At the risk of re-stating what has come before, the purpose of all Jesus-centered leadership is Spirit-empowered mission. If you as a believer have influence in any measure, it is for the sake of people coming to know Jesus and growing up in Him. It is for the sake of Jesus being revealed through you to other people. We cannot discuss leadership without discussing discipleship, and we cannot talk about discipleship without getting to mission. If you are not devoted to Jesus' mission, you are not a leader in His Kingdom. What are you leading people into? Leadership is not an end in itself. It is only a means of Jesus accomplishing His great end.

Now, back to the question: Where do you do mission? And, going a little bit further, how do you bring others that you are leading into that? The good news is that, as a humble servant of the King, you can lead people into this as you are figuring it out. You do not have to pretend you have all the answers up front but can invite those you are discipling into your journey of discovering mission. In fact, walking with you in your process may be the best way there is to launch them into their own Kingdom purposes.

I moved to Tulsa, Oklahoma with my family in 2007 to help begin a discipleship community with a local church. At this time in my life, I suspected the truth of what I have been writing about: that mission must play a vital role in any discipleship endeavor. I was further convinced that God was calling us to bring His love and hope to the poor and marginalized of our city. But I had no idea what I was doing or how to go about this. As the leader, I had a vague idea that I should have a plan, that I should develop a strategy and cast vision for it among those I was discipling. The only problem was I truly did not know what I was doing, and the thought of a mission to the poor intimidated me. Thus, in providential cluelessness and growing desperation, I did the only thing I could think to do. I invited the community to pray for God to reveal and lead us into His mission for us. We gathered early in the mornings for prayer, and it was always on the agenda to beseech the Spirit to lead us into some good Kingdom work. We continued this for nearly two years.

I hasten to add that during this time of praying and waiting on the Lord we were not idle. In fact, we tried many things. We dove into serving in after-school programs and mentoring kids in a local public school and volunteering at various agencies and ministries that worked with the poor. We learned about evangelism and reaching our city from fruitful practitioners. And we continued to pray. One day a couple of the members of our community were walking downtown and were approached by a homeless man asking for money. These young disciples wanted to help in some way but had no cash to offer. Instead, they invited the homeless man to gather a few of his friends and join them for a cook-out at the park. They also brought along a few of their friends, and close to twenty people showed up for the meal. They all had a great time. At the end of the evening as my friends were leaving, one of the homeless men shouted to them, "See you next week?" And so, it happened. Within a few weeks we sensed that this was at least part of the answer to our prayers over the previous two years. It seemed a little bit anticlimactic in some ways, just eating hot dogs and hamburgers at a park once a week with some homeless people. But we felt the Lord's delight and began to believe He had a purpose for this unplanned outreach.

At the time of this writing, folks have been gathering every Thursday evening for the past fifteen years to enjoy a family-style meal and to share the love and power of Jesus. The Father has taught us much, and many of us have been transformed as we've made friends with the poor and the set-aside. But the point I am seeking to illustrate here is that, as a leader, you can include those you are leading in the process of discovering God's mission for you. In fact, I have come to see that this is a powerful way of serving and leading. It highlights again the reality that Jesus is the One true Leader, and we are all His servants. It reminds us that in the big scheme of things, we are not leaders, but servants of a good and powerful God who loves us as His very own children. If I had been better at mission and had planned out exactly how our community was going to serve the Lord in our city, this outreach that has blessed so many people over the years and has revealed the grace of Jesus so beautifully would probably never have happened. Through my weakness and ignorance, and through the God-given gifts and passions of those I discipled, the Father brought about something glorious.

My initial role in all that I described above was to invite friends that I was discipling into my own journey of learning how to be part of Jesus' mission, and to continually put before them the mandate for us to be part of reaching our city. Once it began, I was able to play the roles of chief encourager, committed participant, and occasional advisor. The universal principle in this perhaps is simply that as "leaders," our role is to follow our King and to help others to follow Him with us. It is no good for people to follow me unless I am ultimately leading them to follow Jesus directly, apart from me. Another part of this is that following Jesus always means participating in His mission. My exhortation to you is to not be too proud to lead in weakness. Do not allow false expectations of what a leader should be keep you from desperately seeking the Lord together with your friends about His dreams for your life together and for your city. Be determined to find your part in His work and bring others along with you. As you are leading others, you do not need to be their leader in everything. Allow them to lead you, too, when God ignites passion and empowers them with gifts that propel them into His mission.

Allow me to share another example. The Lord brought into our community a young lady, freshly returning from a disappointing exit from the mission field. Though back in Tulsa, her heart burned with love and compassion and longing for those she had left behind in Reynosa, Mexico. She also carried a conviction that her work in that difficult place was not finished. Up until this point, I had never felt a burden for Mexico or a desire to go there. Even when Emily first described her ministry among prostitutes and drug addicts in a filthy red-light district, I at first felt no compelling desire to be part of it. But I saw in Emily a passion and courage and love for these lost and broken souls that I knew came straight from the heart of Jesus. In time, our small community of disciples fully embraced this mission and these people. We prayed. We took trips. We gave money. We mobilized others. Again, as leader, I did not know how to reach and disciple prostitutes in a Mexican border town, nor did I have the compelling vision and determination to see it happen. But Emily did. So once again, my role in "leading" our community into mission was to champion Emily, to actively participate, and to occasionally advise. In the few years that we were deeply involved in this work, our community was profoundly impacted, and none more so than me.

As a leader, part of your work is to discover the missional passions and gifts that God has put within those you are discipling. You are then to nurture and help to develop your disciples into powerful agents of Jesus' redemption. Help them to find outlets for what the Lord has put in their hearts. You may not have a clue as to how to do the thing God is calling them to do, but you can play an essential role. You are still there to serve and to help bring them to maturity. You are there to see Christ formed in them. Make use of the experiences they will have in mission to this end. The best way you can do that is by joining them in that work, and together seeking God's wisdom and power and grace.

God used our community in His work among the homeless of Tulsa and prostitutes in Reynosa, but the reason I share these stories here is to consider how such missional outreaches have been an essential part in our discipleship process. It is these experiences that have helped us to know Jesus more deeply and to become more like Him. You cannot make disciples apart from missional engagement. This is not true only for certain leaders — for missions-minded leaders or evangelists. This is true for every Kingdom leader. Where is your mission? How can you bring others with you?

A Disciple-Making Movement

It was already quite dark in Kampala, Uganda when my friend Wilson parked his beat-up van in a rather questionable part of town. I timidly exited through the passenger door while a couple of other friends climbed out of the back. I could not see very much of my surroundings, but enough to know that we were in a poor part of town, and enough for me to wonder how safe it was to be here at this time. Wilson had told me we were going to visit one of the "ghetto churches" that had been planted as part of the disciple-making movement he leads. We walked down a path for a short distance until we encountered a group of young men who were listening to music, laughing, talking, smoking, and just hanging out. Some sat on the porch of an old house, while others spread out on the ground or stood in small groups, talking loudly in Luganda. They all seemed happy to see Wilson, and I allowed myself to relax a little. Someone brought a rickety plastic chair for me, and after greeting those present, I sat down and observed.

Before long, more than twenty people had gathered; all young men, with the exception of Alice, a young lady who had accompanied Wilson and me in the van. I found out later that the leader of this group was being discipled by Alice, who had a heart for the poor and the marginalized. Over the course of the evening, through my own observations and with some clarifications and further details supplied by Wilson, I discovered several things about those gathered in this place: (1) Fewer than half were followers of Jesus yet; (2) They were all poor and lived in the "ghetto;" (3) They had been coming together every week like this for several weeks; (4) Four generations of leaders were present (normally this was not the case, but tonight they all came): Wilson, a young man he discipled, Alice (who was discipled by this young man), and the leader of this particular group, who was being discipled by Alice.

For the next hour or so, I sat in awe. The leader, a quiet, unassuming youth, opened the meeting with a word of welcome and prayer. He then asked each person to share about how they did in obeying the scripture from the previous study a week prior. Some had not been at that meeting, so gave no response. Others confessed that they had done nothing. But a surprising number mentioned a specific thing that they had been challenged to do the week before and were able to tell how they had followed through. More than one said that the lesson had been about inviting others to follow Jesus, and in obedience to that word they had brought a friend or family member to be part of the gathering this evening, and there were actually several new people present as a result of these efforts.

After everyone had a chance to speak in this way, we were all asked to share, one by one, something for which we were thankful and something for which we would like prayer. Then we took a moment and prayed for the person next to us. After this, the leader read a passage from the Gospel of John and facilitated a lively discussion about its meaning and implications for us. He then asked each person to share how they were going to obey this passage of scripture in the coming week, reminding them that they would be asked to give a report the next time they met. Finally, everyone was asked to name at least one person with whom they would share the truth just learned over the course of the coming week.

I was very quiet on the ride back to Wilson's house as I pondered all that I had witnessed. In this very rough-around-the-edges church gathering, I saw laid out before me Jesus' pattern of leadership and discipleship. It had all started with Wilson praying and sharing the gospel as he walked the streets of his own neighborhood. As he did this, people came to Jesus, and he began to disciple them with simple methods such as those utilized in the gathering I described. He also brought these new converts with him as he proclaimed the gospel to others, gathered them together, and discipled them. Before long, instead of trying to begin new groups himself, he was challenging his young disciples to do so in their own neighborhoods and among their friends. Soon, disciples were being made in ghettos and among refugee communities, among gang members, drug dealers, and prostitutes. Even now, each person that Wilson disciples participates with him in this simple pattern of gospel proclamation and discipleship. Even as they are learning the basic foundations of the faith, they are being challenged to replicate what is happening in their own spheres, and many of them do so.

Each leader is discipling and being discipled. All takes place in the context and for the purpose of mission, and lives are being wonderfully transformed by the power of Jesus. Disciples learn to introduce people to Jesus at their places of work, in their neighborhoods, among their family members, and anywhere they go. They are trained in gathering spiritually hungry people together and discipling them into mature followers of Jesus, and they always challenge those they lead to go out and do the same. These are not "full-time" ministers in the sense that they work for a church or

172

receive any money for their efforts. They are, however, "full-time" in the sense that they are always on the lookout for opportunities to make disciples in any setting in which they find themselves.

As of this writing, more than 11,000 of these groups have been started, with most of the members being young people who have been introduced to Jesus through people in the movement. Leaders are not given impressive titles or positions of authority. Instead, they are encouraged to love and serve those they lead. They are committed to discipleship and to bringing others to Jesus. They are becoming mature and trustworthy ministers of the gospel within this context of outreach and spiritual family. All of their training is based on an obedience-centered study of the Bible, using a discovery process. The vast majority of those in the movement are poor and not well-educated. They are considered to be the marginalized and unwanted of society. I should also mention that Wilson sacrificed both position and finances to begin and lead this work. He has been beaten and robbed and has endured great financial stress and lack as he attempts to care for his family while leading this out-of-the-box church network. He has little or no worldly power or leadership, but in the Kingdom, he is bearing great fruit. Specifically considering the missional element, allow me to make the following observations that are highlighted in this movement:

As emphasized already, Jesus-style leadership is discipleship and is missionally focused. In this movement, leaders see themselves primarily as servants and disciple-makers, and their inclination is always towards those who are far from Jesus but who express spiritual hunger.

For Kingdom leaders, mission is always a full-time endeavor. Of the thousands of leaders in this movement, very few are full-time in the vocational ministry sense. However, all of them are trained to see their current situation and environment as their place of unique calling and mission. If they are employed, their primary purpose in that job is discipling people. If they are students, the same is true. If they are unemployed, they give themselves to serving and to the work of ministry as they seek whatever work they can find.

The greater their involvement in mission, the less prone leaders are to care about position or title. True missional leaders are not interested in building their ministries or climbing the ecclesiastical ladder. Their passion for the lost and the broken forces their attention away from their own advancement and keeps it on Jesus and His Kingdom.

Discipleship that is based on obedience to the Bible produces observable growth in spiritually hungry people. Although there are many problems and setbacks and disappointments in this movement, they experience much more clear, indisputable growth in maturity among their members than ministries that focus primarily on passing on knowledge through pastor-centered or teacher-centered gatherings.

Missional leaders make raising other leaders a top priority. The movement cannot grow without more leaders being deployed, because no one individual leader is growing a large following. The only way that growth happens is for more disciples to obediently begin serving others, proclaiming the gospel, and discipling the hungry. And this happens at a remarkable rate.

On-the-job leadership training is the best way to equip laborers for the harvest. There is no time to send promising leaders away for a one- or two-year training program, and even if there were, that would not be as effective as the system of apprenticing and discipleship that is being utilized. Leaders, like the first disciples of Jesus, experience great personal growth as they are intentionally trained within the fires of relational ministry.

Missional leaders are devoted to prayer out of a constant awareness of their need for God's power. In the movement being discussed, prayer is not a program that leaders are begged to support or participate in. Out of a clearly felt desperation for God's help, they are committed to seeking Jesus both personally and corporately.

Spiritual family is often the invitation that brings people to Jesus and into discipling relationships. The characteristics we discussed previously of vulnerability, availability, grace, and commitment tend to be the very things that motivate people to join the movement.

Leadership that is focused on mission is costly. I briefly mentioned some of the personal cost that Wilson and his family have been called upon to make, but the reality is much more intense than expressed by my summary. Wilson is confronted with deep brokenness, tremendous needs, and complex relational issues on a daily basis. His family depends on the generosity of the Father for their basic needs, and often help comes at the very last minute. They experience rejection and the overwhelming pain of beloved spiritual sons and daughters falling back into the ways of the world. Still, through all of the stress and hurt, they testify that they would lead in no other way. Jesus continually proves Himself worth it all.

Gospel Leadership is Disciple-Making

Gospel leadership is always concerned with making disciples as its central focus. Disciples are formed through prayer, the Word of God, spiritual family, and mission. There is an intentionality and an organic element to all of this. Looking back to Part One and our study of Matthew 18-20, we can tie some of this together.

Greatness in the Kingdom looks very different than greatness in the world. Children, in fact, are the faces of Jesus-style leadership. The powerlessness of children serves as a picture of the kind of disciple-making leaders we are to be. We are called to purposefully take the low position, following in the footsteps of our Master, "Who, being in very nature God, did not consider equality with God something to be used to his own advantage" (Philippians 2:6).

I remind us of these qualities, attitudes, and actions we discussed in Part One of this book:

* forgiveness
* fidelity
* loving Jesus more than anything
* being last
* humility
* getting our value only from Jesus and what He has done for us
* laying down our lives
* willingness to suffer
* accepting whatever position or role the Father gives us
* being utterly different from worldly leaders, even the greatly successful ones
* not exercising authority
* not trying to be better than others
* being servants — hard-working, invisible, without control
* washing the feet of our brothers and sisters

All of the above apply directly to the kind of leadership that is about making disciples. How will you absorb these qualities and activities into your own life and leadership?

13: DEVELOPING LEADERS

Ralph Nader has said, "I start with the premise that the function of leadership is to produce more leaders, not more followers."[61] In Part One, I attempted to lay the foundation for all leadership in Jesus' revolutionary teaching as recorded in Matthew 18-20. This should be the beginning for every conversation about Christian leadership, because in it, Jesus radically upends all worldly and cultural ideas about what it means to lead. In Part Two so far, we have explored the idea that all Jesus-style leadership is actually discipleship, and I suggested four primary elements that are critical in making disciples: prayer, obedience to the Bible, spiritual family, and mission. Now I hope to offer some very basic thoughts related to the development of other leaders.

Jane Overstreet, in her experience serving leaders in many nations, observes that "Leadership development had been one of the most frequently cited needs among Christian leaders for the last twenty years."[62] Jeff Reed adds this:

Western Christianity is not turning the world upside down as it did in the Early Church. In fact, many of its ministry forms are actually entruncating spontaneous expansion of the Church in Latin America, Asia, and Africa. Many of our Western forms of missions and leadership development are contributing

---

[61] Quoted in Neil Cole, *Organic Leadership* (Baker Books, Grand Rapids, 2009), pg 129.

[62] Jane Overstreet, *Unleader* (Biblica, Colorado Springs, 2011), pg 8.

to the lack of church leadership that plagues the churches in these fast growing parts of the world.[63]

Reed continues:

> In the past, theology was understood to be the orientation of the soul for the purpose of acquiring wisdom, which all men and women need regardless of their station in life. By removing the training from the life of the church and putting it in an institution, it transformed the leadership development process into something very different from the New Testament church... It has created an academic set of criteria for service... Character, ministry skills, and family qualifications are marginalized by degrees and certificates. In addition, this education is very expensive, and slow. And it is distant from the church. It has also changed the very character of biblical truth, framing an understanding of the Bible into a more academic enterprise from a life development enterprise.[64]

There is a lot to unpack in these fairly dense quotes, but there are key issues being revealed here that get at the very heart of the purpose and methods of leadership development. I am only seeking to provide a brief introduction to this important topic in the current book, and I urge you to follow up with more study on your own.

First, let me be clear about what I mean by "leadership development." For our purposes, leadership development refers to the process of identifying, preparing, and sending servants of Jesus to proclaim the gospel, make disciples, and shepherd God's people. In these final chapters, we will consider, in overview fashion, how to identify leaders, prepare leaders, and send leaders. Please note that leaders are not necessarily positional leaders within the church but people who are actively making disciples and leading others in so doing.

Secondly, we need to consider the purpose of leadership development. As should be obvious by now, leadership, and thus leadership development, is not the end goal we are striving for. Leadership in the Kingdom of God is not about attaining a position, creating a successful organization, being impressive, or gaining power. That is clear. To be a leader is not the goal of

---

[63] Jeff Reed, The Paradigm Papers (BILD International, Ames, IA, 2017), pg 292.

[64] Jeff Reed, The Paradigm Papers (BILD International, Ames, IA, 2017), pgs 298-299.

any servant of Jesus. It is only a means to an end. What, then, is that end? As we have been saying all along, the ultimate end is the glory of Jesus through the making of disciples. We develop leaders so that Jesus will be revealed through people believing in Him and being transformed into His likeness. We develop leaders so that more people will be engaged in the work of His harvest and so that they will be faithful and able servants, bearing fruit for the sake of our Lord and King. Leaders do this by connecting others to Jesus so that He may lead and guide them. As Ruth Haley Barton puts it:

> Many define leadership as having a compelling vision, a clear rationale and the ability to influence others. While these are important aspects of leadership—especially if the vision is God-given and there is an anointing by God to lead toward that vision—spiritual leadership is not fundamentally about our leadership. It is about putting ourselves and guiding the group into a position to be led by Christ, who is the true head of the church.[65]

The purpose of leadership development, then, is to glorify Jesus through the making of disciples by guiding God's people to be led by Christ Himself.

Another important issue to highlight is the inadequacy of our current leadership development paradigm. Jeff Reed's claim is that the way we have chosen to develop leaders is actually limiting the expansion of the church rather than helping it. Thus, the very thing we are supposedly developing leaders for is being diminished rather than strengthened by the way we do it. There are several reasons for this. For one, our method of developing leaders puts a great emphasis on academic achievement at the expense of "character, ministry skills, and family qualifications." In other words, we consider a person qualified for ministry, not because of traits emphasized in the New Testament, but because of degrees, diplomas, and certificates. We are appointing people to positions of leadership in a way that is setting them up to fail because they think they have been fully prepared when in fact they have not. If we followed the example of the early church as revealed in Acts and the epistles, we would apprentice young ministers of the gospel into leadership rather than depending solely on academic institutions which are removed from the grit and grind of daily life. Another reason our current system is failing us, again pointed out by Reed, is its lack of capacity to

---

[65] Ruth Haley Barton, *Pursuing God's Will Together* (InterVarsity Press, Downers Grove, 2012), Kindle location 3048.

produce the numbers of leaders needed by the global church. If we were to add up all the current students in every formal seminary or Bible College around the world, the number would be pitifully small as compared to the number of qualified leaders needed. We also need to consider the expense of having every Kingdom leader trained by formal institutions. There must be a better way.

Please understand, I am not saying that there is no need for seminaries and Bible colleges. I am simply making the point that they are insufficient in and of themselves. They cannot, by themselves, produce either the quality or the quantity of leaders that are so desperately needed. They have a part to play, but we cannot rely on these institutions to fill the leadership gap that is so evident in the world and in our churches today.

A final issue to put forward has to do with the job description of Christian leaders. As Nader put it in the quote at the top of this chapter, our job as leaders is not to create followers for ourselves, but more leaders in the service of Jesus. To put it another way, a primary responsibility of every leader is to develop other leaders. This goes far beyond simply delegating. You must take the time to raise up, equip, and provide opportunities for potential leaders. If we are to have anywhere near the number of sound leaders we need in this hour, it will be the work of every current leader to help produce more. This does not mean you have to teach classes or create a training curriculum. It does mean you have to be intentional and that you must reconsider your priorities and your job description as a leader.

In the remainder of this chapter, I will endeavor to give a brief overview of how a leader can develop other leaders and why this should be a priority. I hope this will be a helpful addition to your own growth in leadership and in developing others.

Choosing Leaders

Now the overseer is to be above reproach, faithful to his wife, temperate, self-controlled, respectable, hospitable, able to teach, not given to drunkenness, not violent but gentle, not quarrelsome, not a lover of money. He must manage his own family well and see that his children obey him, and he must do so in a manner worthy of full respect. (If anyone does not know how to manage his own family, how can he take care of God's church?) He must not be a recent convert, or he may become conceited and fall under the same judgment as the devil. He must also have a good reputation with outsiders, so that he will not fall into disgrace and into the devil's trap. — 1 Timothy 3:2-7

An elder must be blameless, faithful to his wife, a man whose children believe and are not open to the charge of being wild and disobedient. Since an overseer manages God's household, he must be blameless—not overbearing, not quick-tempered, not given to drunkenness, not violent, not pursuing dishonest gain. Rather, he must be hospitable, one who loves what is good, who is self-controlled, upright, holy and disciplined. He must hold firmly to the trustworthy message as it has been taught, so that he can encourage others by sound doctrine and refute those who oppose it. — Titus 1:6-9

The overwhelming emphasis in the scriptures regarding choosing and developing leaders is related to character. God is seeking loving, humble servants to do the work of leading others in His Kingdom. We tend to look first for gifts, abilities, charisma, and skills. We seek academic qualifications and impressive resumes. We are enamored by qualities of decisiveness and the ability to exert authority. However, as Oswald Sanders put it, "When Jesus selected leaders, He ignored every popular idea of His day (and ours) about what kind of person could fit the role."[66] I would go further and say that, far too often, when God's people select leaders today, they tend to ignore every direct teaching of Jesus about what kind of person could fit the role, instead relying on the wisdom of the world. We have been fully persuaded by the methods and values of a godless culture. We choose people for leadership based on secular values, and then in a futile exercise of wishful thinking, exhort them to be "servant-leaders," hoping that they will catch something of the power of Christ's own leadership. At best, we choose based on secondary qualifications while ignoring the things that Jesus focused on.

I would like to suggest a few ideas to help us choose leaders in a way that reflects the values and purposes of Jesus. Again, this is meant to be a beginning, a conversation starter.

(1) Take your time. Paul advised Timothy, when selecting people to serve as deacons in the church, that "They must first be tested; and then if there is nothing against them, let them serve as deacons." (1 Timothy 3:10).

---

[66] J. Oswald Sanders, <u>Spiritual Leadership</u> (Moody Publishers, Chicago, 2007), pg 33.

In the same letter, he urged his protégée, "Do not be hasty in the laying on of hands." (1 Timothy 5:22). In this context, the laying on of hands is a clear reference to appointing leaders in the church. All of this points to the need for patience. Do not give people more leadership responsibility than you are confident they can handle. Do not appoint someone to a position of leadership that is greater than their measure of wisdom, humility, and godliness can support. Let them first demonstrate the character that will be needed in order to carry those burdens. Lifting up immature believers to a place of authority and recognition is a dangerous move, and it will likely cause harm both to the newly appointed leader and to the ones they are called to serve.

Having said all of this, I must also acknowledge that patience needs to be tempered with action. You cannot wait forever. You will rarely find the ideal candidate, and you must choose based on who you have been given. There comes a time when you must trust that God has chosen those in your circle to be the ones you run with. You cannot fantasize about a dream team. We see this in Paul's own ministry. In Acts 14:23, Luke shows Paul and Barnabas appointing leaders in churches that were very young indeed. The apostles had spent only a matter of weeks in each place, and everyone in the churches was a relatively new believer. Still, they appointed leaders from among those who were available. It is possible that Titus was in a similar situation on the island of Crete when Paul wrote to him. You will notice that the admonition against choosing a new believer as seen in the Timothy passage is not present in the instructions to Titus. Timothy was serving in Ephesus, an established church that had existed for more than a decade. There were many disciples from whom to choose, and a good number of these had undoubtedly been in the faith for years. Titus, on the other hand, may have been looking for elders from a much narrower pool, and perhaps none had spent significant time as followers of Jesus. The point is that there is a tension between patience and urgency. Do your best to not be hasty in your choices, but at the same time do not hinder the work by dithering about the faults and yellow flags that are evident in the young believers whom you are discipling.

(2) Pray. Luke tells us that before Jesus appointed the twelve apostles, He spent an entire night in prayer (Luke 6:12-16). He had many followers at this time, but he chose twelve to be His primary leaders. The message is clear. Jesus spent significant time in prayer before making this monumental decision. We need to do the same. We tend to be far too confident in our own perception and wisdom. We need to hear from the Father, just as Jesus did. God knows who among your disciples are the best choices for any given leadership responsibility. Look to Him. Be desperate in seeking Him. Remember that He sees into the very heart of people, while we can only see the outside. Prayer is probably the most needed and the most neglected element in choosing leaders. Again, we are limited by what we can see: academic qualifications, obvious gifts and abilities, personality, experience, etc. God sees all of that and a lot more. Spend time seeking the Father. To the best of your ability, empty yourself of your own bias and inclinations and truly seek to hear from the Lord with a willingness to do what He says, trusting in His choices.

(3) Be relational. When Jesus chose those twelve young men, He had come to know them by spending time with them already. When He was ready to appoint leaders, He did not send out advertisements in an effort to attract the best rabbinic students in the land. He chose from among those He already knew. This surely limited His choices, and perhaps many impressive candidates were never given a chance. However, whatever was lost by this narrow field was more than made up for by the element of relationship.

When Paul needed leaders for those young churches of Lystra, Derbe, Iconium, and Antioch, he did not put the word out to the mother church back in Jerusalem. Instead, he chose people from those new communities themselves who were surely already serving and building friendships with others in the churches. Do not be tempted to trade in personal knowledge of upcoming leaders for the fool's gold of "ideal" candidates that nobody in your community really knows.

One of the reasons that relational connections provide the best pool for choosing leaders is that relationships give you the opportunity to assess the key trait of faithfulness. We will discuss this more in a future chapter, but faithfulness sums up the character traits that are so necessary in Christian leadership, and yet it can be the most difficult to measure in those you do not personally know. Faithfulness is measured in the context of friendship and struggle. In addition to faithfulness, you are primarily seeking humility, teachability, and availability. Again, these are traits that can best be discerned through actual relationships rather than by relying primarily on resumes, interviews, and recommendations.

There is no hard and fast rule in this, but generally it is preferable to appoint those you know. You must always allow room for the Holy Spirit to override the norm, but typically speaking friends will be the best choices.

(4) Look for shared values. No amount of giftedness or personality will overcome the lack of unity in values. Are the people you are considering convinced that God is calling them to be servants? Are they focused on using their position, gifts, and influence for the great purpose of glorifying Jesus through making disciples? Are they committed to winning the lost? Do they demonstrate the values of the Kingdom in the way they work and relate to people they lead? Do they prioritize family? Are they gospel-centered? Do they "hold firmly to the trustworthy message as it has been taught" (Titus 1:9)?

(5) Choose servants. If you have made it this far, you surely were expecting this, but it cannot be overstated. Do not choose people who look like leaders but may or may not actually be servants. Choose those who are true servants and develop them as they grow in influence and responsibility.

As has been stated before, leadership does not depend on position. However, there are positions of leadership that are significant and God-ordained. These positions carry with them a degree of authority and responsibility that are important. As a leader, you will at some point most likely be in a place in which you need to share your authority and responsibility, and the choices you make in appointing others are weighty. Do not take the task lightly and do not rely on the cultural expertise of the world. Lean into the patterns and instructions of Jesus and the early apostles, and make it a priority to seek the wisdom of the Lord.

14 - TRAINING CONTENT

There are at least three essential areas of focus in developing leaders in Christ. These are character, biblical literacy, and ministry skills. In this chapter I will introduce each of these broad categories of leadership training, beginning with character.

Character

Do you not know that in a race all the runners run, but only one gets the prize? Run in such a way as to get the prize. Everyone who competes in the games goes into strict training. They do it to get a crown that will not last, but we do it to get a crown that will last forever. Therefore I do not run like someone running aimlessly; I do not fight like a boxer beating the air. No, I strike a blow to my body and make it my slave so that after I have preached to others, I myself will not be disqualified for the prize. — 1 Corinthians 9:24-27

By character, I mean the totality of who one is as a person. It is the *being* aspect of discipleship, while biblical literacy focuses on *knowing* and ministry skills on *doing*. It is important for disciples to give attention to each of these areas if they are to become leaders that bring Jesus glory, but the *being* element is the foundation.

In developing leaders, it is of utmost importance that you do all you can to instill discipline, thus guiding your disciple into intentional character growth. There is nothing more damaging than a person who sits in a position of Christian leadership but who lacks the kind of godly character which points people to Jesus. The most powerful lesson a leader ever teaches is the example of their life, and they must give attention to what kinds of messages they are sending. As a leader who is called to train other leaders, you will want to put considerable thought and prayer and energy into how you can help facilitate a lifestyle of growth in those you develop. If they are not growing in strength of character, they will hinder the work of the gospel rather than increase it.

All of us have witnessed the devastation wrought by leaders who lacked godly character. In their failures, they have driven people from Christ rather than attracted them to Him. Godless traits of greed, ambition, arrogance, sexual impurity, deceit, and the like have caused great pain and harm. And yet, if we pause long enough to search our own hearts, we must admit that these temptations lurk within each of us. Though I long for Christ to be formed in me, I am almost irresistibly drawn to sin.

All this points to an urgent need for us to lend all the aid we can in helping to develop the strength of character in our upcoming leaders that can withstand such onslaughts. They will be tested. They will be tested hard. If we do nothing else for these beloved servants and friends, it is incumbent on us to lead them in the way of continual renewal and growth. As Ruth Haley Barton says, "The best thing any of us have to bring to leadership is our own transforming selves."[67] This is what we offer to those we are developing, and it is what they in turn will offer to others.

There is, of course, much that could be written on this subject alone, but I will confine our discussion to two big ideas. The first is that the key ingredient we are seeking to cultivate could be summarized in the word *faithfulness*. The idea of faithfulness covers an entire complex of related qualities which are essential for Kingdom leadership.

Faithfulness, first and foremost, is related to *faith*. To be faithful as a disciple is to be full of faith in Jesus. It means that all we do flows out of our relationship of trust with Him. It acknowledges that "everything that does not come from faith is sin" (Romans 14:23). As a developer of leaders, you

---

[67] Ruth Haley Barton, *Strengthening the Soul of your Leadership* (IVP Books, Downers Grove, 2018), pg 19.

will be determined to help build the faith of those you are training. Remember, you are emphatically not wanting them to be dependent on you, but on Jesus. Leadership that seeks to attach people to oneself is absolutely not gospel leadership. Our role is to help people be more attached to Jesus Himself, and that happens as people grow in their faith in Him. This is the foundation of faithfulness.

Faithfulness that is rooted in faith in Jesus leads to following the teachings of Jesus. We are called to "keep" and to "guard" the teachings we have received (2 Timothy 1:13-14). These teachings, of course, are not abstract issues of theology that do not touch our daily lives but actually include the way we live: our behavior, relationships, thoughts, and speech. Faithfulness includes purity and generosity and forgiveness and integrity and loyalty. It means that we are committed to modeling our lives after that of Jesus, actively seeking to become more and more like Him.

Faithfulness has a relational aspect to it as well. We are called to be faithful to Jesus and to other people. The leaders you are developing must learn to be people who can be counted on. They have to grow out of all tendencies of flakiness and unreliability. They are going to become people whose commitments are unshakeable. In order to grow in this trait, you must help them develop biblically informed priorities and time management skills. Everyone is busy, but Kingdom leaders are learning to be busy with the right things and for their busyness to be tempered by appropriate margin which helps them to fulfill their primary relational commitments. Faithful people are wise in what they say "yes" to and what they say "no" to. They do not follow every opportunity but are learning to discern the will of the Father.

Faithfulness is a rare but desired commodity in our world today. We are drawn to faithful people. We all want to journey with companions we can trust: people who are consistent in their behavior and responses. We want to attach ourselves to stable people who are not easily shaken; to those who will not give up on us; to people who will demonstrate consistent and even sacrificial obedience to Jesus. We know that we need to rely on others, but we hesitate because we want to know that the ones on whom we rely are trustworthy. As you develop disciples into leaders, always keep in mind that nothing can overcome a lack of faithfulness. Do all you can to cultivate it.

The second big idea regarding character development deals more with the how. How are people strengthened to withstand the attacks of the enemy? How do they grow in faithfulness? At the risk of reducing a complex subject to something simplistic and ultimately unhelpful, let me offer one key element. In order to grow in character and capacity to lead, followers of Jesus must pursue Him through spiritual habits and practices. Fruitful leaders will be devoted to seeking Jesus alone and with others.

The first essential practice of a Christian leader is to make time to spend with Jesus alone. Barton urges us to this pursuit like this:

> Solitude is the foundational discipline of the spiritual life; it is time set aside to give God our full and undivided attention. In solitude we withdraw from our lives in the company of others and pull back from our many distractions in order to give God complete access to our souls. Devoid of the normal interruptions, silence deepens the experience of solitude. It enables us to withdraw not only from the noise and distraction of the external world, but also the "noise" of the inner compulsions that drive us. In solitude and silence, we become quiet enough to hear a voice that is not our own. This is the Voice we most need to hear. Spiritual leadership starts with listening for the one true Voice and learning to distinguish it from all the other voices that clamor for our attention.[68]

This is the key. If your leadership development is pushing people towards a frenetic pace that idolizes busyness and activity and does not drive them alone into the presence of Jesus, you are not doing any good. They will never go further than their own wisdom, ability, and strength can take them, and these will prove to be sadly inadequate for the tests they will face. They need the ongoing, indwelling, recognized presence of the Holy Spirit. This cannot come without seeking Him in solitude. They must learn to strain their ears for the "voice that is not our own."

It could probably go without saying that this solitude can, and should, include an array of actual practices. Essential ones include worship, silence, prayer, and Bible reading. In worship, we surrender our full selves again to our Lord and Master (Romans 12:1-2) and allow Him to fill our vision and focus. In silence, we listen for the One Voice that matters. In prayer, we pour out our heart to our Father and we join Jesus in interceding for the world. In the scriptures we are sustained by the teachings and revelation of Jesus. We get to know Him more so that we can become more like Him and make Him known.

---

[68] Ruth Haley Barton, *Pursuing God's Will Together* (InterVarsity Press, Downers Grove, 2012), Kindle location 597.

Pursuing Jesus also includes corporate habits, and these are also essential. You were not created to manage anything absolutely alone, even your relationship with Jesus. Other people help you in those practices of worship and prayer and Bible study. They also provide the opportunity for other practices such as confession and celebration and remembrance. As you develop leaders, it is essential that you guide them into regular and frequent rhythms of pursuing Jesus with other brothers and sisters.

Spiritual formation must take center stage in our discipleship and leadership development efforts. You are training them to be powerful forces for the gospel without being dependent on you. They must learn to connect to and hear from the Father and to walk in the power of the Spirit. We need to move far beyond training people how to be good at doing stuff and getting things done (though we desperately feel the need for just that kind of person in leadership) and get to the place of valuing true spiritual maturity as demonstrated by the fruit of faithfulness.

Biblical Literacy

Until I come, devote yourself to the public reading of Scripture, to preaching and to teaching. Do not neglect your gift, which was given you through prophecy when the body of elders laid their hands on you. Be diligent in these matters; give yourself wholly to them, so that everyone may see your progress. Watch your life and doctrine closely. Persevere in them, because if you do, you will save both yourself and your hearers. — 1 Timothy 4:13-16

Be diligent to present yourself approved to God as a worker who does not need to be ashamed, accurately handling the word of truth. — 2 Timothy 2:15 (NASB)

He must hold firmly to the trustworthy message as it has been taught, so that he can encourage others by sound doctrine and refute those who oppose it. — Titus 1:9

In passing on the leadership baton to his sons in the faith, Paul urges Timothy to accurately handle the scriptures; to be active in proclaiming them; to be diligent in growing in them. He instructs Titus to be sure those he will appoint are people who "hold firmly to the trustworthy message as it has been taught." We need to do likewise. In fact, we need to give significant time to training upcoming leaders in how to handle the scriptures. This is true whether their leadership will be primarily in the context of church ministry or in the marketplace. All spiritual influencers must be strong in the Word of God.

Several key areas should be included in this training. **First, we need to pass on a deep love for and trust in the Bible.** We have discussed this already to some degree in chapter 22, but it is worth mentioning again in this context. There is, in our time, an assault on the idea of the trustworthiness and authority of the Bible, even within the Church. We are in danger of giving more weight to our own historical and textual analysis than we are to simple faith in the Bible as God's Word. In the first century, Peter urged believers to trust in the Bible, both the Hebrew Scriptures (Old Testament) and the writings that would become the New Testament Scriptures. Speaking of the Old Testament, Peter says:

> We also have the prophetic message as something completely reliable, and you will do well to pay attention to it, as to a light shining in a dark place, until the day dawns and the morning star rises in your hearts. Above all, you must understand that no prophecy of Scripture came about by the prophet's own interpretation of things. For prophecy never had its origin in the human will, but prophets, though human, spoke from God as they were carried along by the Holy Spirit. — 2 Peter 1:19-21

Peter is in no way ambiguous here, nor does he leave room for doubt. When he speaks of the "prophetic message," he is referring to the scriptures as they had been passed down to his generation. This message of the scriptures is "completely reliable" and we would all "do well to pay attention to it." This has not changed. You can rely on the scriptures, and indeed you must pass this unshaken trust in them on to the leaders you are developing. There is too much at stake to trust in human scholarship that does not acknowledge the supernatural formation of the Bible.

Peter also admonishes his readers to trust in the message that eventually came to be the New Testament, saying, "For we did not follow cleverly devised stories when we told you about the coming of our Lord Jesus Christ in power, but we were eyewitnesses of his majesty" (2 Peter 1:16).

The New Testament was written by people who were eyewitnesses of the life and ministry of Jesus or who interviewed and learned from those who were, or, in the case of Paul, received specific revelation from Jesus concerning the gospel and its outworking. Again, Peter is stressing the reliability of the message. "For prophecy never had its origin in the human will, but prophets, though human, spoke from God as they were carried along by the Holy Spirit." (2 Peter 1:21).

The writers of the Bible were indeed human, but they "spoke from God as they were carried along by the Holy Spirit." That is a strong statement! The Bible is far more than a human theological interpretation of the events of history. It is indeed the writings of people who communicated just what God intended, though in their own language and within their own culture. Furthermore, just as the Holy Spirit carried along these biblical authors, we believe that He also has watched over the copying of the texts and even the translation into other languages. If God took such care to cause the original writings to be reliable, we can have confidence that He likewise has been involved in seeing that this Word would be made available to future generations in a way that is trustworthy.

One further thought: I want to encourage you again that in addition to the Bible being trustworthy and authoritative, it is also accessible. You and those you disciple can understand the main thrust of what the biblical authors, carried on by the Holy Spirit, intended to relate. Yes, there are barriers of which we must be aware: time, language, and culture. These all do cause legitimate difficulties in interpreting the text, but with dedication and discipline these barriers can be overcome. As followers of Jesus and servants in His Kingdom, it is imperative that we develop a high level of trust in the Bible and that we put ourselves under its authority as the very words of God.[69]

As we hold high the revelation and authority of the Bible, we need to cultivate a love for it that we pass on to those we lead. I urge you to put the Bible into the very heart of your daily routine. Develop the disciplines of study, meditation, memorization, and devotional reading, both personal and corporate. As you revere the Bible, hold fast to your time devoted to it as sacred work. Look to the Bible every day. Do whatever it takes to cultivate a love of being in God's Word. For some, this will come more naturally than

---

[69] See Timothy Keller, "The Bible and Experience," (*Gospel in Life Podcast*, Episode 586). My brief overview of the authority and reliability of the Bible is largely drawn from this sermon.

others, but no matter how natural or not it is to you, you must do it. In time, you will learn to be more comfortable in it and will grow in your passion for it. The more you read and meditate on the scriptures, the more they will come to shape your worldview. You will find yourself relying on them for encouragement and for correction, for direction and for inspiration. You will grow more and more in your ability to almost instinctively understand what God would say in a given situation, because you are immersed in His words and His thoughts.

Secondly, provide basic training in how to study the Bible. It can be an overwhelming task to learn to read the Bible and base your life on it. How does one do that?

The first step in studying the Bible is choosing where you will begin. You may want to read the Bible through from Genesis to Revelation, take time to go more in depth into a particular book, or study a series of passages designed to teach the foundations of the faith or a particular topic. Wherever you begin, I suggest a simple set of principles to guide your study. The first principle is to look for the author's intention in writing that passage. Now, as straightforward as this is to say, it actually requires a multi-layered approach. First, keep in mind the dual authorship of the Bible: the "little a" author and the "big A" Author. Every book in the Bible was written by a human that was carried along by the Holy Spirit. Thus, you will be able to identify the human characteristics of the human writer: the style, experience, and particular context are all significant. But at the same time, we acknowledge that this author was operating fully under the sovereignty of God, who was able to express through the writer's very human capabilities and limitations the divine truth and revelation He intended to communicate. The divine and human authors share the same intent. God did not dictate word-for-word the message He chose to make known to a willing but ignorant automaton but rather worked through the writer in a way unique to that individual. God revealed the truth and guided the authors as they expressed it in their words. They were humans partnering with God in delivering His message.

As you consider the divine-human partnership in your particular passage, also be aware of the various contexts that come into play. There is the specific historical context of the writer and of the intended readers, the context of the entire book and section of scripture, and of the Bible as a whole. The more you know of these various contexts, the more accurately you will be able to discern the intent of any given passage. This is of course an ongoing process as you grow year by year in your knowledge of the Bible. Even so, wherever you are in that journey, you can legitimately begin to interpret. As you read a passage, seek to discover the main point or points. Is this section you are reading part of a larger story? Is it part of an ongoing argument or set of instructions? How does it fit into the larger message of the book? What is the meaning of the specific verse or set of verses you are considering? Can you put the message succinctly into your own words?

What I am proposing is counter to the methods with which many of us have been familiar. It does not begin with the question, "What does this mean to me?" Nor is it primarily concerned with "what stands out" or "what I like about this." It begins with searching out the intended meaning of the original author to the original audience. This is important, because it keeps us from assigning meaning that is not actually in the text. It helps us to hear the objective Word that is unchanging and true. Many people look to receive truth in a tweet-sized pithy statement, but divine revelation is often more nuanced and complex than that. The writers of the Bible typically did not organize their books into a series of mic-drop statements that are designed to stand out on social media, but instead wrote with one idea building upon another. Being aware of all this can help you to do the work of discovering the intended meaning of any given text.

Of course, once you have a good idea of what a passage means, you are just beginning. The next crucial step is to hear what God is saying to you through that truth. The truth is the same for all people of all times, but the application can be very different. It is essential, then, that you ask what the implications of this truth are in your life and community. This is key. The implication is at once tethered to the universal truth being expressed in the text and, at the same time, very personal and specific to your situation.

As already emphasized, the final steps are to obey and share the truth that you have heard. How is God calling you to respond? What does the text demand that you do? Is there an action to take, a sin to repent of, a habit to end? Is there something about yourself or God that you need to believe, perhaps a lie that God wants you to denounce?

There will, of course, be passages in the Bible that you read but do not understand. There are whole arguments or narratives that will be confusing and difficult, if not impossible, to follow and sort out. Do not use this as an excuse to back away from daily interaction with the scriptures, but instead, let that experience push you further into serious study. There is no need to get frustrated. Remember that the foundational, absolutely need-to-know-now kind of messages in the Bible are clear, and you will have no problem understanding them. Believing and obeying them may be an issue, but not understanding. So, there is no need to panic if you are scratching your head over the meaning of the Levitical sacrifices or an argument in Paul about the sovereignty of God as it relates to the human will. It is not that these are unimportant or irrelevant, but simply that you can still wholeheartedly follow Jesus with the information available to you as you simultaneously (and perhaps slowly) pursue a greater understanding of some of these hard-to-understand portions of the Bible.

With that in mind, dive in. Make use of resources that are provided by people who love and believe the Bible and who have invested a lot in gaining an understanding of it. But don't just look to what others have said, spend time yourself mulling over the difficult passage. Exercise your brain. Search for clarity. And of course, through all of this process, pray and ask the Holy Spirit to guide you and provide insight and revelation as you study the Word.

Thirdly, provide basic instruction in the overall message of the Bible. The Bible can be seen as a great Story, beginning with Genesis and going all the way through to Revelation. As such, it is a unity. There is a continuity that runs throughout, and each book and section is an essential part of the whole. In order to be trained in the scriptures, we need to learn to recognize the big picture narrative and to know how any given passage fits into the larger story. In Acts 8, Philip overheard an Ethiopian eunuch reading from Isaiah 53. Because of his familiarity with the full narrative of the scriptures, Philip was able to give understanding regarding that specific passage and point the eunuch to Jesus. This is the kind of biblical literacy we should aim for. What are the themes that run from the beginning to the end? What are the events that build upon one another as they reveal God's plan for the ages? Get to know the big Story of the Bible, and pass that on to those you lead.

Fourthly, be absolutely sure that those you are raising in leadership are very firm in the gospel, the good news that the early apostles proclaimed. The gospel is the simple message of who Jesus is and what He has done. Through this, it also reveals who we are and how we are to respond to Jesus. It includes the historical facts of Jesus' life, death, burial, resurrection, ascension, sending of the Spirit, and promised return. Leaders in the Kingdom of God must be strong in the gospel, not wavering or diluting, not adding to or subtracting from. The gospel is not a subjective feel-good set of principles that are adjusted for each generation and culture. It is a story of historical fact that is unchanging and solid, yet powerful and relevant in every human situation and context. Kingdom leaders know the gospel and are experienced in applying it to all the realities of daily life. They are becoming adept at sifting all of their actions and decisions through the grid of the gospel.

Finally, focus on obedience to God's message as revealed in the Bible. It is not enough to teach the Bible or even methods of Bible study. You must always lead those you teach to personal and corporate obedience. We live under the authority of what God has said. If we do not accept the authority of the Bible in our lives, we are drifting in dangerous waters. If we do accept it, we need to demonstrate this through obeying it. Remember that Jesus did not instruct the original apostles merely to teach everything that He had taught, but to teach people to obey all that He had taught.

This has been a very brief and insufficient introduction to how to read and train others in studying the Bible, but it should be enough to at least get started. I recommend making use of the Discovery Bible Study method as related in Chapter 10. Also, there are many Bible study aids that you can search out and different methods of study that are helpful.

The Bible is an amazing gift and an essential tool in making disciples and developing leaders. Do not be guilty of misusing or under-using this powerful resource. As I close out this topic, I feel compelled once again to emphasize the incredible importance of following through and taking the scriptures as your daily bread. The world in which we live is full of ideologies and lifestyles that are not only different from the Bible, but in direct conflict with it. These voices are all around us. Indeed, the very atmosphere is thick with ungodly worldviews, values, and practices. These very easily seep into our thinking, our families, our churches. This is part of what Paul urges us to guard against.

> See to it that no one takes you captive through hollow and deceptive philosophy, which depends on human tradition and the elemental spiritual forces of this world rather than on Christ. — Colossians 2:8

Let us take our stand with the truths of the Bible: the ones we naturally love and the ones that frighten us, offend us, and confuse us. The issue is not with the Bible. It is with us and with our culture. These are God's thoughts, and they can never be irrelevant or outdated.

Leadership Skills

I nervously but excitedly waited to be called to the front of the small gathering. Seated on hard, backless benches in the late-afternoon African sunshine, the small crowd was ready to hear from the American missionary. As a nineteen-year-old college student, I was about to preach my first ever sermon, out of which my career as the next Billy Graham would be gloriously launched. I had been in Uganda for close to two months by this point, and my turn as the main speaker had finally come. Our small summer mission team was helping to plant a new church by proclaiming the gospel and encouraging the saints. I knew I would remember this moment for a very long time.

I gave it my all that day, lacking neither in zeal nor confidence. I believe I was faithful to the scriptures and that my heart truly yearned for Jesus to be glorified through this act of ministry. And yet, there was a haunting suspicion, which I desperately tried to suppress, that I was not a very good preacher. I prayed for God's anointing. I studied and prepared and tried my best. But the truth is, I was still an unskilled, inexperienced novice. Now, there is a beautiful grace that Jesus gives His unimpressive servants to enable them to bear fruit and bring glory to His Name. What a gift! In fact, even the most eloquent and gifted minister of the gospel must rely on the anointing of the Spirit far more than on his or her own experience or talent. After all, leadership in the Kingdom is a spiritual work and it requires spiritual power. Still, though, we must acknowledge that there are skills and abilities which propel ministry efforts into greater usefulness and success. The good news is that we can get better. We can improve and grow and develop. And you, as an equipper of other leaders, can play an important role in that process for those you are raising up.

As you develop leaders, in addition to focusing on growth in character and in the scriptures, you also must give attention to the honing of skills. Depending on the context and the type of work being done, there are many things that leaders need to do, and as representatives of the King, it is imperative that they learn to do them well. Leaders in the Kingdom of God may need to counsel, lead small groups, share the gospel, pray for the broken, do administration, preside over meetings, preach to crowds, teach the Bible, manage their time, organize events, build teams, communicate details, oversee the work of others, and many other things. People will be naturally good at some of these activities and naturally not very good at others, but in each, they can and must improve.

Your first line of training, and this can be quite intimidating, is your example. As a leader developing others, it is inevitable that how you do things will impact those you are raising up. What is especially disconcerting about this is the fact that most of us truly only excel in a very few skills. There are maybe two or three things that we do in which we feel very confident and assured. There are a number of other duties in which we feel moderately competent. And then there are things we must do but we know we have never mastered the knowledge or skills required to do them particularly well. However, though all this is true, your example is still going to be noticed and followed to some degree, so you need to make the most of it. As I write this, I am preparing to teach a group of emerging leaders how to facilitate small group Bible studies. I am somewhat apprehensive about this, because each of these leaders has observed me many times doing this very thing. I am aware that there is a gap between the ideal that I will teach and the practice that they have observed in me. However, both are still good and helpful: the observation and the instruction — even though I know myself to have come up short many times in actual ministry.

Of course, the first implication of this is that you yourself must be continually growing in your own skills and abilities. Always seek to improve yourself. Take classes, read books, attend retreats, observe others, listen to podcasts, be mentored. Do not be satisfied with whatever level of competence or expertise you have attained. Robert Clinton, after studying the lives of hundreds of leaders, made this observation:

> Leaders who plateau early reveal a common pattern. They learn new skills until they can operate comfortably with them, but then they fail to seek new skills deliberately and habitually. They coast on prior experience.[70]

---

[70] Robert Clinton, The Making of a Leader (Second Edition, NavPress, Colorado Springs, 2012), pg 76.

Kingdom leaders cannot afford to coast! There is too much at stake. For the sake of Jesus, we must push on to higher levels of skill and competence. In so doing, we are not only growing in fruitfulness ourselves, but we are setting an example to those we lead in how to never stop developing. We are demonstrating to them the value and the way of lifelong learning.

Another implication is that you need to be aware of your strengths and weaknesses. In areas where you are weak, try to point your disciples to other leaders who may be able to help them more. This is no time for petty jealousies and ministry competition. For the good of the Kingdom, lay down your pride and provide the best opportunities you can to help your disciple grow. At the same time, do not hesitate to engage with your trainees even in areas of your weakness. Sometimes the person who has doggedly learned and practiced doing something in which they have little natural affinity or ability makes a better teacher than the expert who cannot relate to the struggles of less talented people. For example, I have learned much about evangelism and prayer from people who at one time were not very good at those very things. They understand my fears and the weakness of my flesh and are therefore able to help me overcome. Of course, I have also learned a lot from those who are naturally inclined to those activities as well. However, please note that when you are teaching a skill in which you know that you excel, you may need to be extra aware of your need to be patient with your trainee's weaknesses.

Finally, be intentional with your example. Invite developing leaders to accompany you as you do the activities of your ministry. Give them as many opportunities as you can to witness you in action in the real-life context of leadership. Jesus did this very clearly with the first apostles. They were present when He preached, healed, raised the dead, confronted sin, and drove out demons. They observed hours' worth of leadership and ministry before being given the responsibility themselves.

As you demonstrate the skills you are passing on, **it is also essential that you provide instruction**. Point out not only the final result but the process that got you there. Invite your trainees into your preparation and all the behind-the-scenes stuff. Give instruction along with your example, and allow them to ask questions. I recently had an appointment with my doctor. At the outset of our time together, he asked if a medical student could join us in order to observe. Every now and then, the doctor would take a moment to explain to the student what he was doing and why. This is a simple but powerful way of training. It allowed the student to see how the knowledge he was gaining in the classroom and the lab is applied in real-life situations. Students do not gain skills in the classroom. They do get important knowledge, but they also need the skills to go along with that.

Observation and instruction are both important, but **skills are ultimately developed through practice**. You must therefore provide opportunities for those you are raising up to actually do the works of ministry and leadership. In Matthew 10 and Luke 9-10, we see Jesus sending out His disciples to do the very things they had been observing Him do. There is no substitute for this. It can be frightening for a leader to thus empower his followers, knowing their weaknesses and faults so well, but it is absolutely essential. They must be given opportunity to put into practice in actual, real-life settings the things they have learned in more formal contexts. And this experience needs to be followed up by encouragement and further instruction. You will of course find the need to correct, but be careful not to be overly critical. Try to give more encouragement than correction, and when you do correct, do so in love and patience. Be specific with what the person could have done differently and do not be exasperated by their failures. Over time, continue to instruct, demonstrate, and send out to practice. Give more responsibility as they achieve greater levels of competence. Eventually, you will need to debrief less, though you will still want to be available for encouragement, questions, and feedback.

As I've mentioned before, a number of years ago my friends started an outreach to the homeless. From the beginning, I wanted to encourage them and to also be a helpful part of what they were doing. Unfortunately, on my first evening out with the team, I realized I was woefully unskilled in anything that would be a legitimate help. I found that I was incredibly awkward in my attempts to strike up conversation and develop friendships with the men and women who were experiencing homelessness, addiction, mental illness, and other challenges. In each attempt at conversation, my mind was racing in an effort to overcome judgementalism and fear, insecurity and ignorance. After one day, I despaired at ever being able to fully join in with this good work. I just was not any good at it. And frankly, it scared me. However, I knew deep inside that the Father wanted me to be part of this. The only thing to do was to simply get better. Over the following weeks and months, I watched my friends closely as they initiated conversations, de-escalated conflict, and shared truth. I began to practice what I saw them do. I developed a few tentative friendships with men who lived in a tent near the highway. I practiced and practiced. Eventually, my ability to engage in a meaningful way improved.

Over the years, I have continued to stretch myself in this ministry. Amazingly, I have been able to help others who have come with apprehensions and deficiencies similar to my own. My ability to initiate others into this outreach has been greatly enhanced by my own struggles. I easily recognize the timidity, confusion, and inner turmoil that newcomers sometimes experience and am able to walk them through it with grace and patience (most of the time). I am still certainly not "gifted" in homeless ministry or evangelism in general. In addition to the prejudices which I have largely overcome, I still face an inherent shyness and timidity that threaten to keep me silent. However, by the grace of God and the encouragement and example of my friends, I became a fruitful member of this team and have been able to help train others.

Training in the skills of ministry and leadership is an important part of your work in developing leaders. Do not be quick to write people off as incompetent without at least first attempting to help them learn. Even with those who are naturals in a particular field of service, know that they have much to learn from your wisdom and experience.

15 - TRAINING METHODS

Having discussed the three major areas of training needed for every disciple-making leader, we will now turn to the methods of passing on that content. Again, I am going to focus on three primary means of growing leaders: apprenticing, teaching, and mentoring. Ideally, all three of these will be happening at the same time and will continue throughout the various stages of development. We'll begin with apprenticing.

Apprenticing

Jesus went up on a mountainside and called to him those he wanted, and they came to him. He appointed twelve that they might be with him and that he might send them out to preach and to have authority to drive out demons. — Mark 3:13-15

But you know that Timothy has proved himself, because as a son with his father he has served with me in the work of the gospel. — Philippians 2:22

Apprenticing as a means of training leaders is a clear pattern in scripture. By apprenticing, I mean training someone by utilizing on-the-job experience in real-life scenarios. It means that the context of development is ministry itself. You make use of the three tools mentioned in the previous chapter: instruction, your example, and practice — all in the fires of actual ministry. Obviously, entire books can and have been written on this subject, and it would probably be beneficial to study some good ones. Here I will offer a few thoughts.

As already mentioned, apprenticing begins with providing ample opportunities for observation combined with the giving of clear instruction. Throwing a trainee into actual ministry without having provided sufficient quantities of both of these is neither fair nor likely to produce the results you yearn to see. Having done your best with that, begin to add the potent ingredients of service, responsibility, sacrifice, and learning from failure. Of course, it should go without saying that you never stop making use of your example and direct teaching, but in so doing, you begin to add in the others.

Service. As a leader developing others, at some point you must take the plunge and provide opportunities for younger or less experienced ministers to serve in genuine ways. At first, if possible, you will want to do so in a safe and somewhat controlled environment. Ask them to lead a portion of the small group meeting or give one part of the presentation or do some basic administrative work. Based on how they do in these introductory level settings, add on more and more challenging and significant work. No matter what the level of difficulty or skills required, do be sure that the work you are assigning has genuine value. Busy work just for the sake of having them do something does not seem to have the same impact. It is when a person has confidence that they are contributing to the big picture that they are most likely to grow. Of course, as you discover various aptitudes, skills, and interests in the person you are training, you will want to both provide more opportunities for them to grow in those areas while at the same time challenging them to develop in skills that come less naturally to them.

Responsibility. Entrusting a trainee with real responsibility is perhaps the greatest tool in your leadership development belt. This is often the key that unlocks a person's potential and launches them into years of fruitful and wise leadership. Even so, giving responsibility can be the most frightening part of developing leaders, and some harbor such fear of this step that they never fully take it. They may give the appearance of handing over leadership in some area, but in reality, they never remove their hands from the levers of power. They remain in control, micro-managing or manipulating at every turn. Some are paralyzed by the fear that the trainee will fail, and the ministry assigned to them will come to naught. They are so aware of the weaknesses and immaturity of the new leader that they cannot bring themselves to take the risk. There seems to be so much at stake, and it is just safer to do the work oneself. Others fear the opposite — that the young minister will succeed and succeed gloriously, thus diminishing the light of the one training and perhaps even taking some of the spotlight or the resources or the honor and acclaim that is normally reserved for the senior leader. Needless to say, this fear is rooted in pride and selfish ambition rather than a devotion to Jesus and a desire for His Kingdom to advance. It must be annihilated from the soul of any leader who wishes to bear lasting fruit in the Way of Jesus.

After boldly — and naively as the case proved — stepping into missionary life at the tender age of 23, I returned to the States defeated and forlorn just three years later. Nothing had gone right. I had failed at assimilating into the culture and had little to no fruit in the ministry to which I had been assigned. I had been often depressed, sick, and scared. In fact, after two years of slugging it out, I had come to the desperate conclusion that the whole thing had been a mistake and that God had probably never intended for me to be a missionary and that the best thing for me to do would be to return home and forget the whole thing. I had failed and was beginning to define myself as a failure. At the counsel of our mission leaders, we stayed in Africa for another year before the inevitable return, and I must say that during those long twelve months the Lord began to restore my hope and desire for gospel work. Still, my confidence was shaken, and it was a defeated young man who stepped off the plane back onto American soil.

Then something happened that surprised me. The director of our mission offered me a position of significant responsibility in the home office. Three years earlier I had been downright cocky as I rode off to save the world, but now I could not imagine what he saw in me after the debacle of my first term on the field. And yet somehow, he convinced me that he did see something that was worth investing in and even that I had something to offer right now. Looking back on this more than twenty-five years later, I am still dazzled by the wonder of it all. It touched something deep within me to be believed in at that vulnerable moment. A long-dormant part of me came awake. What a gift! By the grace of God, I returned to Africa with my family after a brief intermission in the States and served joyfully and fruitfully for years thereafter.

Giving responsibility in spite of the risks and the battles of the flesh is a powerful thing. Something beautiful happens in the soul of one who has been entrusted with significant responsibility, especially one whose pride has received a well-needed thrashing. As a leader determined to develop other leaders, you will surely make mistakes. At times, you will hold back too long before entrusting an up-and-coming leader. At other times, you will act prematurely, weighing down a disciple with a burden still too heavy due to lack of maturity or adequate preparation. Yet with all that being said, it is worth it. There is nothing like the experience of beginning to share your load with a trusted disciple and watching him or her develop into a mighty co-worker and leader.

I find the example of Paul and Timothy in this matter to be frankly stunning. Beginning with Acts 16-17, an amazing story unfolds. After some time in the city of Antioch, Paul sets out with Silas to visit the churches he had planted on his previous mission. In one of these communities, they come across a young man named Timothy, whom Paul recruits for his team. Timothy is at this time probably a teenager, or at the very most in his early twenties. Continuing to travel, they reach areas not touched on the previous mission. One such place is the city of Thessalonica, where within three weeks of ministry many people come to faith and begin to follow Jesus. However, a fierce and violent opposition arises, and very soon the situation deteriorates to the point where Paul and his friends have to flee the city for their very lives. Picking up the story in 1 Thessalonians 3, we learn that Paul is understandably distressed and anxious about the young church in Thessalonica. He longs to go and see the situation for himself and to encourage and bolster the faith of this fragile beachhead. But this is impossible. His presence would only cause more trouble for the fledgling community, probably putting their lives (and his) at even greater risk. Yet what can he do? He had been able to spend no more than a few months with them on that initial visit, and there are still many deficiencies in their development. Can they who have been in the faith for so little time endure in the face of such intense opposition?

Paul's inspired answer to this dilemma is shocking. He sends Timothy! Timothy the teenager. Timothy who himself has benefitted from Paul's teaching and training for only a matter of months — certainly less than a year.[71] And this is the job description Paul gives to his young apprentice:

---

[71] For a general timeline of Paul's ministry, including this story, I relied on: Jeff Reed, <u>Pauline Epistles</u> (BILD, Ames, IA, 2001), pgs 31-34.

We sent Timothy, who is our brother and co-worker in God's service in spreading the gospel of Christ, to strengthen and encourage you in your faith, so that no one would be unsettled by these trials. For you know quite well that we are destined for them. — 1 Thessalonians 3:2-3

This assignment is not only fraught with danger and risk of all kinds, but it is also of incredible importance. This is a weighty responsibility, and Paul trusts Timothy to carry it out. And so, he does. Paul's inspired example encourages me, too, to take that risk and give significant responsibility to those I am serving and equipping.

Sacrifice. Walking alone on a beach in the South of England, a young man wrestled with God. He was in deep agony of soul as he struggled with the horrible weight of this burden he knew had come from God. The inner conflict was terrible, and he felt he could bear it no longer. On one side, he daily felt the call of millions of unreached Chinese who were perishing apart from Christ. He had lived among them and given himself to bringing the gospel to them at great personal cost. He was more than willing — even anxious —- to return and continue his work despite the personal sufferings that would entail. He could not do it alone, however, and he knew that God wanted to send more laborers. Furthermore, he had an unwavering confidence that, if he asked, God would send these workers to go with him. But on the other hand, he knew the cost. He understood the extreme difficulties and dangers that would be faced by any who agreed to go with him. And at this, he balked. How could he call men and women to such sacrifice? How could he call them to face the difficulties and sufferings and dangers that he had known? What if it proved too much? What if they were not equal to the challenge? In his own words, Hudson Taylor relates what happened on the beach that day:

> In great spiritual agony, I wandered out on the sands alone. And there the Lord conquered my unbelief, and I surrendered myself to God for this service. I told Him that all the responsibility as to the issues and consequences must rest with Him; that as His servant it was mine to obey and to follow Him, His to direct, care for and guide me and those who might labour with me. Need I say that at once peace flowed into my burdened heart? Then and there I asked Him for twenty-four fellow-workers, two for each of the eleven provinces which were

without a missionary and two for Mongolia; and writing the petition on the margin of the Bible I had with me, I turned homeward with a heart enjoying rest such as it had been a stranger to for months, and with an assurance that the Lord would bless His own work and that I should share in the blessing ...[72]

The laborers were indeed given — and hundreds more in the ensuing years — and a great work was done in China and beyond. Here is another example: When the great missionary Adonirum Judson sought permission to marry Ann Hasseltine, he wrote thus to the father of his beloved:

I have now to ask, whether you can consent to part with your daughter early next spring, to see her no more in this world; whether you can consent to her departure for a heathen land, and her subjection to the hardships and sufferings of a missionary life: whether you can consent to her exposure to the dangers of the ocean; to the fatal influence of the southern climate of India; to every kind of want and distress; to degradation, insult, persecution, and perhaps a violent death. Can you consent to all this, for the sake of Him who left His heavenly home, and died for her and for you; for the sake of perishing immortal souls; for the sake of Zion, and the glory of God? Can you consent to all this, in hope of soon meeting your daughter in the world of glory, with a crown of righteousness, brightened by the acclamations of praise which shall redound to her Savior from heathens saved, through her means, from eternal woe and despair?[73]

Somehow the loving father did consent.

As leaders who love Jesus and live to see Him known and glorified, sacrifice is part of the calling. Not only that, but as faithful followers of the Lord, we must be ready to lead and send others to share the gospel in ways and in places that will extract a price. It is not loving or beneficial to try to shield gospel workers from the reality of sacrifice. Jesus Himself was very clear about this with his first followers, and without hesitation sent them into harm's way, expecting that they would make sacrifices for the sake of the work He gave them to accomplish. "Then you will be handed over to be

---

[72] Dr and Mrs Howard Taylor, Hudson Taylor's Spiritual Secret ( ), pg 101.

[73] Vance Christis, Adonirum Hudson: Devoted for Life (Christian Focus Publications, Ross-shire, Scotland, 2013), kindle location 574.

persecuted and put to death, and you will be hated by all nations because of me" (Matthew 24:9).

> Then he said to them all: "Whoever wants to be my disciple must deny themselves and take up their cross daily and follow me. For whoever wants to save their life will lose it, but whoever loses their life for me will save it." — Luke 9:23-24

It is a privilege to suffer for Jesus, and He gives the grace to stand firm amid suffering, oppression, persecution, and all kinds of hardship. "The apostles left the Sanhedrin, rejoicing because they had been counted worthy of suffering disgrace for the Name" (Acts 5:41).

It is necessary in service to Christ that we are willing to suffer and to lead others into difficulties, challenges, pain, and trouble of all kinds. This sacrifice is not only necessary for the work, but it is useful in forming us and our disciples into the image of Jesus. In God's loving grace, we are strengthened in hardship. But there is something more. In suffering we come to know Jesus more intimately and experientially. That mystical fellowship with Him for which we long is profoundly deepened in suffering. "That I may know Him and the power of His resurrection and the fellowship of His sufferings, being conformed to His death" (Philippians 3:10, NASB).

Having said all that, the simple but difficult truth is that we must trust Jesus with those we raise up and send out, just as Hudson Taylor learned to do on a lonely beach that Sunday afternoon. It is He who has the authority and the right to send them and us into any situation. It is He who is able to call people to offer personal sacrifices for His sake. We must not stand in the way of Him doing so with those we love and in whom we have invested so much.

Learning from failure. I have mentioned previously how I returned to the US at the end of my first missionary term after having more or less failed in all I had set out to do. I wish I could report that everything was good after that. But the truth is that my first taste of ministry failure was by no means the last. A few years later I was back in the city of Kampala, eager to do better this time around. My assignment this time was to plant a church. Once again, I was filled with rather exalted images of what this was going to become. Surely after my initial taste of bitter defeat I was ready for a great victory.

About ten months after arriving in Uganda, I spoke with Dr Ron Meyers — a valued mentor and missions leader from the US. He was visiting to check in on us and see what kind of encouragement he might bring. On this day as the two of us drove across the East African plain, the conversation felt anything but encouraging. He dared to suggest, "This just isn't working for you, is it?" *Come on! Not again?!* But it was all too true. Strike two.

The church plant did not make it, but fortunately for me, Dr Meyers had more to offer. He pointed out something with which I'd been involved in my spare time — a kind of side gig. I had been teaching in and helping to lead a small Bible School, and it was actually going quite well. Through this I had discovered that I loved teaching and was decent at it. I was also developing a passion for equipping and encouraging rising ministers of the gospel. Dr Meyers keyed in on this and suggested I do something with those passions and gifts. After the devastation caused by his blunt assessment of my current work had time to dissipate somewhat, I turned to the idea of beginning a new track. Within a month I was excited. Within two months we were off and running, and years of fruitful ministry followed. My point is this: failure can be a fantastic tool that God uses to develop us. I was very fortunate to have wise mentors walk me through my failures, ones who recognized the good that could come out of them. Looking back over the decades, I am now so thankful for these failures that occurred at the outset of my missionary life. Not only did they help to shape the direction of my future work and ministry, but they also played a great role in shaping my character.

Through these initial failures, I became stronger and more determined. Of course, at the time I was miserable. Failure is no fun for anyone. It is humiliating. It can bring self-doubt and deep discouragement. But in the long run, if we allow the Spirit of God to use it, it will strengthen us. Through failure, I became more resilient and faithful. I learned more about how to listen for and follow God's direction. I became more open to wise counsel from godly men and women. I became less arrogant and idealistic. I was reminded that I am dust. I came to understand that failure is not the end, and it has helped me to be more bold and fearless in trying new things and taking risks. After all, I have survived failure before, so even if my current plan does not go well, I will learn from it and move on. The list could go on and on. I am grateful for failure. And, by the way, those early experiences have by no means been the only times I have failed. Not by a long shot. My life has continued to be a confusing mixture of success, failure, and a lot of *sort-of-goods* and *not-so-bads*.

As a leader helping others along in the development process, you have a very important role in helping your apprentice to navigate failure. You can gently but directly give words to the truth of the situation, as Dr Meyers did for me. "This isn't working, is it?" Indeed. You can point out the good that God may be doing through the unpleasant experience. Most of all, perhaps, you can give encouragement. Share your own experiences of failure and disappointment. Give hope that there are greater things ahead. Be an understanding and caring presence in the trying moment. Your apprentice will benefit greatly, because God does not waste anything that happens in our lives.

Teaching

And teaching them to obey all that I have commanded you… — Matthew 28:20a

And the things you have heard me say in the presence of many witnesses entrust to reliable people who will also be qualified to teach others. — 2 Timothy 2:2

Apprenticing provides many opportunities for on-the-job instruction in response to life's ups and downs and the challenges of ministry. However, Jesus did not rely solely on spur-of-the-moment, spontaneous opportunities. There were things He needed to pass on, and He made intentional time to do that. An example of this is shown in John 13-17, in which Jesus pulls His disciples aside the night before His crucifixion for some essential teaching. We can see something similar with the early apostles. For example, Paul says to Timothy:

What you heard from me, keep as the pattern of sound teaching, with faith and love in Christ Jesus. Guard the good deposit that was entrusted to you—guard it with the help of the Holy Spirit who lives in us. — 2 Timothy 1:13-14

He reminded the Ephesian elders that he had "not hesitated to proclaim to you the whole will of God" (Acts 20:27). There is a pattern of teaching, discernible in the writings of the New Testament, that we are responsible for passing on to those we disciple. You may think of these teachings in two different but related types. The first type of teaching is the core of the gospel itself — the foundational teaching about who God is and what He has done. This is what Paul is referring to when He says to the Corinthians:

> Now, brothers and sisters, I want to remind you of the gospel I preached to you, which you received and on which you have taken your stand. By this gospel you are saved, if you hold firmly to the word I preached to you. Otherwise, you have believed in vain.
>
> For what I received I passed on to you as of first importance: that Christ died for our sins according to the Scriptures, that he was buried, that he was raised on the third day according to the Scriptures, and that he appeared to Cephas, and then to the Twelve. — 1 Corinthians 15:1-5

Here, Paul uses a brief summary outline to remind his disciples of the gospel he had taught them before. Some refer to this message as the *kerygma*: the *proclamation*, or the preaching, of the apostles. Related to this, the second type of teaching revolves around the appropriate response to the *kerygma*. We may simply refer to this as the *teachings*, and we could say that if the *kerygma* is focused on what God has done, the teachings center on what we are to do. Or, another way of looking at it: the *kerygma* is what we believe, and the teachings are how we live out those beliefs.

"Guard the good deposit that was entrusted to you," says Paul (2 Tim 1:14). As leaders developing other leaders in a world that is hostile to the gospel, it is essential that we take the responsibility of guarding and passing on the deposit, just as the first apostles did. The deposit is the essential truths of the gospel along with the teachings in how to live that out. The church continued to prosper and to grow for the first few centuries after the resurrection of Jesus, because in each generation there were leaders who willingly carried the burden of responsibility to pass on the genuine faith to the coming generation.

You may be thinking that this is the job of pastors and theologians, of bishops and missionaries and Bible School teachers. But do not be so quick to pass the buck. As a Christian leader — within any vocation or calling — you cannot shirk this duty. Too many times we leave the teaching to the "experts," and those we are leading suffer because of it. Of course, Sunday sermons are good and useful, and we should probably not stop giving them. But they are not enough. Once-a-week preaching for 30 minutes is not what the apostle had in mind when exhorting his apprentice to "guard the good deposit" that had been entrusted to him. You, as a disciple-making leader, have a good deposit to pass on to those you disciple. And the stakes are high. Most of the books in the New Testament contain some kind of warning against false teachers and false prophets. This is because we humans are shockingly susceptible to lies and because the consequences of following these lies are dire indeed. As a gospel leader, you are expected to protect those you lead from these deceitful doctrines and help them to be able to stand firmly so that they in turn can strengthen others.

> I know that after I leave, savage wolves will come in among you and will not spare the flock. Even from your own number men will arise and distort the truth in order to draw away disciples after them. So be on your guard! Remember that for three years I never stopped warning each of you night and day with tears. — Acts 20:29-31

> But there were also false prophets among the people, just as there will be false teachers among you. They will secretly introduce destructive heresies, even denying the sovereign Lord who bought them—bringing swift destruction on themselves. Many will follow their depraved conduct and will bring the way of truth into disrepute. In their greed these teachers will exploit you with fabricated stories. Their condemnation has long been hanging over them, and their destruction has not been sleeping. — 2 Peter 2:1-3

There is much to pass on to ensure that your disciples are equipped and ready for the good work prepared for them to do. As mentioned, this begins with the gospel itself. Nothing is more vital for followers of Jesus than holding firmly to the gospel that we have received. The world and the devil have a way of slowly picking away at one's confidence in the gospel, eroding it drop by drop until what is left is hardly recognizable as Christian faith. And yet, in the gospel alone lies our hope. The gospel is the message of who Jesus is and what He has done. It is rooted in historical realities. It is about events that really happened in a specific place at a specific time.

Jesus was born miraculously to a virgin mother and lived a perfect life. He revealed to us exactly what the Father is like. He also demonstrated what we as humans are meant to be. He never gave into temptation; never faltered in His commitment to His Heavenly Father. He worked miracles and spoke the truth and made disciples and loved others like nobody ever has before. He was cruelly killed on a cross, intentionally surrendering His life to save ours. In dying like this, He took our sins and shame and guilt upon Himself, and He gave to us His perfect righteousness and goodness. He rose from the dead, ascended to heaven, and sent the Holy Spirit to be with us. He promised to come again and make all things right, gathering His followers to live with Him forever. This is the gospel. We believe that it is true and that we are called to trust this Jesus to forgive our sins and grant us true and eternal life. Those who do not believe in Him will be separated from Him forever. In Him alone is salvation. In Him alone is eternal life and deliverance from death.

Such is the *kerygma* — the proclamation of the apostles. Now for the teachings: instructions on how to live in response to the gospel. Just as the gospel is centered on who Jesus is and what He has done, so the teachings bring to light who we are as a result of this and what we are to do. Regarding these basic doctrines of the faith, Paul has this to say:

> As for other matters, brothers and sisters, we *instructed you how to live in order to please God*, as in fact you are living. Now we ask you and urge you in the Lord Jesus to do this more and more. For you know what *instructions we gave you by the authority of the Lord Jesus.* — 1 Thessalonians 4:1-2 (emphasis added)

> In the name of the Lord Jesus Christ, we command you, brothers and sisters, to keep away from every believer who is idle and disruptive and does not *live according to the teaching you received* from us. — 2 Thessalonians 3:6 (emphasis added)

The enemy is very crafty in separating belief from practice in the lives of professing Christians. Would-be disciples somehow take on the false understanding that salvation is all about checking the boxes of orthodox creeds or statements of faith and is fully unrelated to the way one lives. Godly behavior is seen as a kind of bonus level for over-achievers but something that is not required for salvation. This is emphatically not the view of Jesus or the first apostles.

> Not everyone who says to me, "Lord, Lord," will enter the kingdom of heaven, but only the one who does the will of my Father who is in heaven. — Matthew 7:21

Or do you not know that wrongdoers will not inherit the kingdom of God? Do not be deceived: Neither the sexually immoral nor idolaters nor adulterers nor men who have sex with men nor thieves nor the greedy nor drunkards nor slanderers nor swindlers will inherit the kingdom of God. — 1 Corinthians 6:9-10

Disciple-makers cannot afford to just hope their followers catch on to righteous living without intentional instruction. Experience simply does not bear that out. Nor do we see the apostles taking that line.

He is the one we proclaim, admonishing and teaching everyone with all wisdom, so that we may present everyone fully mature in Christ. To this end I strenuously contend with all the energy Christ so powerfully works in me. — Colossians 1:28-29

My dear children, for whom I am again in the pains of childbirth until Christ is formed in you,… — Galatians 4:19

Strenuously contend. Pains of childbirth. The apostle is describing a great conflict in which the forces of darkness array themselves against the works of God. Their weapons are deceit, shame, the temptations of the flesh, and so on. Their goal is to hinder the very work Paul describes — bringing God's people to maturity so that they may live holy, godly lives in the image of Christ. Leaders in Jesus' wonderful Kingdom carry a responsibility to help people obey His commands; to help them live pure, godly lives in the midst of a depraved culture.

Of course, I am not advocating a kind of spiritual nagging or pharisaical manipulation of behavior. That is of no value at all. We must avoid on one side the ditch of overbearing, control-based instruction that seeks to dominate and manipulate people into right behavior. And on the other side we need to equally be cautious of the ditch of *laissez-faire*, do what you want, the Holy Spirit will tell them the truth in His time and so there is nothing for me to do kind of wishful thinking. Of course, we do rely on the Holy Spirit and He does the heavy lifting in all our disciple-making. But He has also reserved a significant part of the work for others. For me and you. Remember the "*strenuously contend.*"

So how do we do this? Instruct people into spiritual maturity without manipulating? Partner with the Holy Spirit without neglecting our duty to teach? Strenuously contend without being overbearing and without usurping the role of the Holy Spirit? A few thoughts and then we'll move on.

1) Pray. Pray a lot. Pray more.

2) Lean on the power of guided discovery. The DBS (Discovery Bible Study) I described in Chapter 10 is a wonderful tool that helps us to navigate these tensions. We teach by selecting appropriate scripture passages for the development of our disciples, by participating in the discussion, and by following up with accountability and grace. At the same time, we demonstrate our trust in the work of the Spirit by allowing the disciple to listen for His guidance in setting obedience goals and sharing with others. We refrain from making obedience suggestions or applications on their behalf. We also persevere in spending time with people even when they do not seem to be getting it — again trusting that the Holy Spirit is at work in ways we do not see. We strenuously contend through perseverance, consistency, availability, study, Spirit-lead exhortations and instructions, prayer, and love.

3) Another aspect of utilizing the Bible in discipleship and instruction is through developing "ordered learning" plans for those you disciple. Again, the apostles had a body of teaching that they intentionally and consistently passed on to new believers. The New Testament refers to this in various places as "the teaching,[74]" "sound doctrine,[75]" "the faith,[76]" "the traditions,[77]" "the good deposit,[78]" etc. Paul claims that he passed on what he had "received" from the Lord.[79] This deposit was not random or completely situationally based. Of course, in their letters the writers of the NT applied these teachings to the particular circumstances of the community to whom

---

[74] See 2 Thess 2:15, 2 Thess 3:6, 1 Tim 4:6, 2 Tim 1:13, 2 Tim 3:10

[75] 1 Tim 1:10, 1 Tim 4:16, 2 Tim 4:3, Tit 2:1,

[76] Jude 1:3

[77] 1 Cor 11:2

[78] 1 Tim 1:13-14

[79] 1 Cor 11:23, 1 Cor 15:2-3

they were writing, but the content was based on teachings that had been delivered already to each church. In the letters, the apostles were reminding their disciples what they had already learned and helping them to apply in specific situations what they had previously been taught. This teaching had been given deliberately and, probably, systematically.

The idea of ordered learning can be intimidating. I understand that. Some people are wired to geek out about teaching plans and curriculum and training materials. They love to think through the issues involved and come up with something that is tethered to the Bible and the wisdom of others in the Church. I confess to being one of these. But many people would rather do lots of other things than sit around thinking about how to teach a certain doctrine or passage of scripture. Others may have the temperament for it but just do not have the time. Once again, there are many resources developed by people who have put in the work to create wonderful tools to help as we seek to pass on the deposit to those we disciple.

4) Another essential resource as we attempt to pass on the good deposit is the family of believers itself. Again, in the context of biblical discovery, our brothers and sisters in Jesus are an immense help. Having biblical discussions with others who are like-minded and filled with the same Spirit helps us to get at the intended meaning of the biblical text and to apply that to our own lives. The biblical community checks our errant conclusions while providing deeper insight, greater inspiration, and clearer revelation. Reading the Bible alone is absolutely wonderful and very helpful, but reading it in community is essential. In my current context in Africa, many people in our disciple-making networks either do not have a Bible or cannot read at a sufficient level to truly understand it. Many others have such poor eyesight that they can no longer make out the very small print in their Bibles. However, all of these can come together with others to read the scriptures, and they often have remarkable understanding and depth of insight even though they cannot read it for themselves.

5) Returning to the first point, we must be devoted to prayer. We must pray for those we are discipling with confidence, passion, and persistence. We truly do trust that the Holy Spirit is doing the work of strengthening the faith of those we are serving. We believe it. And the way we demonstrate this confidence in the Lord is through prayer. Praying for others to grow up in

Jesus is a mystery. I do not know how it works. I do not know what happens in the heavenly realms when I lift my voice in supplication. But something does happen. The Lord, who drew my heart to prayer in the first place, responds to that prayer on behalf of those He loves. There are other factors at work — the fallen nature and sinful passions of the person as well as the forces of darkness who are opposed to God. I do not understand how my prayer enters into that conflict, but I am confident that the Lord calls us to this ministry of intercession and that somehow it makes a difference.

This has been a quick survey about the essential teachings of our faith and how we are to pass those on, but hopefully it will stir you to consider these ideas further. Of course, there are other things to be taught in addition to these most essential doctrines — things like ministry skills, leadership lessons, and so on. These were covered in previous chapters, though, so here I have given attention to the essential biblical foundations that must be passed on.

Mentoring

To Timothy, my true son in the faith… — 1 Timothy 1:2

To Titus, my true son in our common faith… — Titus 1:4

Before I share some thoughts about mentoring, allow me to define terms. One book on the subject defines mentoring in this way:

Mentoring is an intentional relationship in which a mentor is invited to share their life, experiences and God-given resources with another. It is a holistic process that nurtures character and self-awareness, promoting the work of the Holy Spirit in empowering the mentee to become all that God wants him or her to be as an effective Christ-like leader.[80]

I have found that in various literature and teachings, there is an array of terms that are used to express similar ideas, though perhaps with subtle differences in focus. These include mentoring, spiritual direction, coaching, counseling,

---

[80] Wolf Riedner, Doug Sparks, and Michele Breene, The Ministry of Mentoring, Version 2.5 (Development Associates International: Colorado Springs, 2016), pg 9.

teaching, and mentoring. In a sense, each of these is a synonym of discipling — though, as mentioned, with variances of emphasis and methodology. All of them highlight specific aspects of disciple-making. I tend to use mentoring almost interchangeably with discipling, but always emphasizing the personal relational element. As the above definition states, "Mentoring is an intentional relationship." Those two words express what I mean by mentoring. It is intentional. There is specific growth that is being pursued. It does not rely solely on the spontaneous or the situational. There is something specific to be imparted. Remember the "good deposit" we discussed earlier. Mentoring is intentional, but it is also relational. It is not only a curriculum, a program, or a class. I cannot be mentored by a book or a lecture. Mentoring is personal. It is a powerful blend of the spontaneous and the planned, of directive and discovery; of admonition and encouragement.

With that in mind, let us look into some scripture passages that will help us to better understand and grow in our ability to mentor. Afterward, I will summarize with some general thoughts regarding good mentoring as an essential element of disciple-making.

Deuteronomy 6:4-9.

> Listen, O Israel! The Lord is our God, the Lord alone. And you must love the Lord your God with all your heart, all your soul, and all your strength. And you must commit yourselves wholeheartedly to these commands that I am giving you today. Repeat them again and again to your children. Talk about them when you are at home and when you are on the road, when you are going to bed and when you are getting up. Tie them to your hands and wear them on your forehead as reminders. Write them on the doorposts of your house and on your gates. (NLT).

What a beautiful picture of mentoring discipleship! This passage begins with an affirmation of who God is. All true Christian mentoring is rooted in God Himself and an understanding of who He is. Furthermore, it is rooted in a firm commitment to Him. "The Lord is our God." We relate to Him appropriately based on who He is: our Lord and our God. Mentoring is also built upon our love for God. This is the driving motivation of both mentor and mentee. It is our *why*. Mentoring is costly and it is difficult, and often very slow, painstaking work. But we have a compelling reason to do it regardless of all that. It is because we love God. Our hearts burn with devotion to Him, and we long to participate in His great cause. We love Him.

Likewise, those we are mentoring love Him and are motivated to grow by that love. They may fail and make mistakes and be slow to learn, and they may slip backward and disappoint and at times want to give up. But they genuinely love Him and are willing to stick with the process for His sake.

While mentoring someone into wholeness and maturity is rooted in who God is and is motivated by love for Him, the action or the effort of mentoring is focused on obeying Him. "Commit yourselves wholeheartedly to these commands." The revelation of who God is leads us to love Him. And the way we express love to God is by obeying Him. This is where the work of mentoring comes in: helping another to obey Jesus. In this passage, we see a potent picture of how we accomplish this. We spend a lot of time talking about God's Word. God's commands are definite and objective. They do not issue from our feelings, our culture, or our human wisdom. They are revealed to us through the Bible. And, as I have stated before, making disciples is dependent upon the scriptures. This passage describes a robust determination and almost constant effort to speak about God's laws. "Repeat them again and again." Yet it does so in a very relational, practical, everyday kind of way. We are to talk about God's Word together in settings both formal and casual. We are to do all we can to remind ourselves and our mentees of this Word. Our job as Christian mentors is to labor to see that God's Word makes its way into the hearts of those we serve.

1 Corinthians 4:14-17

> I am writing this not to shame you but to warn you as my dear children. Even if you had ten thousand guardians in Christ, you do not have many fathers, for in Christ Jesus I became your father through the gospel. Therefore I urge you to imitate me. For this reason I have sent to you Timothy, my son whom I love, who is faithful in the Lord. He will remind you of my way of life in Christ Jesus, which agrees with what I teach everywhere in every church.

Paul refers to both the Corinthian believers and the young man Timothy as his spiritual children. Mentoring is akin to parenting, as discussed in Chapter 11. As such, it is built on such things as commitment, sacrifice, availability, and affection. It also highlights the important element of example. A mentor is not only someone who passes on information and urges his disciple towards growth but is also one who offers the example of his own life. A mentor fosters growth through both words and actions. This means, of course, that the mentee is invited into the life of the mentor so that he might observe as well as listen.

John 10:11-18.

> I am the good shepherd. The good shepherd lays down his life for the sheep. The hired hand is not the shepherd and does not own the sheep. So when he sees the wolf coming, he abandons the sheep and runs away. Then the wolf attacks the flock and scatters it. The man runs away because he is a hired hand and cares nothing for the sheep.
>
> I am the good shepherd; I know my sheep and my sheep know me— just as the Father knows me and I know the Father—and I lay down my life for the sheep. I have other sheep that are not of this sheep pen. I must bring them also. They too will listen to my voice, and there shall be one flock and one shepherd. The reason my Father loves me is that I lay down my life—only to take it up again. No one takes it from me, but I lay it down of my own accord. I have authority to lay it down and authority to take it up again. This command I received from my Father.

Jesus, of course, is the One true Shepherd and has a unique role that no one else can fill. However, His is also an example of how we are to under-shepherd His people. This passage highlights several more important elements of how to do that well. The great challenge here is that "the good shepherd lays down his life for the sheep." In saying this, Jesus was referring to Himself going to the cross. At the same time, He is giving an important principle. Anyone who would join with Him in the work of developing others must be willing to lay down their lives as well for the sake of those to whom they minister. The fact that Jesus demonstrated this by actually dying for our sake only emphasizes the point that this is a serious business. In an earlier chapter, we discussed Jesus' call for us to be slaves to all. The point here is similar. We are to willingly lay down our lives for those we disciple. This is the calling of a mentor. We lay down our lives by making whatever sacrifices Jesus leads us to make for the sake of our mentees. We do this because we are true shepherds, not mere hired hands. We have a genuine love for those we lead, and we have a very real calling from the Lord to serve them. We have no ulterior motive. We are not working for money, control, notoriety, or to feel good about ourselves. None of those motives will prove enough to fortify us to be faithful in the midst of the trials that must come.

This passage also speaks to the relational aspect again. "I know my sheep and my sheep know me." This one line speaks volumes about the types of mentors we are to be. To know and be known by those we mentor. Mentors have a genuine interest in the lives of their mentees. They are not interested only in the ministry part or the work part or whatever area they would like to specialize in. They are interested in the whole person. They care about the history of the mentee. About their hurts and failures and disappointments, their victories and their breakthroughs. They are also vulnerable and available to be known. It is not a one-way street. The mentor does not set himself above the other, maintaining a "professional distance" from which to instruct and advise. Nor does he only allow his strengths and successes to be seen while carefully keeping the less attractive parts hidden. To know and be known is essential in good mentoring.

A few more general comments about mentoring:

(1). Listening is an essential skill in mentoring. A great listening tool can be described with the acronym L.E.A.P. The "L" stands for "Listen" — an active, engaged attention to the one speaking. True listening refuses to give in to the temptation of using mental space to formulate a response while the other is still talking. It does not allow the mind to wander. It proves engagement through good non-verbal communication. Its eyes do not wander but are locked in on the speaker. The "E" is to "Empathize." This is to put oneself in the other person's shoes. Before making judgments or giving advice or pointing out errors, the good listener seeks to enter into the mental and emotional space of the one speaking. Experience the situation or the understanding from the other's perspective.

The "A" is to "Ask." Good question-asking is a wonderful part of listening, as long as it follows the first two elements of *listening* and *empathizing*. To question well is not to interrogate and not to get off subject. It is to clarify, to show you were listening, and to help the person think through possible responses or solutions. Finally, the "P" stands for "Pray." A great response to anything that has been shared is to bring it to the Lord together in prayer, asking for insight, direction, and His perspective.

(2). Mentoring is most ideal with more than just one other person. For many people, the idea of mentoring conjures up pictures of two people sitting over a cup of coffee or something similar. This is a good approach, but I have found that adding at least one other person to that common scenario can enhance the mentoring experience. Now, this is not always the case, and it is not always feasible. However, I do ask you to consider the idea of small group mentoring. Neil Cole suggests that "Three, in fact, is the ideal number for a group to experience real growth through community."[81] Three or four people coming together can be beneficial in several ways. It provides another perspective and will often lead to questions and insights not present with just the two. Practically, it also allows you to mentor more people because you save time by meeting with different ones at the same time. Another practical advantage is that the group can still meet when one person is not able to make it, allowing you to keep momentum and consistency. A small group is also beneficial because it can be more engaging and natural. There is less pressure on each person to come up with something to say and to fill the silence. It also provides more practice in listening well.

(3). Adding some degree of structure is very helpful. Many mentoring sessions degenerate into complaint sessions or times to only casually talk about life. While maintaining the relational dimension, structure helps with the intentionality part. Again, the DBS talked about previously is a good tool. Anything that can assure the inclusion of the various elements of prayer, scripture, sharing about life, and accountability is truly beneficial.

(4). Your personal story is a powerful mentoring tool. Spend time thinking through your story: how God has brought you from where you were to where you are. Think about the hardships and the pains, the successes, the highlights, and the disappointments. What are the key things in your history that have helped you to become the person you are? As you think about these on your own, be ready to utilize them to help others. You have perhaps faced similar things to what your mentee is facing now. You have learned how to leverage experience and all the good and bad situations of life into your own growth and development. Be willing to share these nuggets with the others in your mentoring group.

---

[81] Neil Cole, <u>Cultivating a Life for God</u>, (CMS Resources, 1999), pg 42.

(5). Cultivate a genuine confidence in the ultimate working out of God's purposes in your mentees. In the words of Wolf Riedner and Doug Sparks:

> The mentor must genuinely believe in the potential of the mentee. A mentor cannot do serious thinking about the needs of the learner or spend the necessary time without believing in that person's potential. There may be times when the learner loses confidence in himself, particularly after a failure, and he will need the mentor to restore his confidence.[82]

Mentoring, teaching, and apprenticing are indeed powerful tools in raising up a new generation of leaders. When these methods are used to pass down biblical fluency, ministry skills, and faithful character, you have a recipe for fruitful leadership development.

---

[82] Wolf Riedner, Doug Sparks, and Michele Breene, The Ministry of Mentoring, Version 2.5 (Development Associates International: Colorade Springs, 2016), pg 158.

CONCLUSION: THE MOST EXCELLENT WAY

Now eagerly desire the greater gifts. And yet I will show you the most excellent way. — 1 Corinthians 12:31

The only thing that counts is faith expressing itself through love. — Galatians 5:6b

In the closing verses of his gospel account, the Apostle John describes a powerful encounter between Peter and the risen Jesus. After fishing all night and catching nothing, Peter and some of the other apostles see a man on the shore. When the man tells Peter to cast his nets from the other side of the boat, the weary fishermen haul in a huge catch of fish. This clues Peter and his friends into the fact that the man on the shore is Jesus Himself. Peter jumps into the water and swims ashore. He finds Jesus cooking fish, and all are invited to join Him for breakfast. After the meal, Jesus takes a walk with Peter on the beach.

> When they had finished eating, Jesus said to Simon Peter, "Simon son of John, do you love me more than these?"
> "Yes, Lord," he said, "you know that I love you."
> Jesus said, "Feed my lambs."
> Again Jesus said, "Simon son of John, do you love me?"
> He answered, "Yes, Lord, you know that I love you."
> Jesus said, "Take care of my sheep."
> The third time he said to him, "Simon son of John, do you love me?"

Peter was hurt because Jesus asked him the third time, "Do you love me?" He said, "Lord, you know all things; you know that I love you." Jesus said, "Feed my sheep." — John 21:15-17

It is not clear what the "these" are that Jesus is referring to when He asks, "Do you love me more than these?" Some argue that He is asking if Peter loves Him more than the other apostles love Him. Others suggest that perhaps He is asking if Peter loves Jesus more than He loves his fellow disciples. A good case can be made that Jesus is referring to the fish. Peter, do you love me more than you love these fish? Again, if referring to the fish, is He asking if Peter loves Jesus more than he loves the miracles or the provision of Jesus? Does he love Jesus Himself or merely what Jesus can do for him? That would certainly be a provocative and revealing question. I think, however, that Jesus is asking Peter if he loves Him more than he loves his old way of life. The fish are a metaphor representing the thing from which Peter in the past earned his living, built his identity, and provided for his family. They represent Peter the self-sufficient, Peter the competent, Peter the successful. And before they go any further, Jesus needs to know — and perhaps more so He needs for Peter himself to know — that Peter loves Jesus more than anything. That is it. I think that Jesus is simply asking Peter, "Do you love me more than absolutely anything?"

I have a friend who moved to the United States as a refugee with his family when he was twelve years old. After living in the States for a number of years, my friend and his family became American citizens. My friend, now a young adult, told me that one day he had a conversation with another friend named John. They were discussing what it means to love God, and how a person can truly love Him with all of his heart and soul and mind and strength. After some conversation back and forth, John looked at my friend and asked a pointed question: "Would you give Jesus your passport?" John knew my friend's history and what that American passport likely meant to him. Stability. A future. Security. Perhaps the chance to live a life not marred by military conflict or persecution. It was something that had taken years to obtain. "Would you give Jesus your passport?" "Do you love me more than these?" Jesus has a way of piercing through generalities to the thing that a person values the most. "Go and sell your possessions and give to the poor" (Matthew 19:21).

My friend confessed that this question troubled him deeply, and he had no ready answer at the moment. But the question burned even more deeply when, a few months after this conversation, John gave his life as a martyr. He was killed trying to bring the gospel to a primitive people who had never heard the Name of Jesus. He had given his passport and so much more.

"Do you love me more than these?" An essential question for us to answer as we come to the close of this study on leadership. What is it that you love the most? What do you value? From where do you get your identity? What gives you meaning? What makes you feel good about yourself? What gives you security or happiness or pleasure? Do you love Jesus more than these? That is the essential question in gospel leadership. Do not skip over it. Do not take it lightly, as if the answer is obvious. This is the burning issue. Heaven is waiting for our response.

"Feed my lambs."

Having settled the question of love (three times no less!), Jesus gives Peter a commission. The Lord has work for Peter to do — and even so He has work for all who love Him more than anything. It is a great work. To feed His sheep. As a follower of Jesus called to lead others, you have an important work to do. Jesus has given you a commission. Be faithful to it. John continues the story, with Jesus addressing Peter in this way:

> "Very truly I tell you, when you were younger you dressed yourself and went where you wanted; but when you are old you will stretch out your hands, and someone else will dress you and lead you where you do not want to go." Jesus said this to indicate the kind of death by which Peter would glorify God. Then he said to him, "Follow me!" — John 21:18-19

I believe that in this moment, Jesus was aware of all the amazing things Peter would do for the sake of the Kingdom. He knew that Peter would stand as a leader among the apostles, that thousands upon thousands would believe because of his preaching, that he would perform great miracles — such as people being healed by just the apostle's shadow falling on them and others even being raised from the dead — that he would be the first to preach the gospel to Gentiles. So many incredible accomplishments and victories.

Yet Jesus does not speak of any of this. Instead, He tells Peter "the kind of death by which [he] would glorify God." Could it be that Peter's greatest moment of bringing glory to his Lord would not be any of the magnificent and powerful triumphs of his ministry, but in his death? Could it be that Peter would most glorify Jesus when his hands would be stretched out and "someone else will lead you where you do not want to go?" At the moment when he is least in control. The moment when he is weak and feeble and by all appearances defeated? It is there that Peter the apostle would in fact be at his greatest.

To glorify Jesus, at least in part, means to reveal Him. It means to show the world who He is and what He is like. Peter would do this most powerfully in his death. What about you and me? How will we most glorify God? How will we reveal Jesus to the world? Will it be in the moments that we are most proud of? In the business deal that brings great wealth? In promotions? In winning an election or a championship? Will it be in gaining a million followers or selling many books or building a successful church? Or will it be in a moment of anonymous, hidden sacrifice in which you lay down your life — your desires, your passions, your dreams — for the One you love? Will it be when you turn away from the fish? When you give Jesus your passport?

Leaders do not glorify Jesus primarily through wielding great power or reaching the pinnacle of success in their field or exercising spiritual gifts with dramatic effect. They glorify Jesus by laying down their lives for those whom He loves. The greatest thing you have to offer the world is to love Jesus more than anything. The greatest thing you have to offer the Kingdom of Jesus is to love Him above all else.

Do you?

RESOURCES

This book is not meant to provide anything like a thorough look at such topics as studying the Bible, leadership development, missions, making disciples, or indeed, Christian leadership. I am offering here a number of resources that have been helpful to me and I believe may be useful for you as well. Some of these have been referenced within the book in footnotes, while others were not used specifically in this book, though I want to recommend them because of their benefit to me personally in my leadership and disciple-making efforts.

Biography

Christie, Vance. *Adonirum Judson: Devoted for Life*. Ross-shire, Scotland: Christian Focus Publications, 2013.

Greig, Pete, and Dave Roberts *Red Moon Rising: Rediscover the Power of Prayer*. Colorado Springs: David C Cook, 2003.

Houghton, Frank. *Amy Carmichael of Dohnavur: The Story of a Lover and Her Beloved*. Fort Washington, PA: CLC Publications, 1953.

McClung, Floyd. *Living on the Devil's Doorstep*. *2nd ed*. Seattle: YWAM Publishing, 2001.

Taylor, Howard, and Mrs Howard Taylor. *Hudson Taylor and the China Inland Mission*. 1919.

Taylor, Howard, and Mrs Howard Taylor. *Hudson Taylor's Spiritual Secret*, 2013.

Prayer

Bounds, Edward M. *Essentials of Prayer and Power Through Prayer*. Chandler, AZ: Brighton Publishing.

Greig, Pete, *How to Pray: A Simple Guide for Normal People*. Colorado Springs: NavPress, 2019.

Greig, Pete, *God on Mute: Engaging the Silence of Unanswered Prayer*. Grand Rapids: Zondervan, 2020.

Murray, Andrew. *With Christ in the School of Prayer*. Merchant Books, 2013.

Missions

Allen, Roland. *Missionary Methods: St Paul's or Ours?* Grapevine India, 2023.

Allen, Roland. *The Spontaneous Expansion of the Church: And the Causes That Hinder It.* Jawbone Digital, 2012.

Farah, Warrick, Editor. *Motus Dei.* Littleton, CO: William Carey Publishing, 2021.

Garrison, David. *Church Planting Movements.* Monument, CO: WIGTake Resources, 2004.

McClung, Floyd. *You See Bones, I See An Army.* Seattle: YWAM Publishing, 2008.

Prinz, Emanuel. *Movement Catalysts: Profile of an Apostolic Leader.* 2022.

Smith, Steve, and Ying Kai. *T4T: A Discipleship* Re-*Revolution.* Monument, CO: WIGTake Resources, 2011.

Trousdale, Jerry. *Miraculous Movements.* Nashville: Thomas Nelson, 2012.

Trousdale, Jerry, and Glenn Sunshine. *The Kingdom Unleashed: How Jesus' 1st-Century Kingdom Values Are Transforming Thousands of Cultures and Awakening His Church.* Murfreesboro, TN: DMM Library, 2018.

Spiritual Formation and Biblical Literacy

Carmichael, Amy. *If.* Fort Smith, PA: CLC Publications, 1938.

Comer, John Mark. *Live No Lies.* Colorado Springs: Waterbrook, 2021.

Emerson, Alain, and Adam Cox. *The God Story: Encountering Unfailing Love in the Unfolding Narrative of Scripture.* SPCK Publishing, 2024.

Fee, Gordan, and Douglas Stuart. *How to Read the Bible for All Its Worth.* 4th ed. Grand Rapids: Zondervan, 2014.

Foster, Richard. *Celebration of Discipline.* New York: HarperCollins, 2018.

Manning, Brennan. *The Signature of Jesus.* New York: Multnomah Books, 1996.

McClung, Floyd. *The Father Heart of God: Experiencing the Depths of His Love for You.* Eugene, OR: Harvest House Publishers, 1985.

Murray, Andrew. *Humility.* Fig Books, 2012.

Patz, Mike, and Brian Sanders. *Different: Reimagining Holiness for a Wandering Church in a Watching World.* Underground Media, 2014.

Tozer, A.W. *The Pursuit of God.* Christian Publications, Inc, 1948.

Other Books on Leadership and Disciple-Making

Barton, Ruth Haley. *Pursuing God's Will Together.* Downers Grove: InterVarsity Press, 2012.

Barton, Ruth Haley. *Strengthening the Soul of your Leadership.* Downers Grove: IVP Books, 2018.

Chan, Francis. *Letters to the Church.* Colorado Springs: David C Cook, 2018.

Chan, Francis, and Mark Beuving. *Multiply: Disciples Making Disciples.* Colorado Springs: David C Cook, 2012.

Clinton, Robert. *The Making of a Leader,* Second Edition. Colorado Springs: NavPress, 2012.

Cole, Neil. *Cultivating a Life for God.* CMS Resources, 1999.

Cole, Neil. *Organic Leadership.* Grand Rapids: Baker Books, 2009.

Hull, Bill. *Jesus Christ Disciplemaker.* Grand Rapids: Baker Books, 2004.

Mallison, John. *Mentoring to Develop Disciples and Leaders.* Australian Church Resources, 2010.

McCallum, Dennis, and Jessica Lowery. *Organic Discipleship: Mentoring Others into Spiritual Maturity and Leadership.* New Paradigm Publishing, 2006.

McClung, Floyd. *Follow: A Simple and Profound Call to Live Like Jesus.* Colorado Springs: David C Cook, 2010.

McClung, Floyd. *Leading Like Jesus: 40 Leadership Lessons from the Upside-Down Kingdom.* Follow Publications, 2015.

Nouwen, Henri. *In the Name of Jesus.* New York: Crossroad Publishing, 2002.

Overstreet, Jane. *Unleader.* Colorado Springs: Biblica, 2011.

Petersen, Jon. *Unraveled: Reform the Church Transform the Culture.* Castle Rock, CO: City Force Media, 2018.

Petersen, Jon. *Unveiled: What a Pirate, a Pot Farmer, and a Gaggle of Prostitutes Taught Me About Being the Church.* Castle Rock, CO: City Force Media, 2019.

Reed, Jeff. *The Paradigm Papers: New Paradigms for the Postmodern Church.* Ames: BILD International, 2017.

Reed, Jeff. *The Encyclicals: A Global Return to "The Way of Christ and His Apostles."* Ames, IA: BILD International, 2017.

Riedner, Wolf, Doug Sparks, and Michele Breene. *The Ministry of Mentoring, Version 2.5*. Colorado Springs: Development Associates International, 2016.

Sanders, Oswald J. *Spiritual Leadership*. Chicago: Moody Publishers, 2007.

Spurgeon, Charles. *The Complete Works of Charles Spurgeon*, Volume 55. Delmarva Publication, 2013.

Tozer, A.W. *Lead Like Christ: Reflecting the Qualities and Character of Christ in Your Ministry*. Bloomington, MN: Bethany House Publishers, 2021.

Watson, David and Paul Watson. *Contagious Disciple Making*. Nashville: Thomas Nelson, 2014.

About the Author

Tim Way is a passionate and flawed follower of Jesus. He has been married to the love of his life, Jill, for 32 years. Together they have 5 amazing children and 2 wonderful children-in-law. Tim has been a pastor, missionary, disciple-maker, and equipper of leaders for more than 25 years. He and Jill currently reside in Masaka, Uganda.

For more information about their work in making disciples and mobilizing for prayer and mission, go to iamsent.net.

www.ingramcontent.com/pod-product-compliance
Lightning Source LLC
LaVergne TN
LVHW051401080426
835508LV00022B/2920